IMAGES
of America

AROUND CHILLICOTHE
ILLINOIS

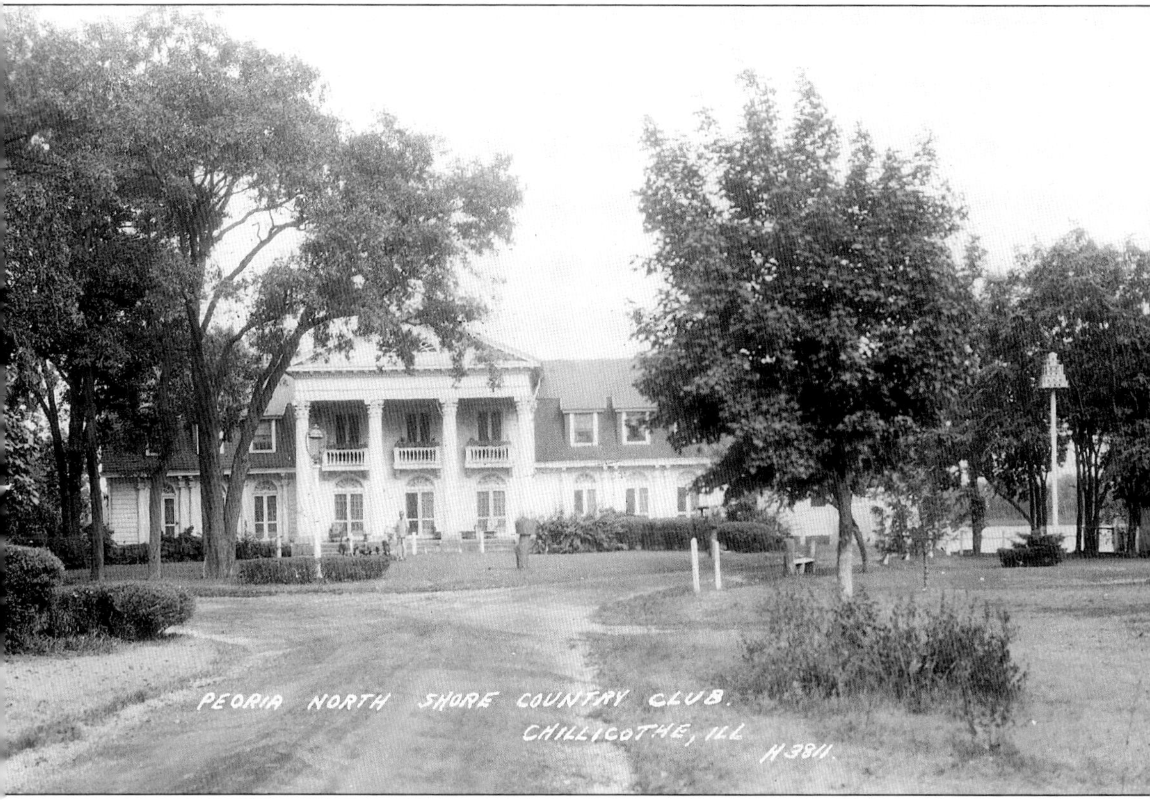

Pictured above is the clubhouse at Shore Acres. Built for the Peoria Auto Club in 1915, it became the North Shore Country Club in 1925, Shore Acres in 1936, and was leased by the park district in 1948.

IMAGES
of America

AROUND CHILLICOTHE ILLINOIS

Chillicothe Historical Society

ARCADIA
PUBLISHING

Copyright © 2000 by Chillicothe Historical Society
ISBN 978-0-7385-0725-5

Published by Arcadia Publishing
Charleston, South Carolina

Printed in the United States of America

Library of Congress Catalog Card Number: 00103959

For all general information contact Arcadia Publishing at:
Telephone 843-853-2070
Fax 843-853-0044
E-mail sales@arcadiapublishing.com
For customer service and orders:
Toll-Free 1-888-313-2665

Visit us on the Internet at www.arcadiapublishing.com

Contents

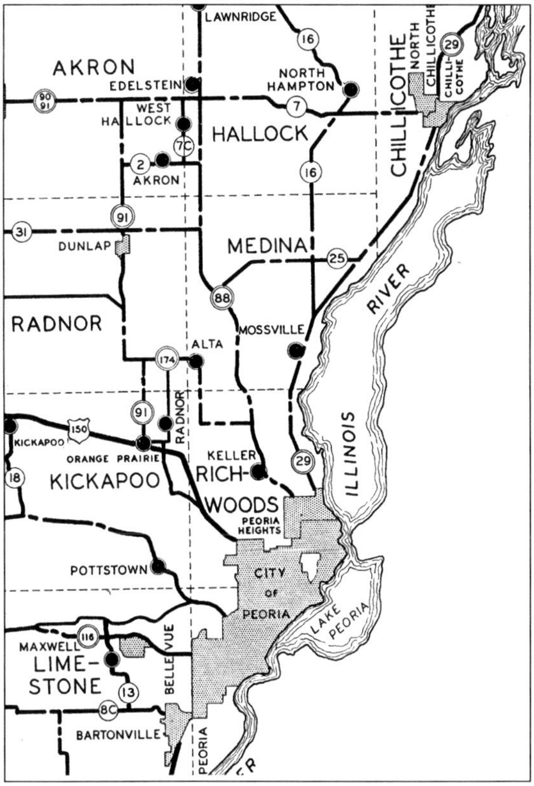

Pictured here is a map of Northeastern Peoria County, Illinois.

INTRODUCTION

A Short History of Our Corner of Peoria County

The history of Chillicothe, Hallock, and Medina townships—the three northeastern townships of Peoria County—is intertwined. Today we forget that this area once was the frontier.

These townships were home to many prehistoric or Native American residents, with the two most obvious reminders of them being the mounds north of Mossville, and geographic names such as Senachwine Creek.

The French passed through the area, starting with Marquette and Joliet in 1673, but have not left behind many reminders of their presence in our area.

The first recorded presence of the United States government in our area was the 1811 visit by Captain Samuel Levering from St. Louis to Gomo's village—north of Chillicothe—to discuss "certain Indian murderers." The next visit was for the destruction of Gomo's village in the fall of 1813 by Illinois Rangers under Brigadier General Benjamin Howard.

The first American settler in this area was Lewis Hallock, who arrived in 1820. He built a cabin in Hallock Hollow and than spent most of his time roaming with the Indians, living as a hunter and trapper. He bequeathed his name to the creek, the hollow, the township, and a settlement.

The next settler to arrive was George Love, who started Love's Settlement in Medina Township on November 10, 1824. Love was soon joined by John Ridgeway. Love was also one of the first to be buried in the La Salle Cemetery in Medina Township. His settlement was renamed Mossville in 1854 by the Peoria and Bureau Valley Railroad. Supposedly there are three houses in Mossville that date back to the 1840s.

The first settlers of what became the settlement of La Salle Prairie arrived in 1825. They were the three Averys, along with Stephen French, Stephen Carl, Resolve and Hiram Cleveland, who moved into empty bark Indian houses on section 4 of Medina Township with their families. Simon, Aaron, and Samuel Reed came to Hallock Township that same year. Simon settled at Union, building a two-room log house about 500 feet southeast of Hallock's cabin. Aaron settled at Northampton, and Samuel went to Buffalo Grove, northwest of Dixon. Closely following the Reeds were Moses and Samuel Clifton, Joseph Meredith, Cornelius Doty, Rev. Gershom Silliman, his son, M.B. Silliman, and William Wright. The second post office in the county was established in the Silliman home in 1832.

The first settlers in Chillicothe Township were Mahlon Lupton in the fall of 1829 and John Hammett on June 10, 1830. They settled north of Senachwine Creek, in section 9. The first cabin in the town proper was built by Jefferson Hickson, a blacksmith who built a shop on the riverbank. Edwin Jones built the second cabin with two rooms right after the town was platted in 1834. One room was stocked with goods to become the first store in the town.

The first village of Rome in Chillicothe Township was platted with 23 blocks on December 24, 1832, by Jefferson Taliaferro. There was no legal survey on the plat, so the exact location is not known. It is said that Rome initially failed. In 1835, Taliaferro sold his holdings at Rome to Isaac Underhill of Peoria. On October 10, 1835, Underhill laid out a larger village of 44 blocks, also named Rome, but again without a specific legal description. Underhill was able to get the second post office in the county moved from LaSalle Prairie to Rome on October 16, 1835. An article in the *Peoria Register and Northwestern Gazetteer* of January 20, 1838, states that Rome was 18 miles from Peoria by stage and had 25 houses.

Chillicothe was founded November 28, 1834, by Samuel McKean when he platted a village—the name was not recorded—of four blocks and four extra lots. It is reported that

McKean's village did not succeed. On June 6, 1836, it is claimed that Harrison Jamison and Joseph Hart platted a new, larger village, which they named Chillicothe after Chillicothe, Ohio—supposedly ignoring McKean's earlier plat, but including the four blocks. An article in the *Peoria Register and Northwestern Gazetteer* of January 20, 1838, states that Chillicothe was 21 miles from Peoria by stage and had 30 houses. At this time, Chillicothe mail was coming to the post office in Rome, three miles to the south. A post office was established in Chillicothe on February 13, 1841. The first businesses were organized along the river, but in 1854 the Rock Island Railroad was built through Chillicothe, and the business district began to move away from the river. In 1887, the Santa Fe Railroad was constructed north of Chillicothe and led to the establishment of a new town—North Chillicothe.

The village of Northampton in Hallock Township was platted in July of 1836 by Reuben Hamlin of Peoria. Hamlin was Aaron Reed's son-in-law and had supplied lumber for the first Peoria County Courthouse in 1834–36. Northampton received the third post office in the county on March 19, 1836.

Lawn Ridge—originally called Long Ridge in 1845—was never formally platted, but was the largest settlement in Hallock Township. The 1880 population was about 500 and contained churches, stores, hotels, etc. When the Santa Fe Railroad bypassed the settlement, the population fell as businessmen moved towards the railroad. By 1900, the population was down to about 200 and has continued to fall since.

Other settlements started in Chillicothe Township were Allentown in 1832, and the village of La Salle in 1837. Medina Township contained Mt. Hawley Post Office in 1837, Helena Post Office in 1842, and Alta in 1873. Hallock Township included West Hallock by 1845, with a post office in 1864; Southampton perhaps as early as 1824, with a post office in 1847; Hallock Post Office in 1860, and Edelstein in 1887. Some of these settlements survive today but most are only vague memories.

One

Area Business

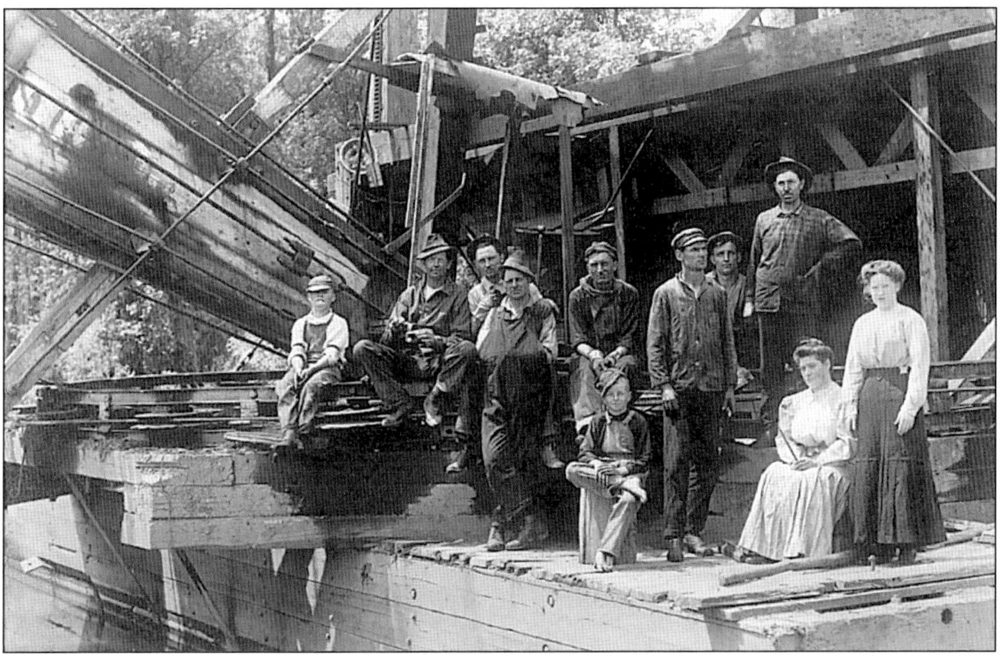

Workers and friends at one of the Carroll ice houses are pictured here. In 1896, one ice house was at the foot of Cedar and the other was at the foot of Chestnut.

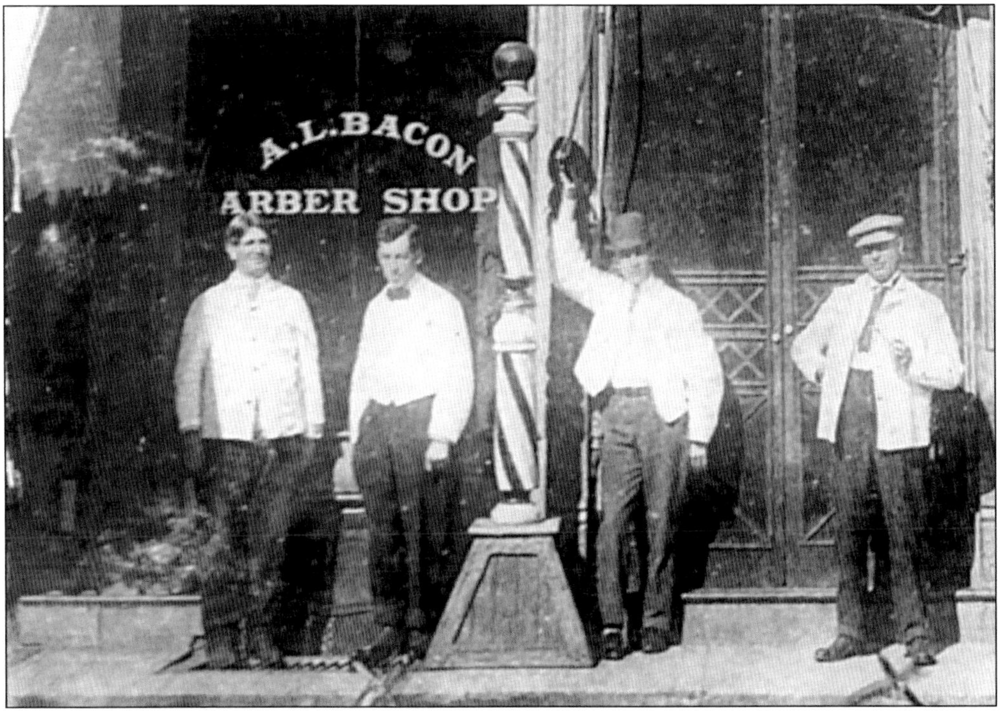

This photo depicts the exterior of the A.L. Bacon Barber Shop in 1913. A.L. Bacon was the father of Wilber L. Bacon, who was also a barber, and Frank Bacon, an electrician.

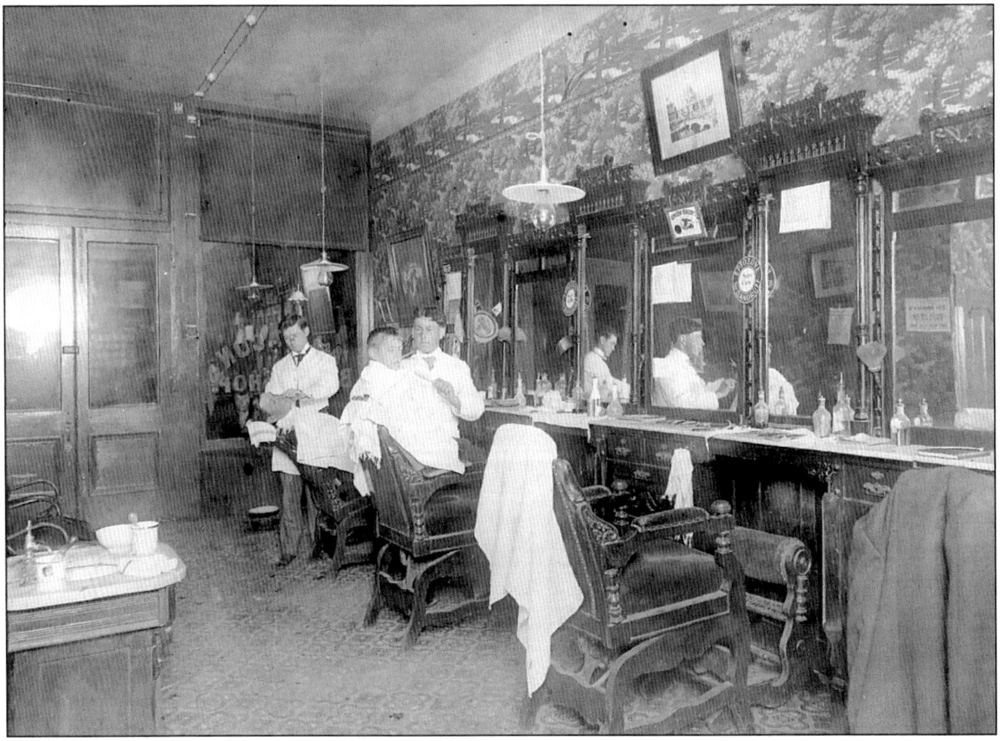

This is the interior of the A.L. Bacon Barber Shop.

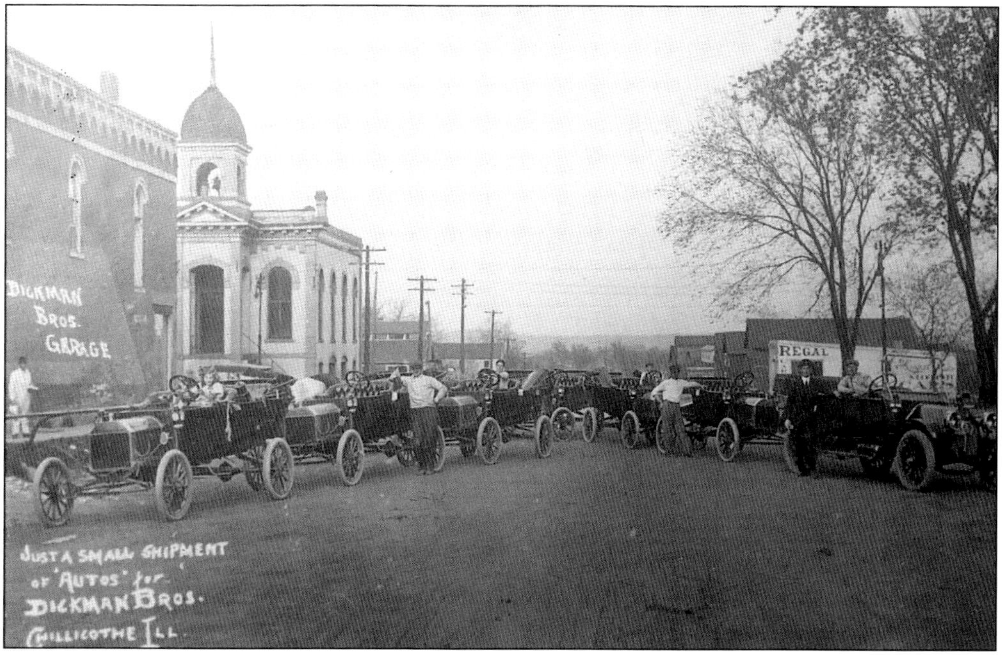

This picture is of an easterly view on Walnut Street looking towards the intersection of Second Street (1910–1915 era) before the library was built. The old city hall sits on the northeast corner. Dickman Brothers was located where the Bacon Building stands today. Phil Matthews' Regal Auto Sales was located east of the library site.

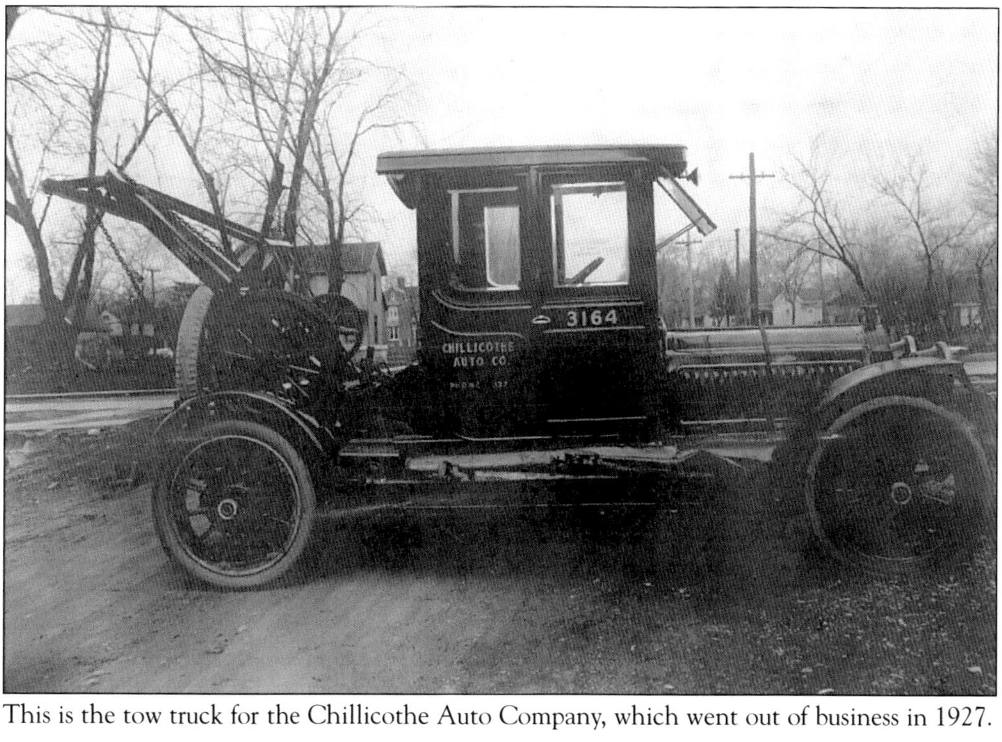

This is the tow truck for the Chillicothe Auto Company, which went out of business in 1927.

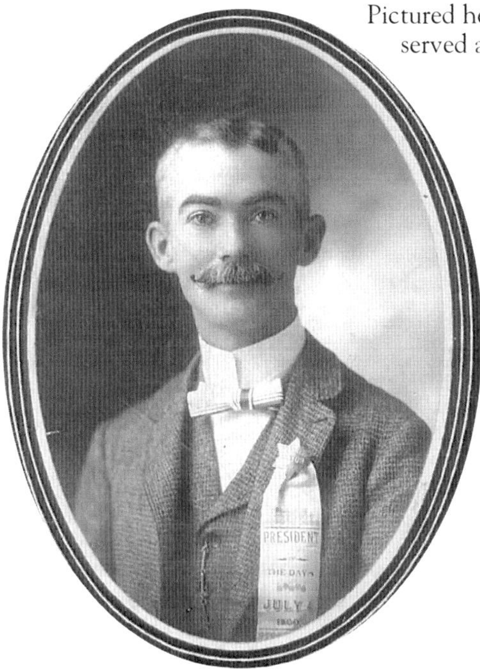

Pictured here is M.C. "Mick" Kelly on July 4, 1900. Kelly served as mayor and civic leader for many years.

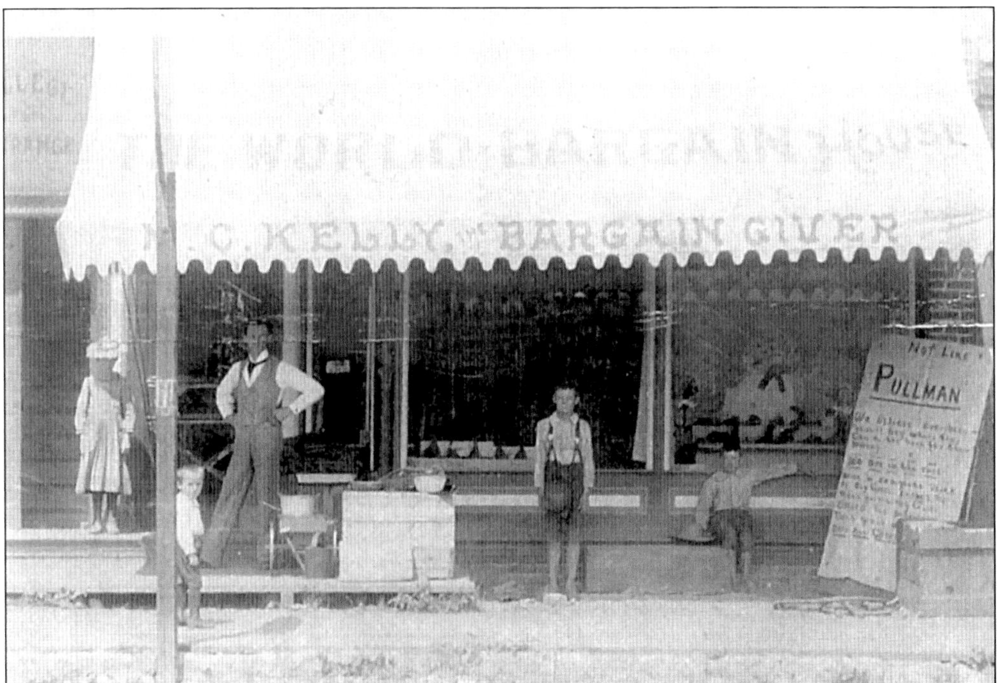

Kelly opened his first store in what is now the American Legion on August 4, 1891. The sign here reads: " Not Like Pullman. We believe everybody should buy where they can do the best for their money. We are in the race with a complete stock of dry goods, ladies' and mens' furnishings. Good shoes for everybody. Don't pass by. We defy all competition."

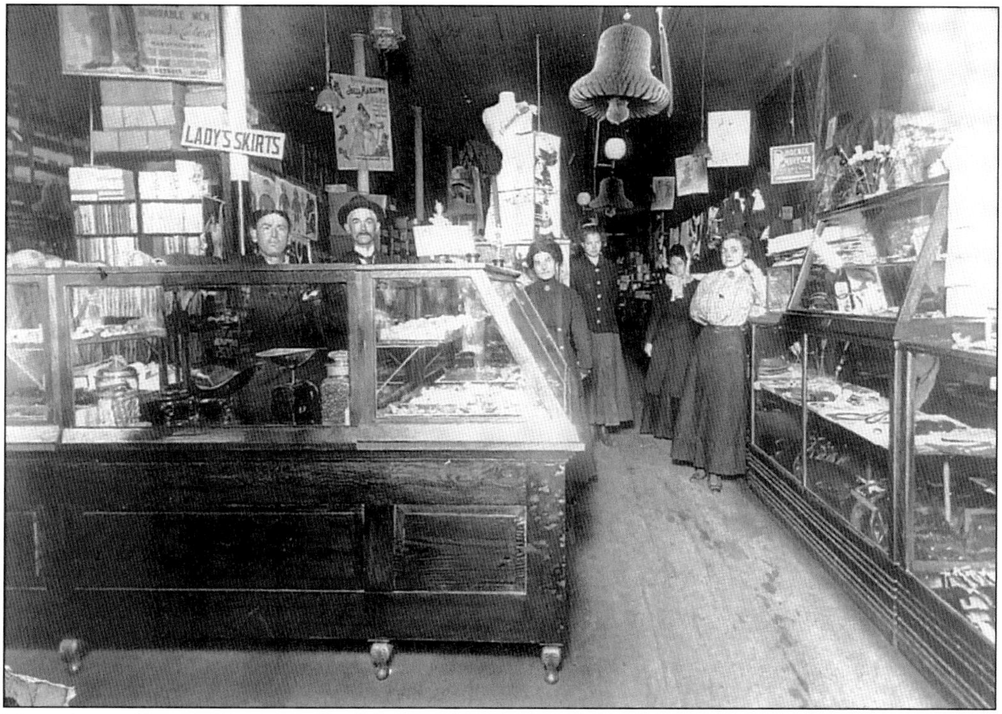

This photo depicts the interior of the M.C. Kelly store; Mick is wearing the hat and standing behind the case.

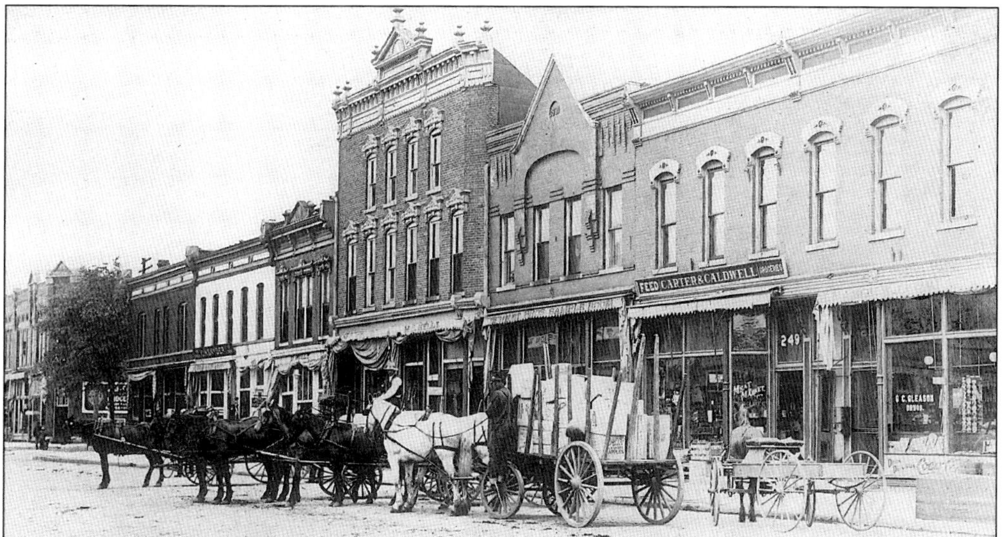

The west side of Second Street is pictured above in about 1910. The sign on the front of the white building, whose address is now 1017, is C.H. Snyder—a baker. The next building, which is now Haymart at 1021, reads D. Kelly. The three-story Kelly Opera House, located where the Town Theater now stands, was where M.C. Kelly organized his second dry goods store. Next is Bennett Bros. Sample Room—a saloon—which is now Haymart at 1035. Carter and Caldwell Feed and Groceries follows at 1037, and G.C. Gleason drug store is shown where the American Legion stands today.

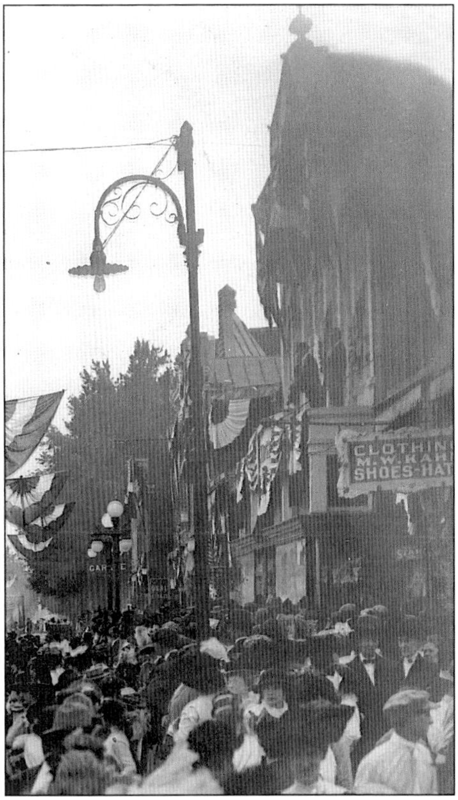

Pictured above is the 1914 Harvest Festival crowd on Second Street. M.W. Kahn sold mens' clothing for many years, and was located at 949 Second Street at this time. Note the projecting entrance with men standing on the roof of the Matthews store—now Sew and Such.

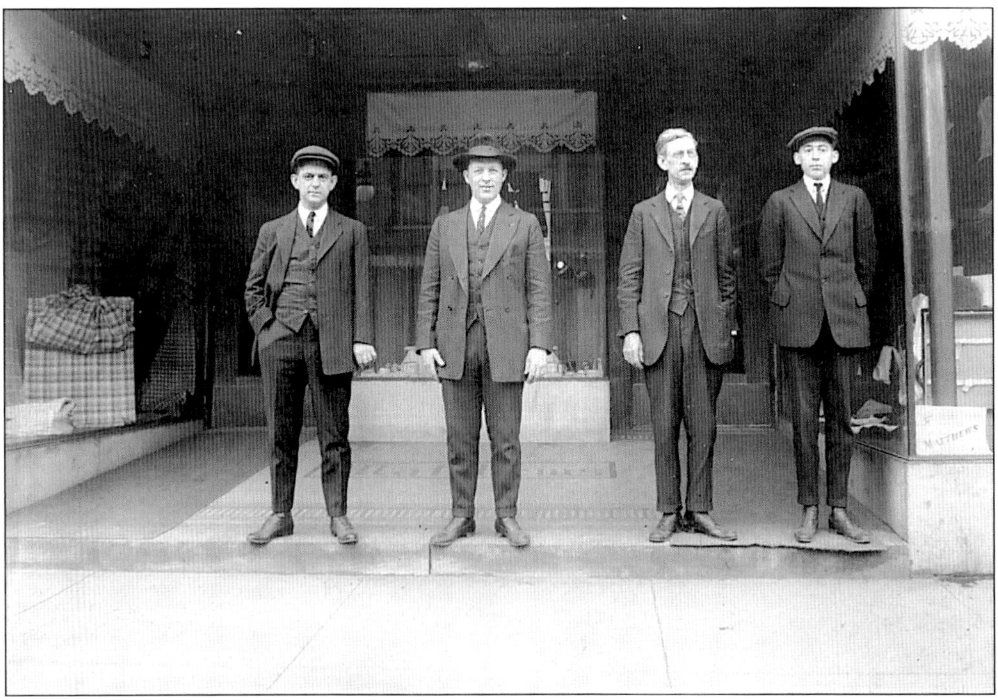

Pictured above is the projecting entrance of the Matthews Store with a mosaic tile walkway.

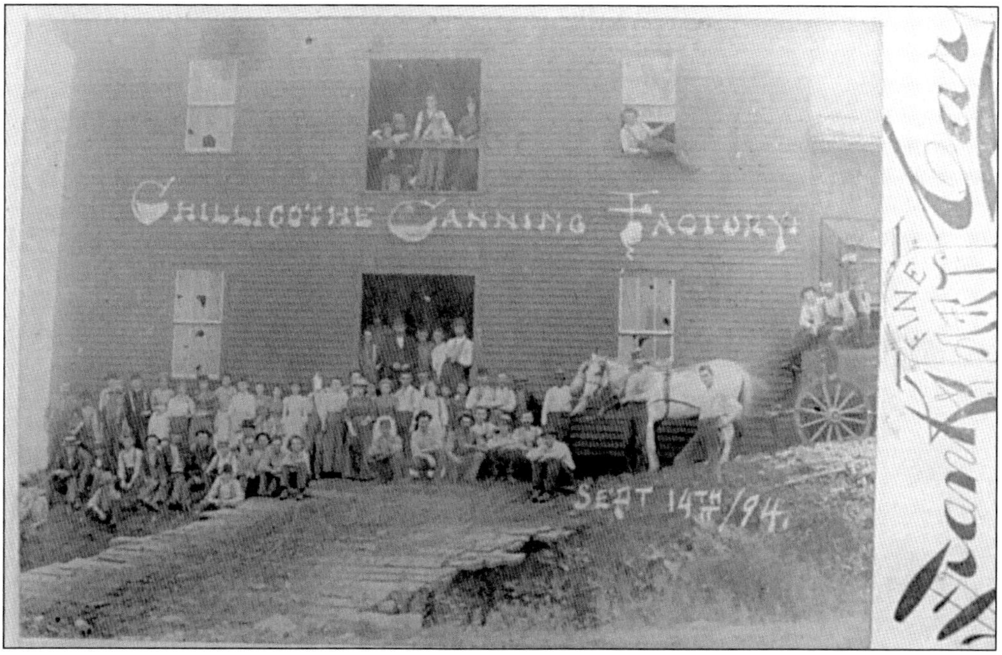

The Chillicothe Canning Company is pictured here on September 14, 1894, and is now Cutright Park. The company was opened in 1883 by Nathaniel Cutright and was torn down in 1922.

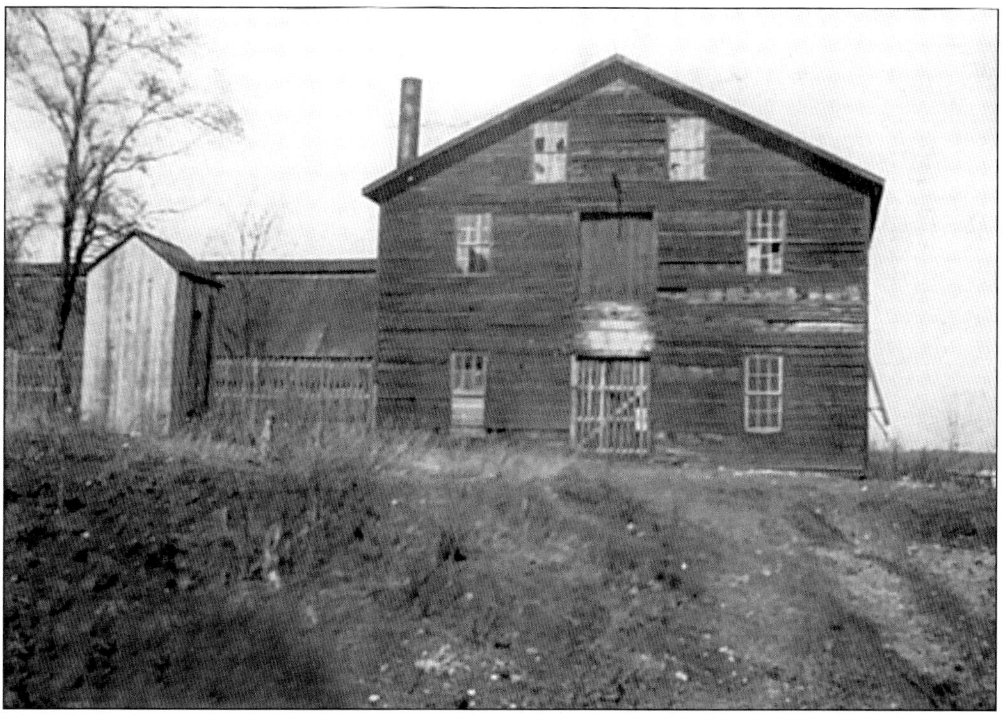

This photo depicts the south side of the canning plant.

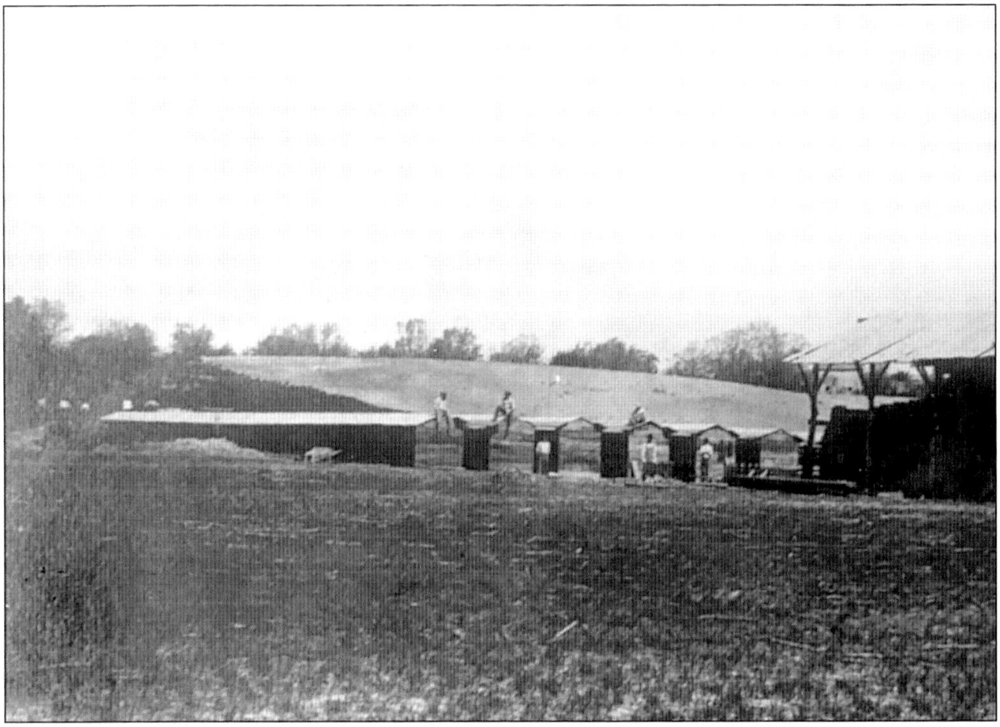

Pictured above is the Northampton Brickyard of old in Hallock Township.

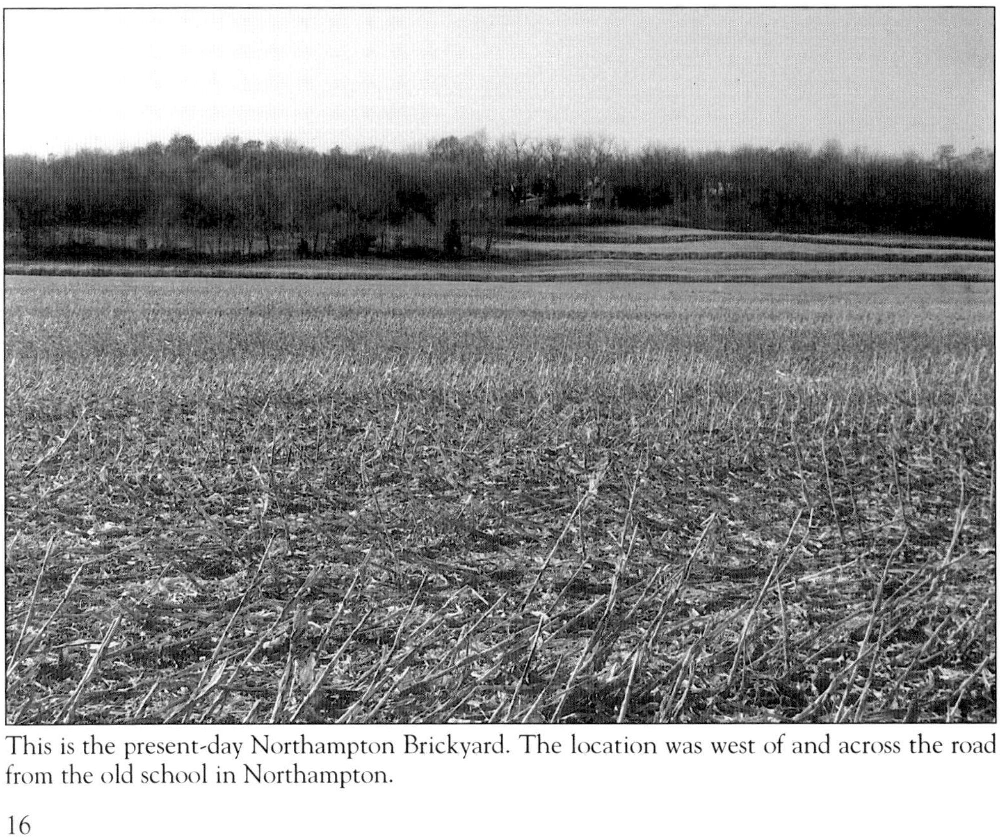

This is the present-day Northampton Brickyard. The location was west of and across the road from the old school in Northampton.

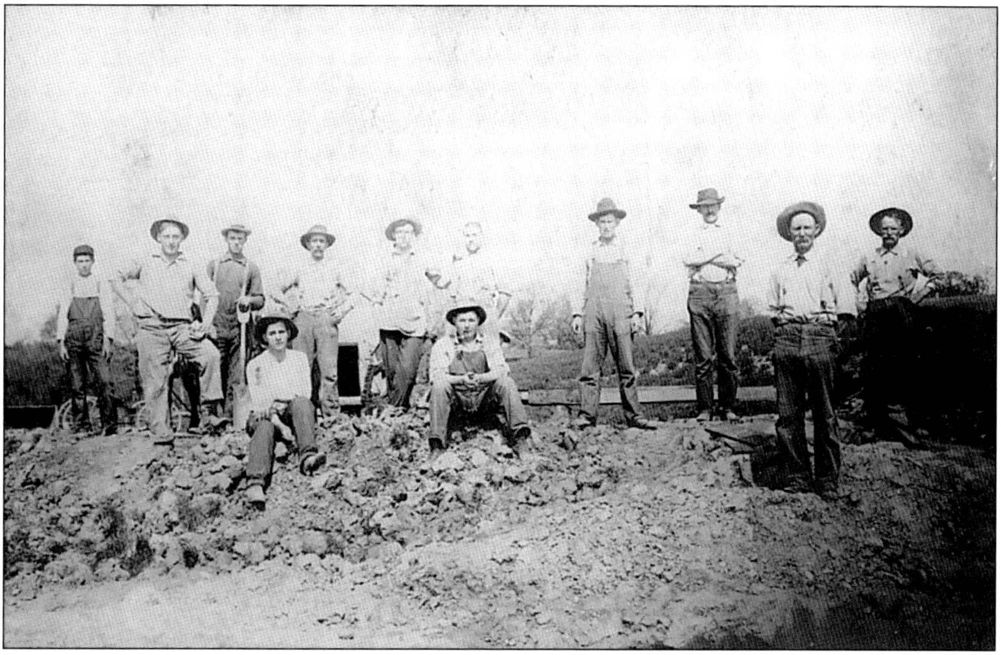

Workers at the clay pit of the Northampton Brickyard in Hallock Township are pictured here.

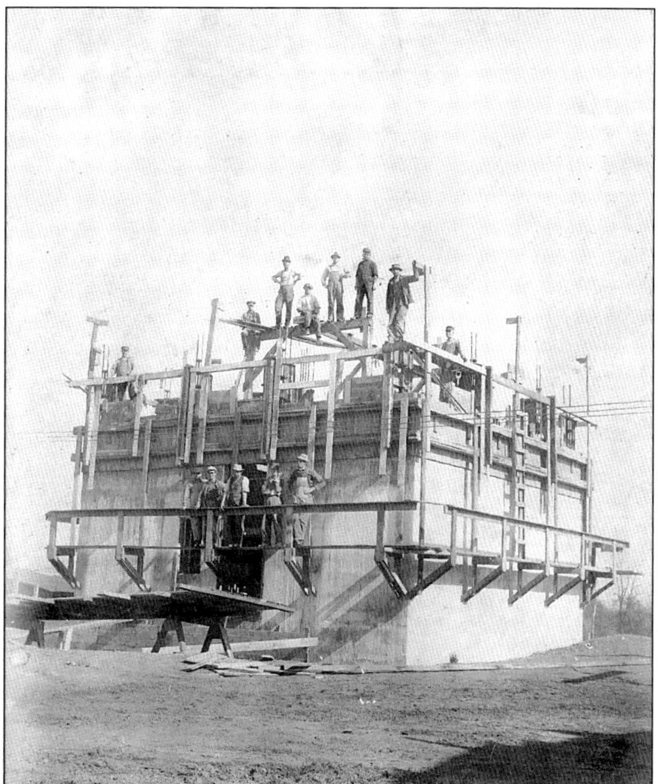

This photo depicts the 1915 construction of the Chillicothe elevator at the foot of Elm Street by a crew for Burrell Engineering and Construction of Chicago for the Turner Hudnut Company of Pekin.

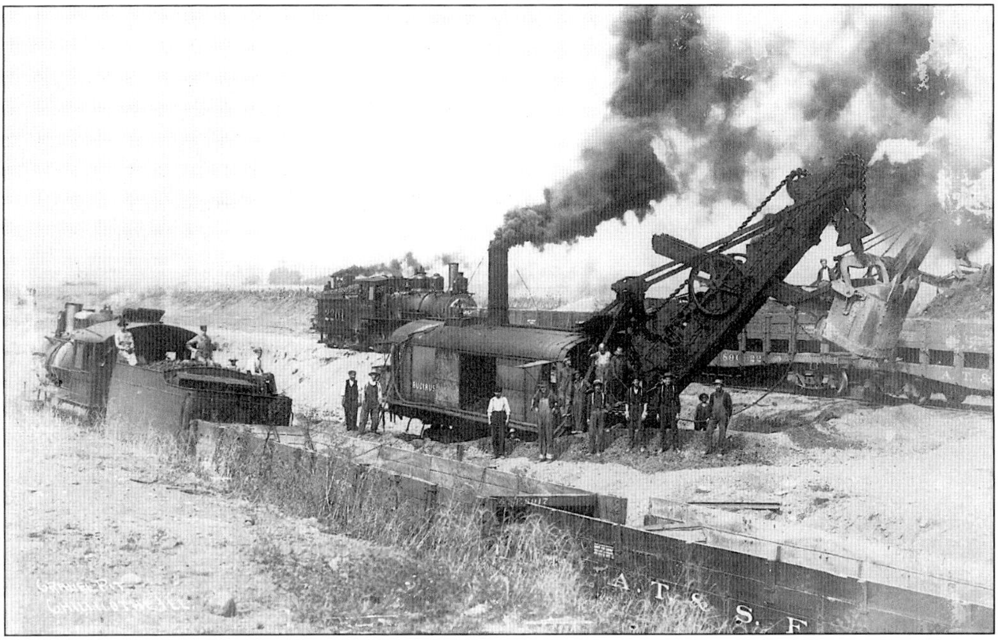

Pictured here are steam shovels mining gravel in the Santa Fe "Pits" north of North Chillicothe in the early '20s.

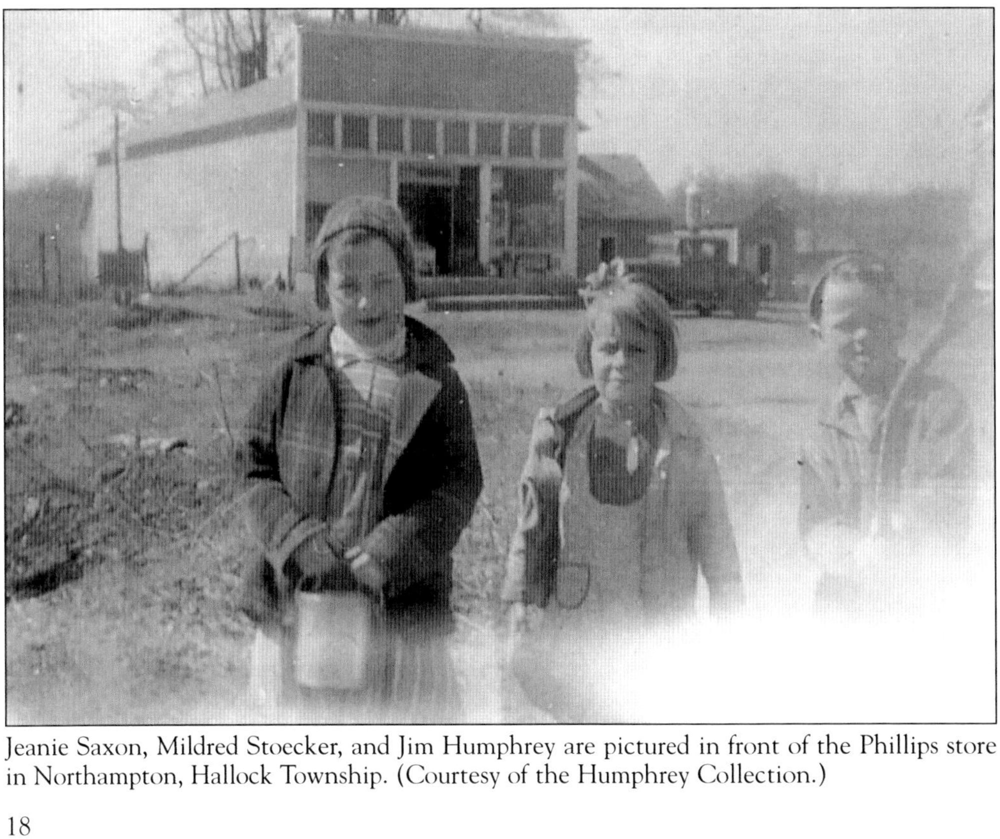

Jeanie Saxon, Mildred Stoecker, and Jim Humphrey are pictured in front of the Phillips store in Northampton, Hallock Township. (Courtesy of the Humphrey Collection.)

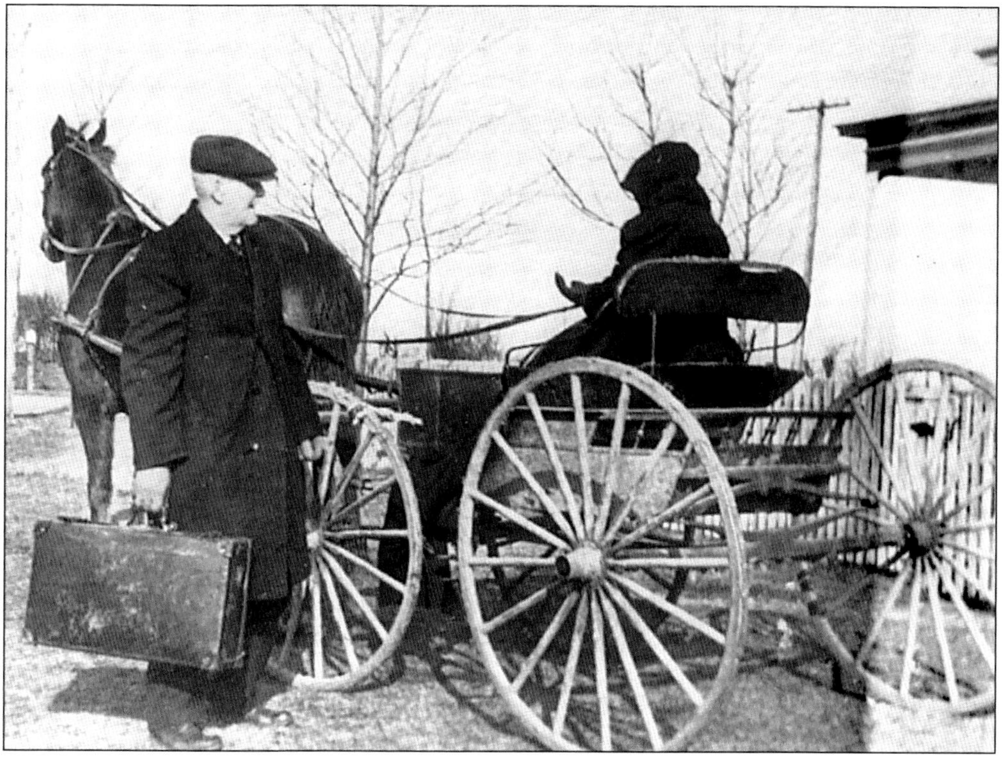

This is a couple in 1902 preparing to travel in a buggy made by the Chillicothe Wagon Works.

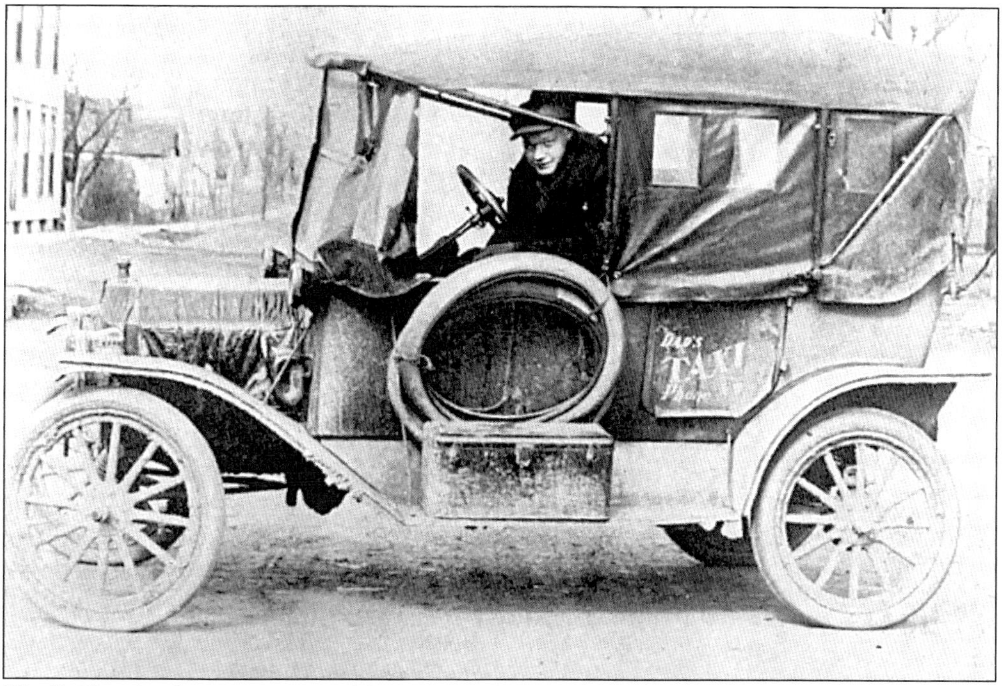

"Dad" Cleveland's taxi is pictured here driven by "Red" Donath.

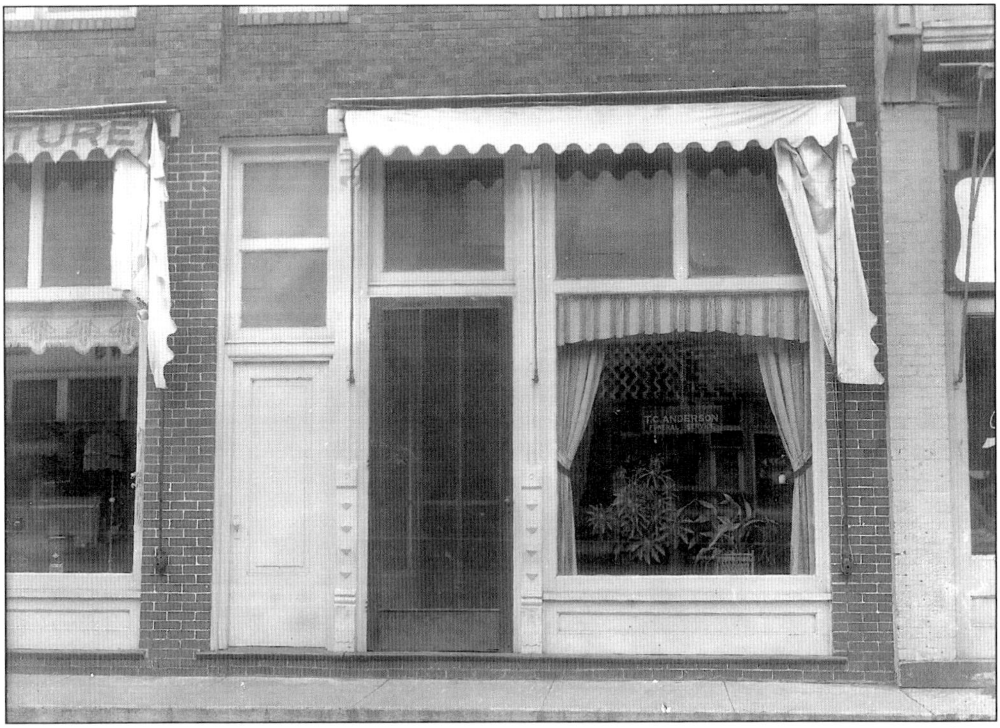

Chris Kauf joined the Weber undertaking parlor and furniture store in 1895, and later opened his own business at 934 and 940 Second Street. In 1915, he was joined by Tom C. Anderson. This photo depicts the funeral parlor at 934 Second Street after Anderson assumed sole ownership.

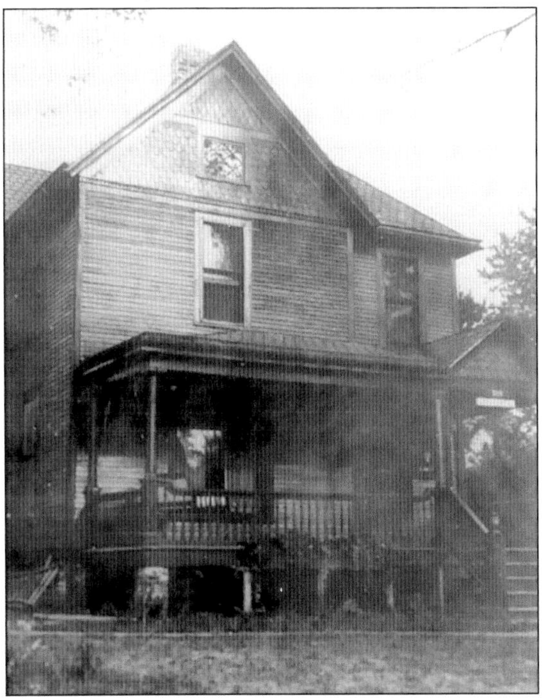

Anderson moved the undertaking parlor to 815 Fourth Street in 1932, and sold it to Robert Anderson in 1953. The building now houses Davison-Fulton-Anderson Chapel. Tom Anderson served as fire chief for many years.

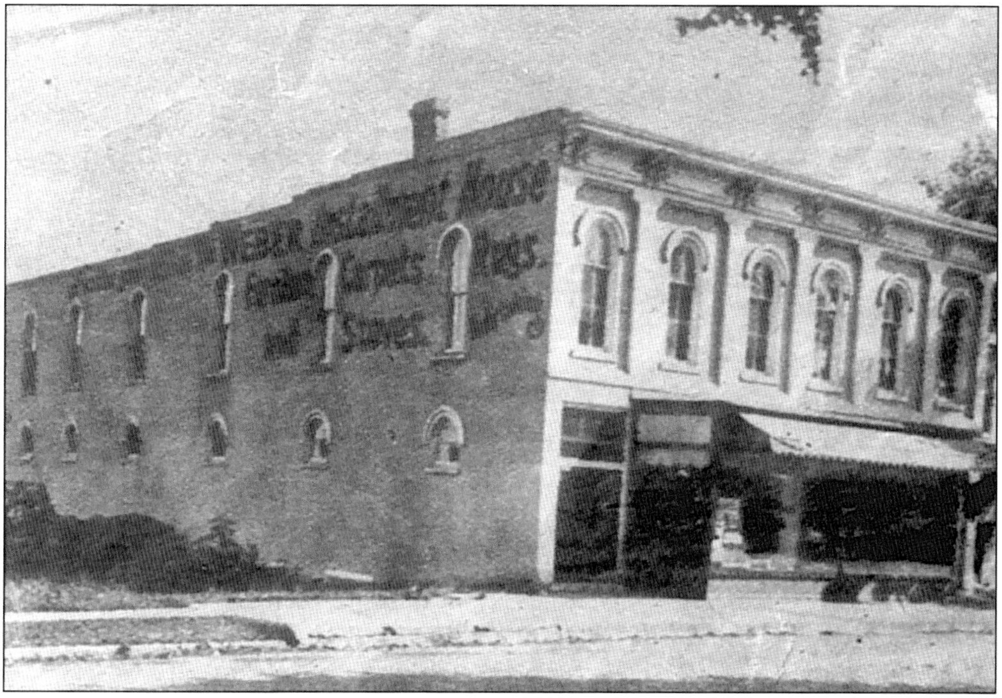

The Weber Building is pictured here at its location south of the library on Second Street. Andrew Weber arrived in 1852, opening a cabinet-making and undertaking business. Andrew's son Pete, grandson Gene, and great-grandson Jack continued the business until 1984. By 1895, the Weber family occupied this triple building on Second Street, selling furniture in the north part and operating the funeral parlor in the south part.

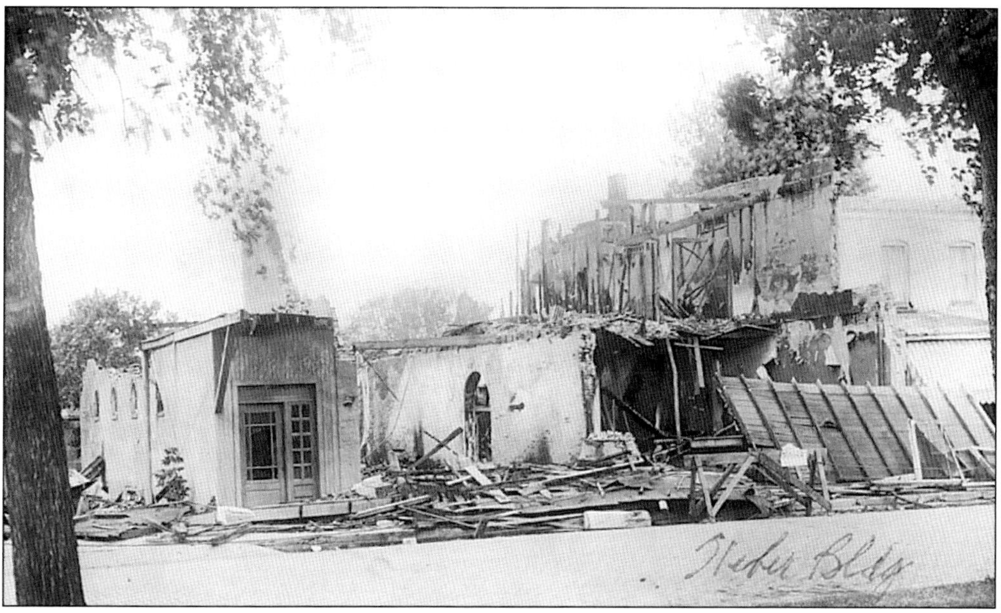

The Weber Building burned in 1934, and the business then moved to the former Sidney Wood/ Darb Woodruff home on Fourth Street. Jack Weber sold both the name and the business to Jack McCann in 1984.

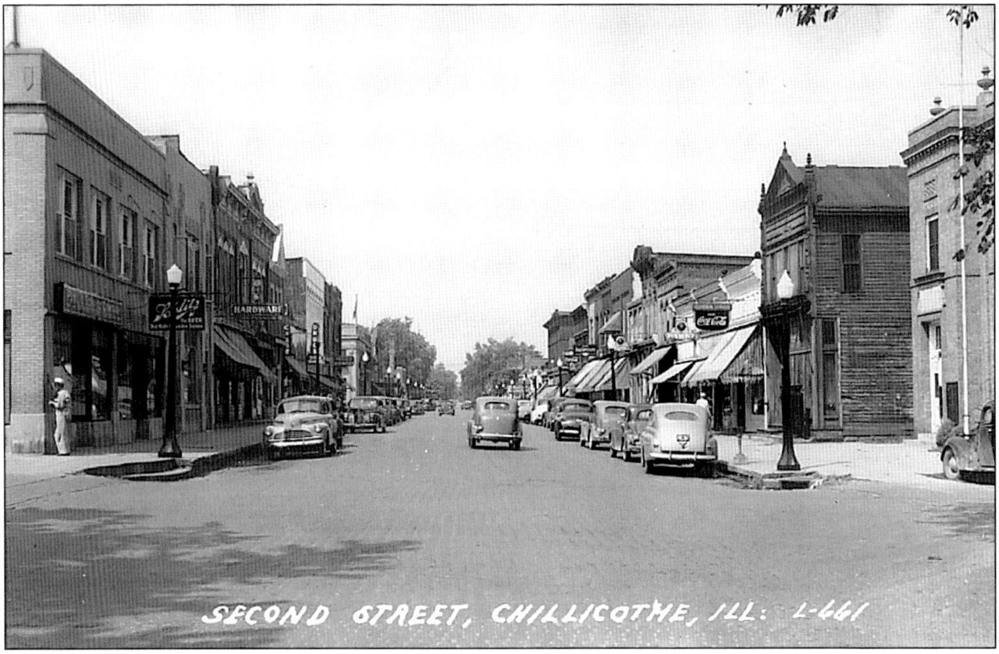

Second Street is shown here in the late '40s looking north. (Courtesy of Mr. and Mrs. Phil McAlearney.)

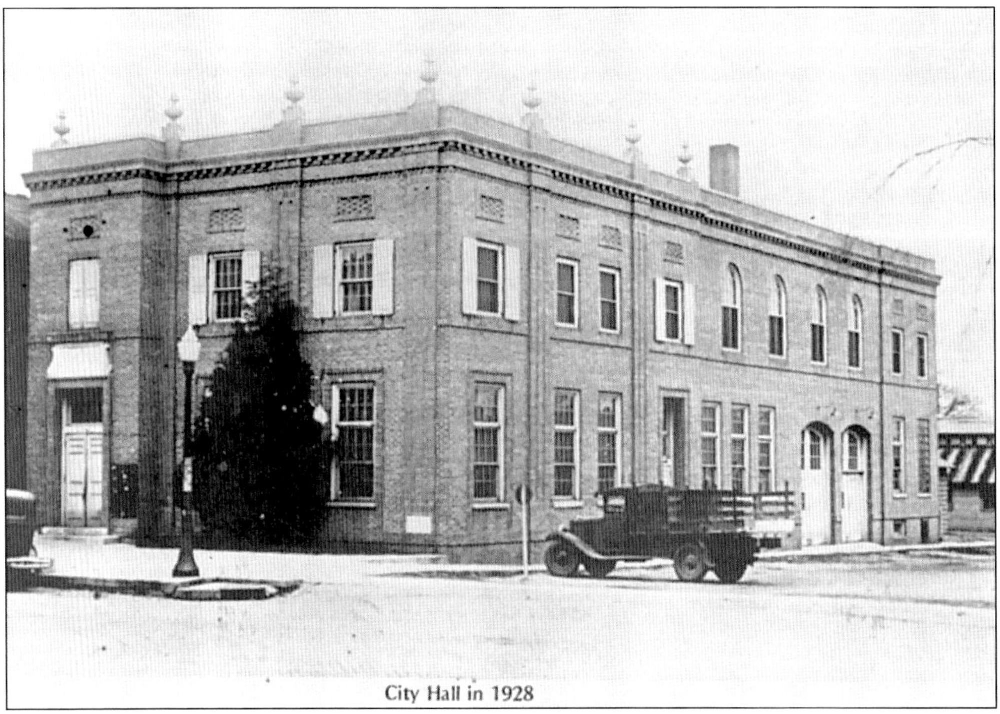

City Hall in 1928

Pictured above is city hall in 1928.

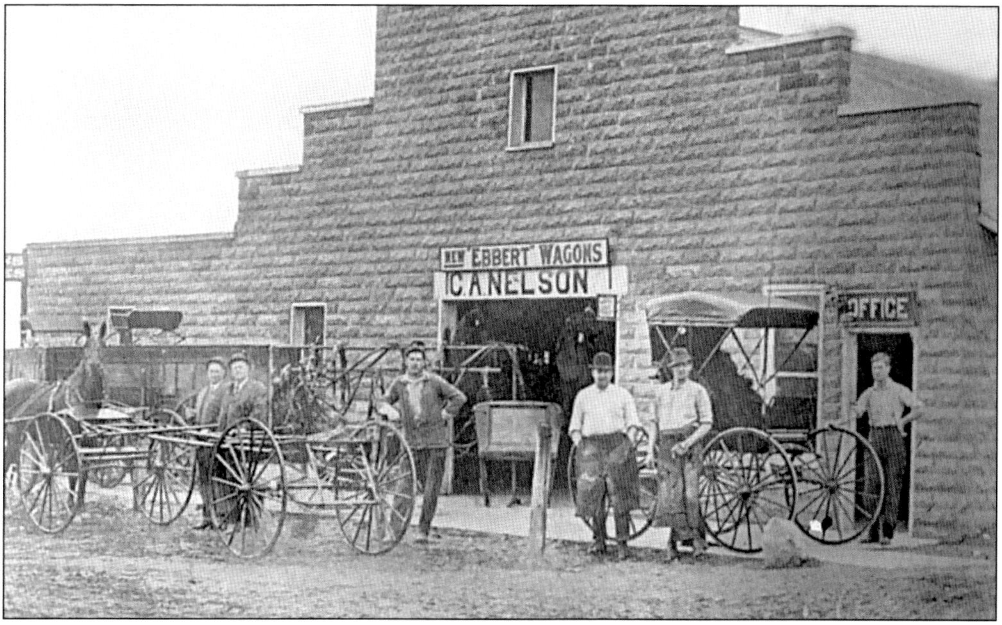

This photo depicts Nelson's livery stable east of the library. The building later housed the George Mattice Ford Garage, was then occupied by J&J Manufacturing, and is now owned by Carl Gross.

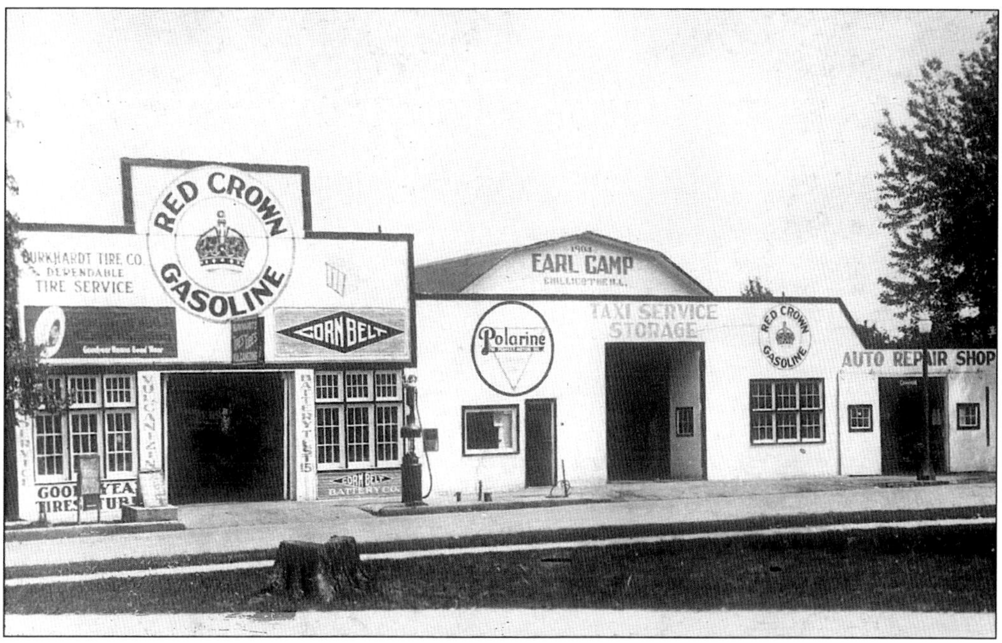

The Burkhardt Tire Compnay was located where John's Autobody now is at 1120 Second Street, and Camp's Taxi Service became the parking lot for the post office.

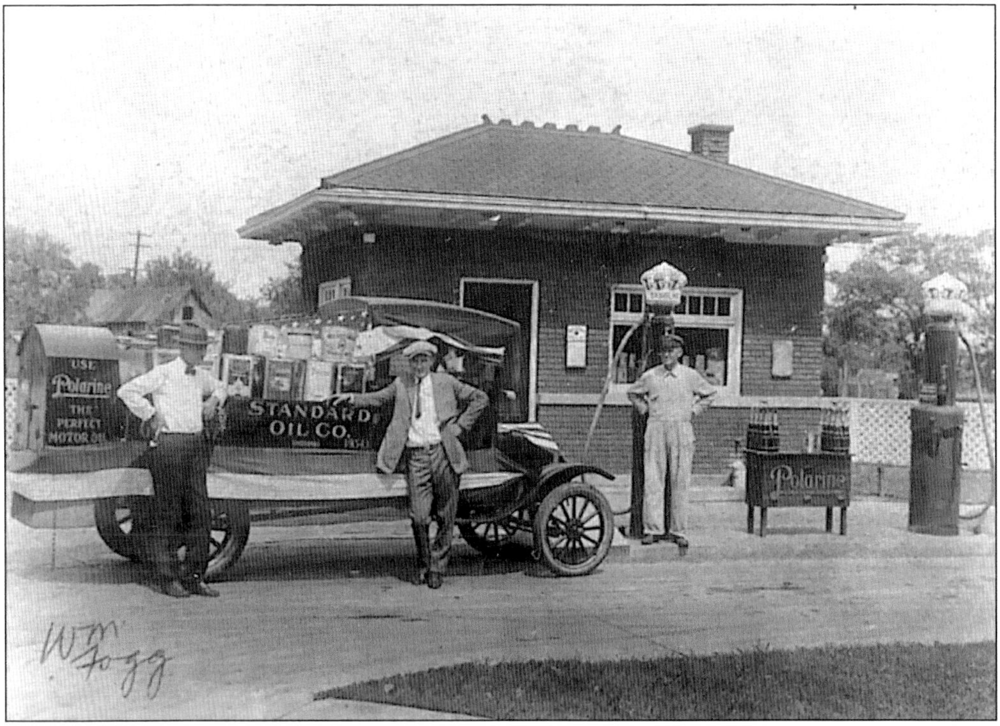

The Standard station with its delivery truck is pictured above. William Fogg became an agent for Standard in June of 1919.

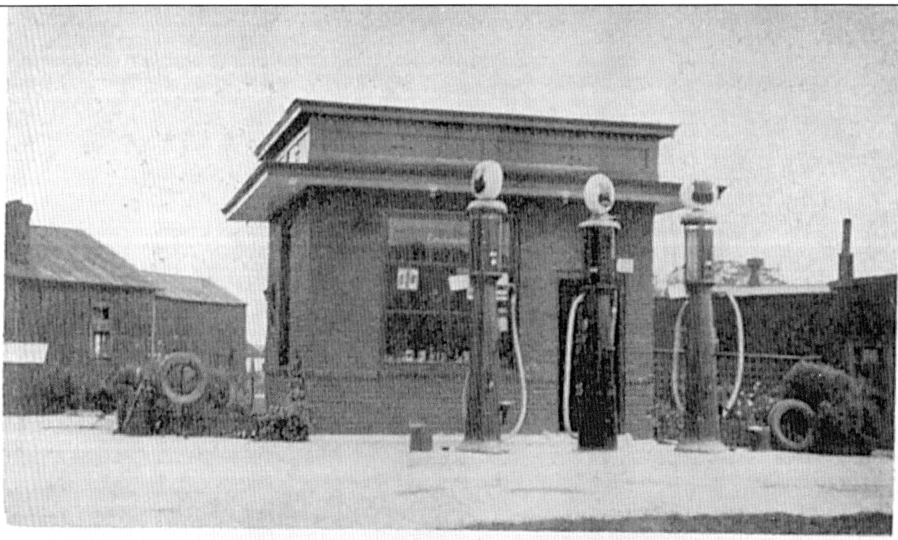

STUMBAUGH'S PHILLIPS "66" STATION

G. L. Stumbaugh has been operating the Phillips "66" Station at the present location the past eight years, having been employed at the station for the past fifteen years. The station sells Phillips "66" products, Lee Tires and Specialized Lubrication. The motto of the station is "Service with a Smile".

Stumbaugh's Phillips "66" Station is shown here in 1936.

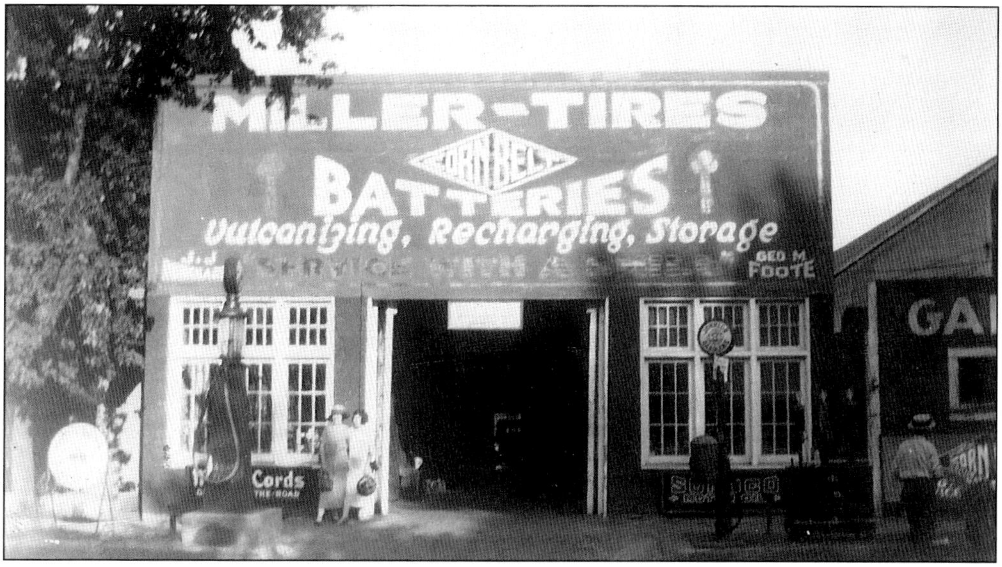

George Foote started the Corn Belt Battery Company in October of 1921, and he was joined by John J. Burkhardt in July of 1922. The building at 1120 Second Street now houses John's Autobody.

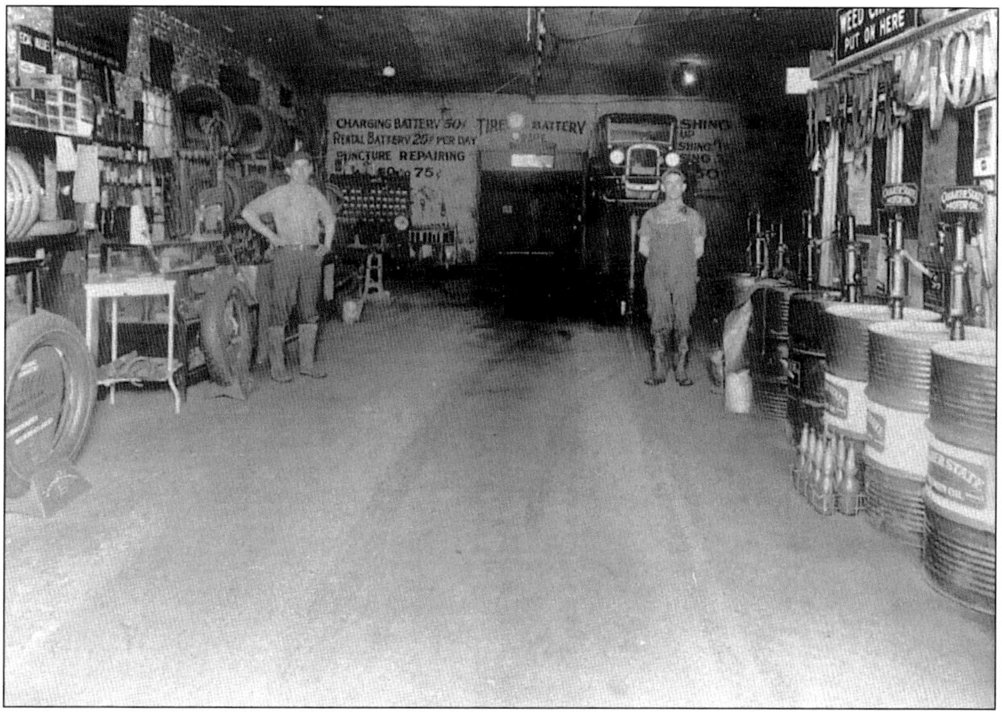

John J. "Johnnie" Burkhardt and George Foote are pictured here in their tire and battery shop.

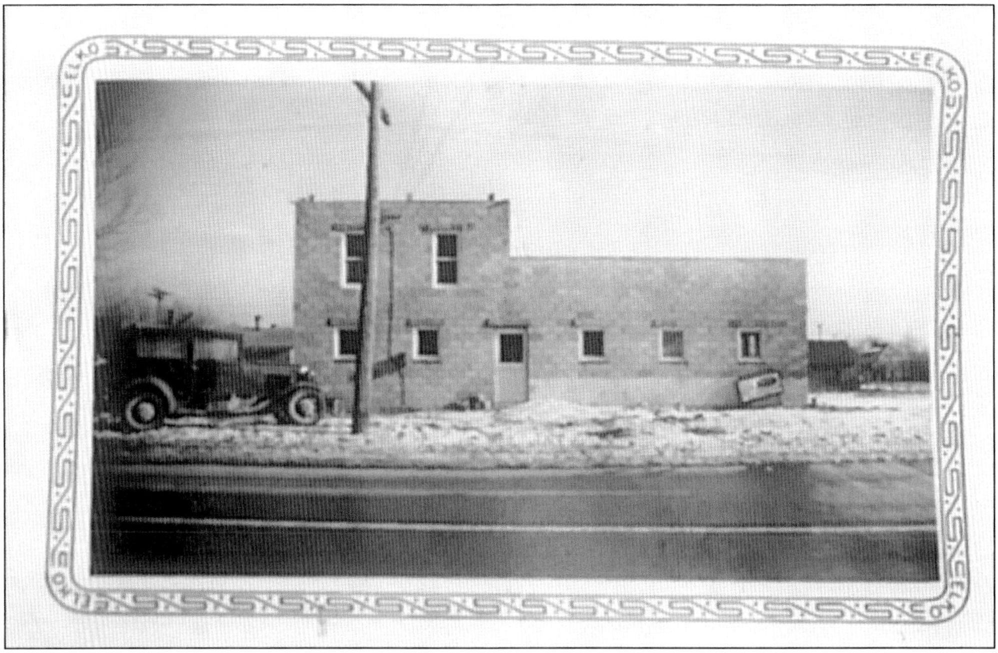

This photo depicts the "old" Barker Bowling Alley on Fourth Street, which is now Peter's Floral. Barker opened this business in 1941.

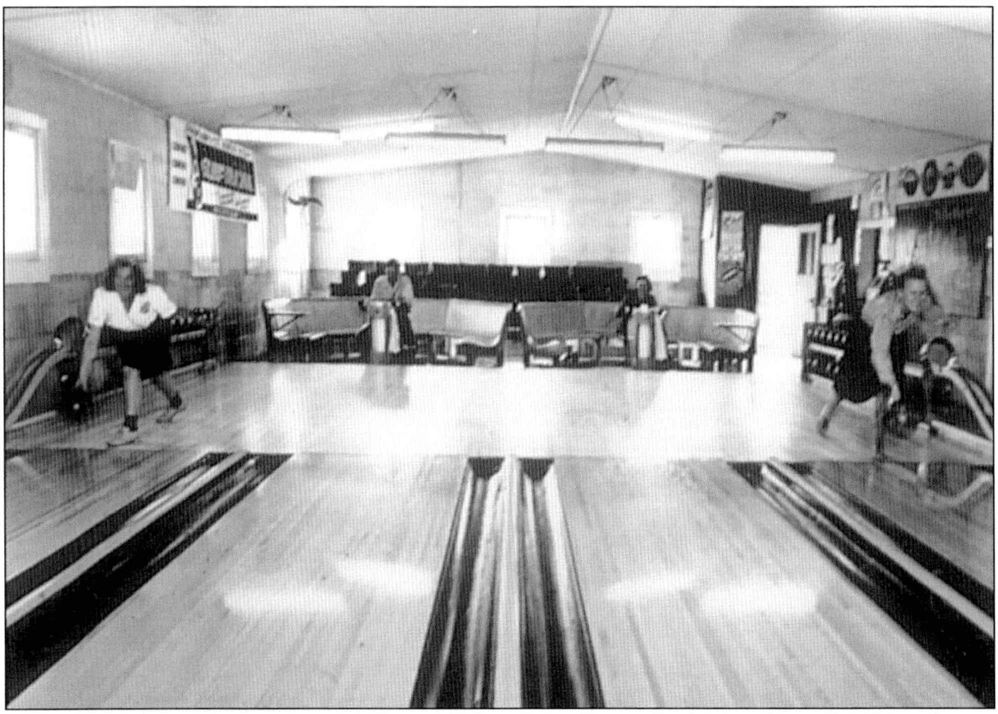

This photo shows the interior of the "old" bowling alley, which closed in the '50s. Graves Chevrolet built a new showroom on the site and moved there in 1961.

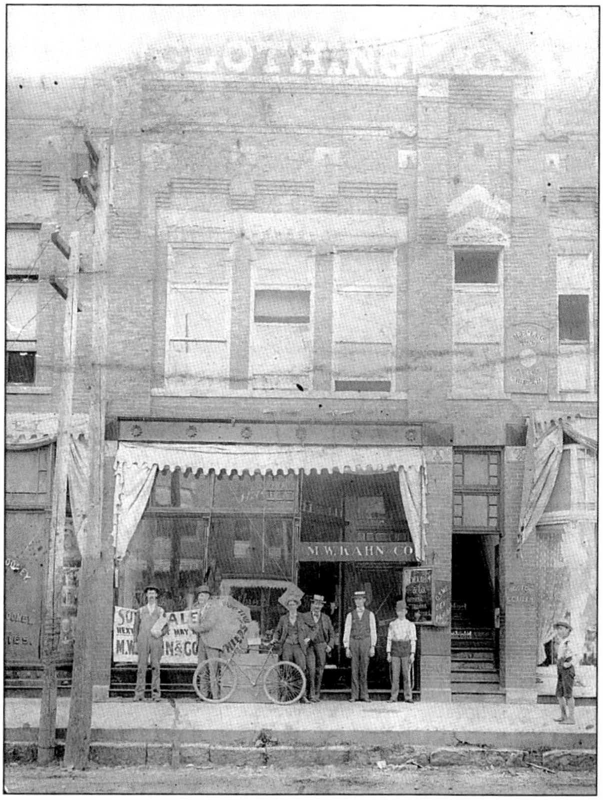

M.W. Kahn opened for business as a merchant tailor in a rented room in August of 1888. In September of 1889, he moved to the building at 932 Second Street—now Fedora's Pizza. The double brick wall of this building actually stopped the 1890 fire. In May of 1891, he moved his business into a new building at 949 Second Street. At that time, he employed 10 tailors to make suits.

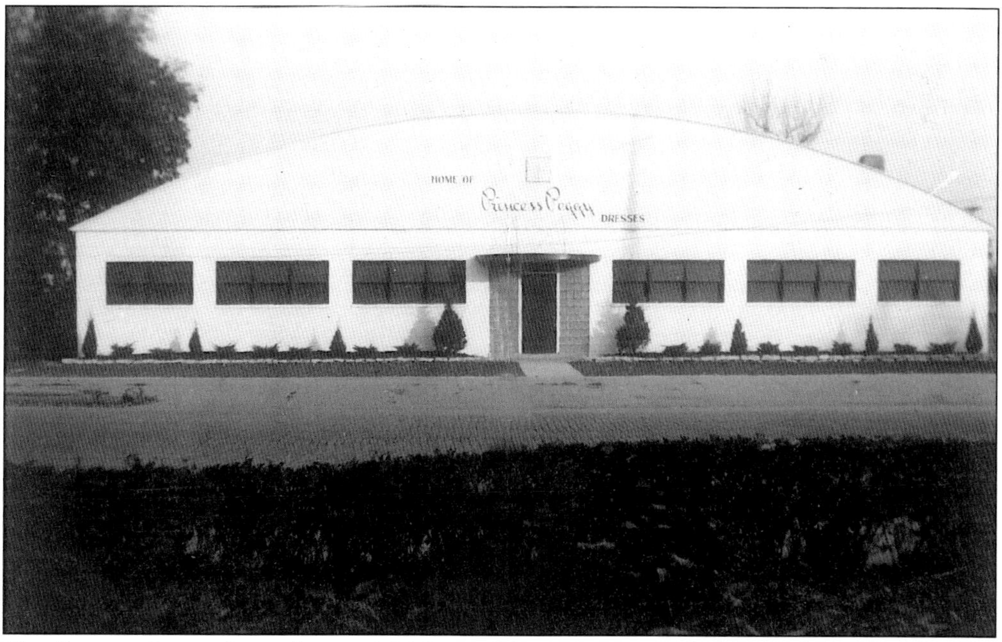

The Princess Peggy dress plant at 806 Second Street is pictured above. Chic Manufacturing Company began operations at its new plant in the former Seward Motor Company building in 1944. The plant closed permanently in 1958.

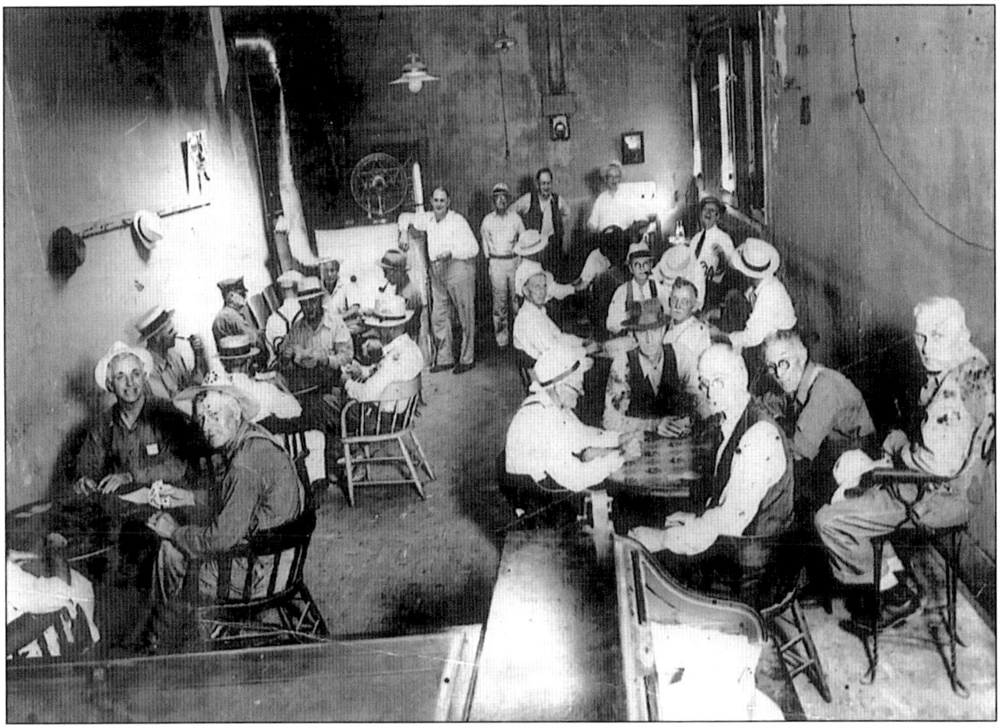

The back room of Nixon's Pool Hall at 920 Second Street is pictured above. (Courtesy of Lillian Cox Allen.)

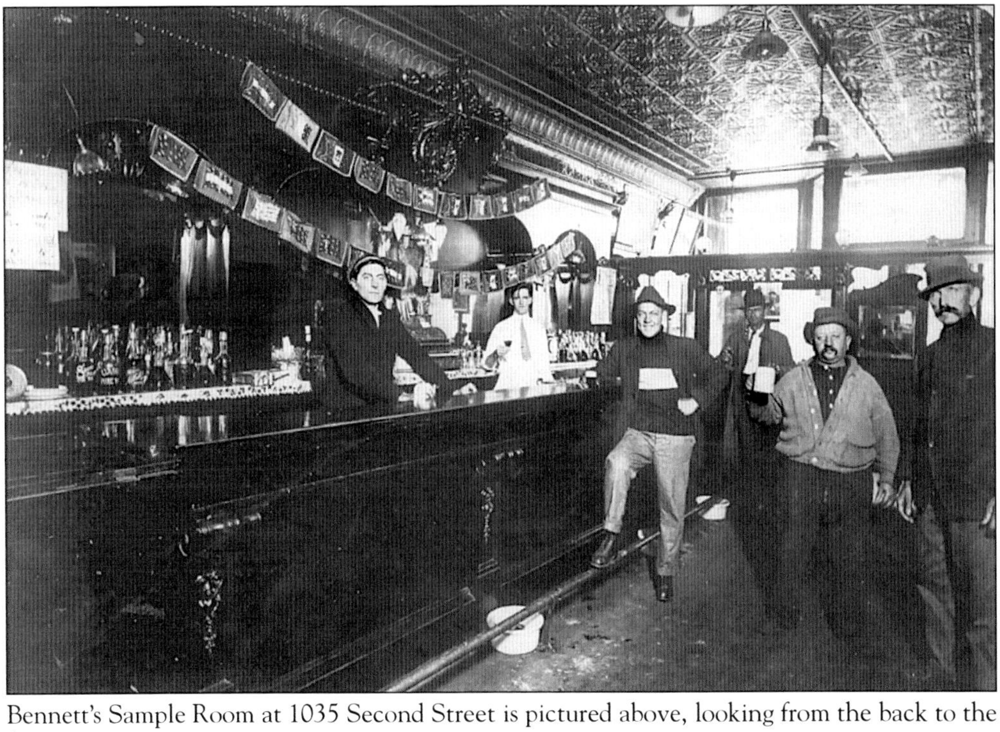

Bennett's Sample Room at 1035 Second Street is pictured above, looking from the back to the front.

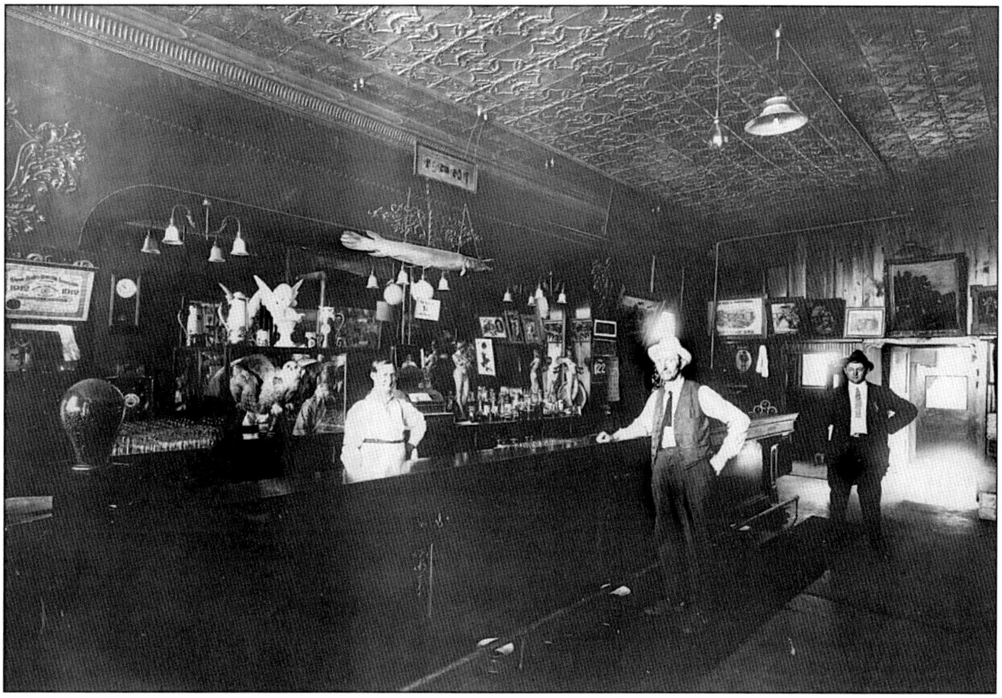

This photo depicts a 1912 saloon.

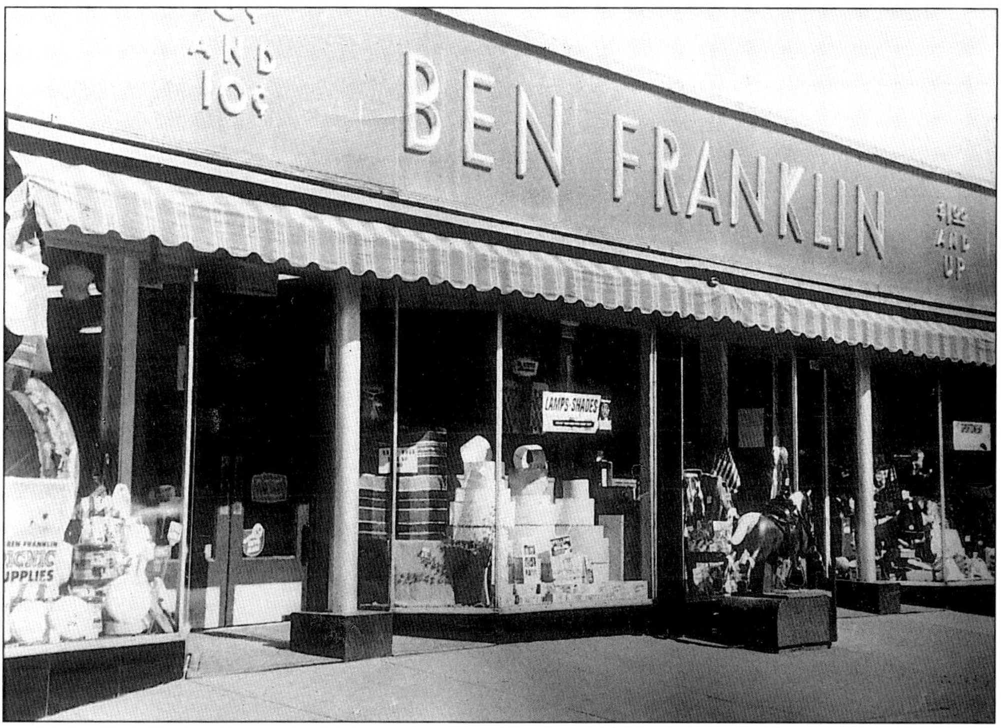

The Matthews store closed and became Smith Variety Store in 1937. John Lee bought the building in 1944 and turned it into a Ben Franklin variety store, and in 1997 the building became Sew & Such.

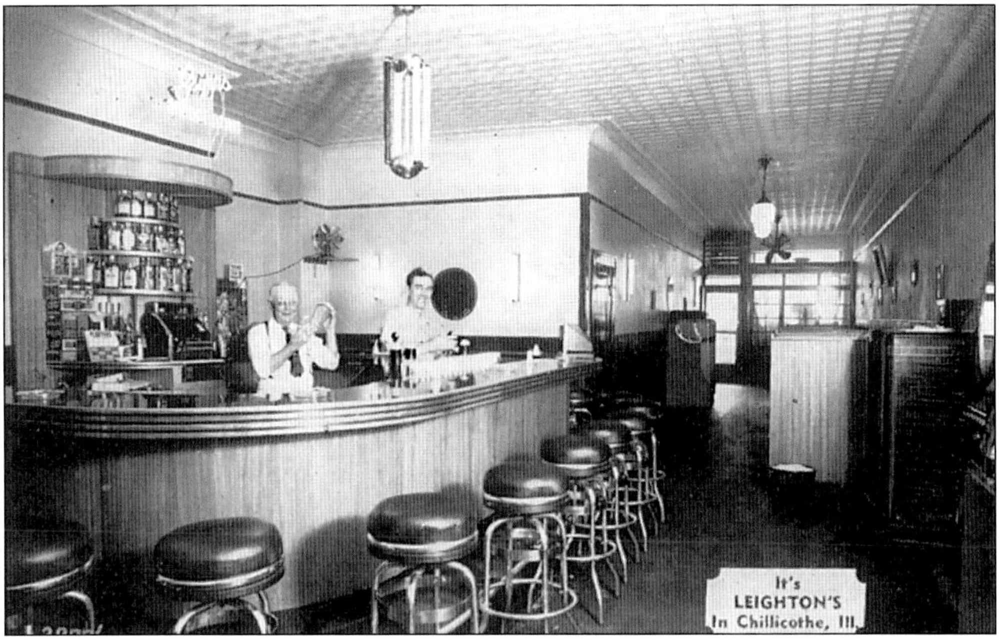

Leighton's Cocktail Lounge opened in 1941 at 911 Second Street in the Bacon Building. Pictured here are Harvey Crutchfield (left) and Chuck Leighton (right). (Courtesy of Tom Proctor.)

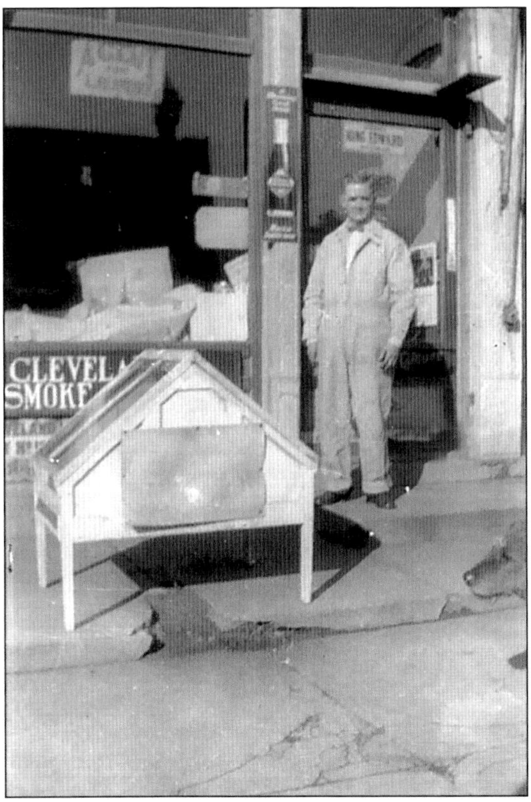

Henry Cleveland and his smoke shop are pictured at left. Cleveland initiated business in January of 1904, and in 1920 his shop was located in the building last used as Traub Real Estate—now a vacant lot north of the American Legion.

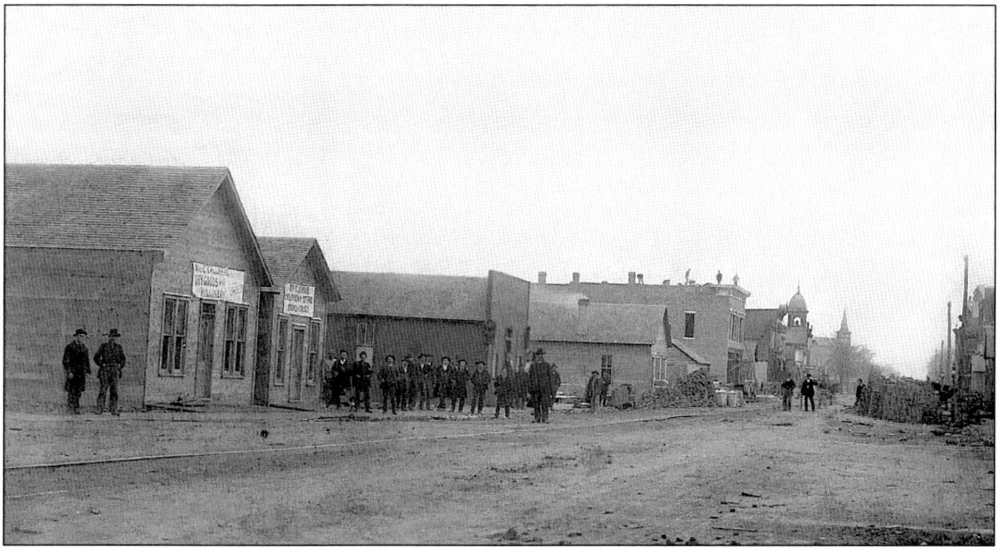

The east side of Second Street is pictured here looking south from Chestnut, rebuilding after the 1890 fire. The first store was Celcia Callahan's Dry Goods and Millinery and next to that was Dr. C. Johns' Books and Drugs. The brick building at the corner—under construction here—was built by John F. Lynch for a hardware store in 1903. Visible in the background is the bell tower on the old city hall and the St. John's Episcopal Church at Second and Elm Streets.

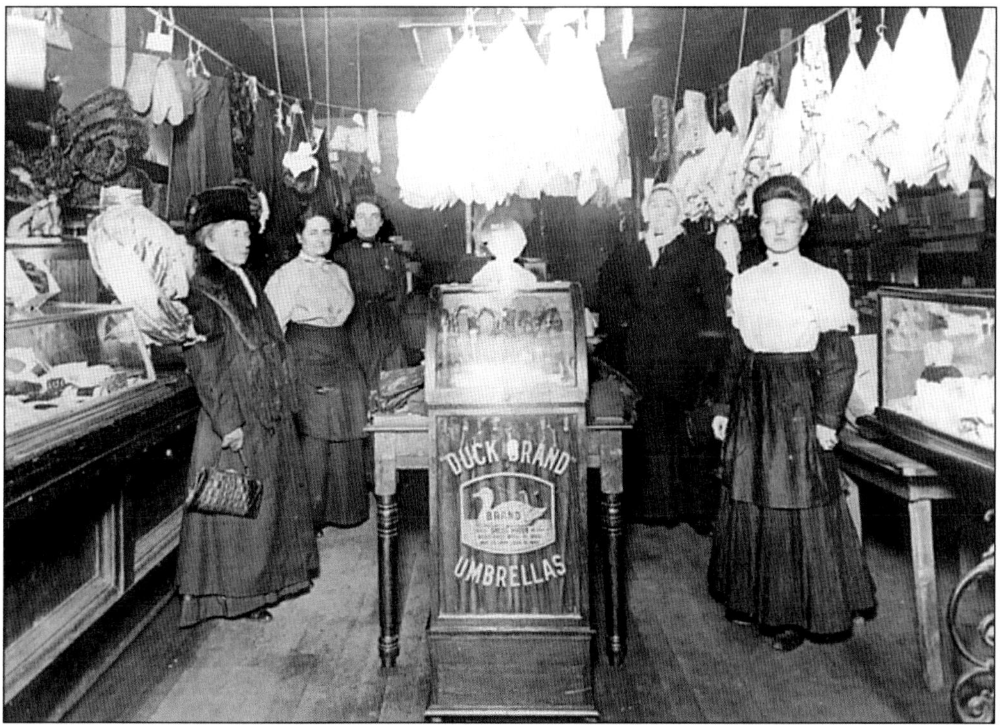

This photo depicts the inside of Celcia Callahan's store. Before the 1890 fire she ran a millinery store, and after rebuilding at 1044 Second Street she carried dry goods as well as millinery. She became affiliated with John Cash Penney and operated one of his Golden Rule Stores, which finally became a J.C. Penney store.

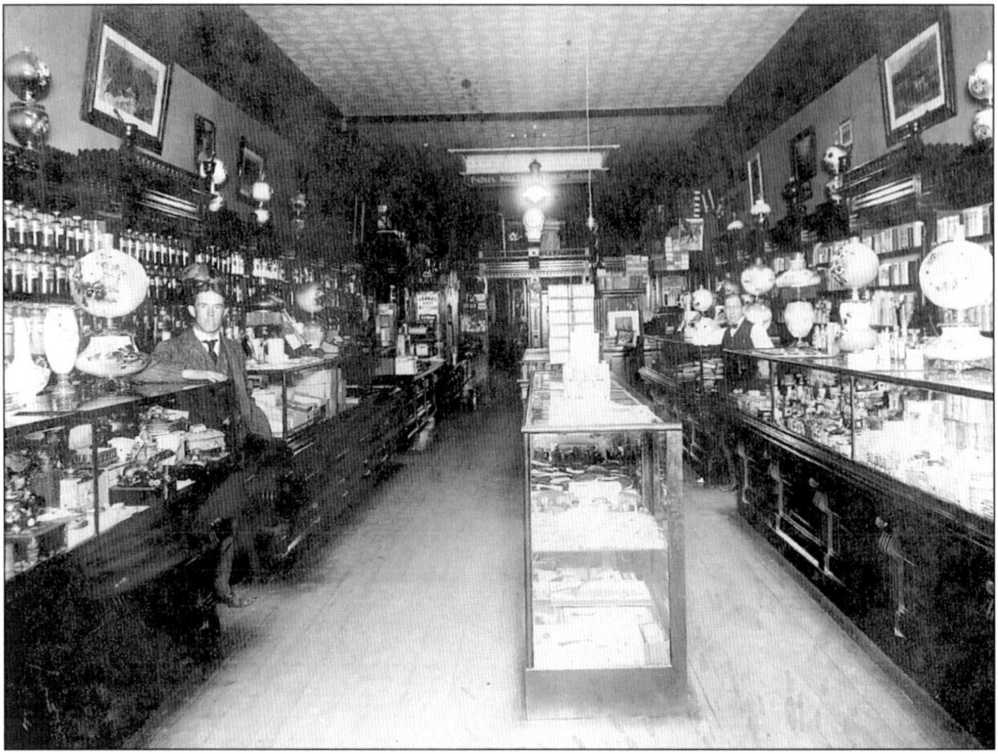

This photo depicts the interior of the Mead Drug Store at 941 Second Street in about 1905. Fred Mead is on the left and Hugh Nurse is on the right. William Mead opened a drug store in 1868, and the store was sold to Willie Moffitt in 1910. (Courtesy of Mary Nurse Meyer.)

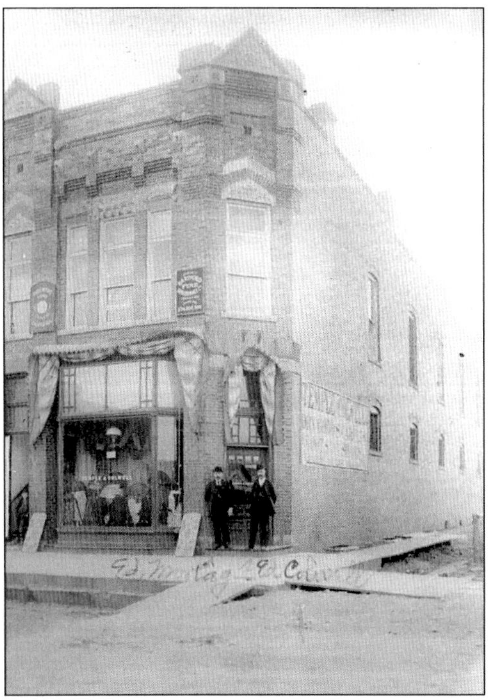

Temple and Colwell Dry Goods is pictured at what is now 953 Second Street—the old Truitt-Matthews Bank. This corner building was next door to the M.W. Kahn Company building. In 1897, E.B. Colwell sold the business to E.F. Mortag.

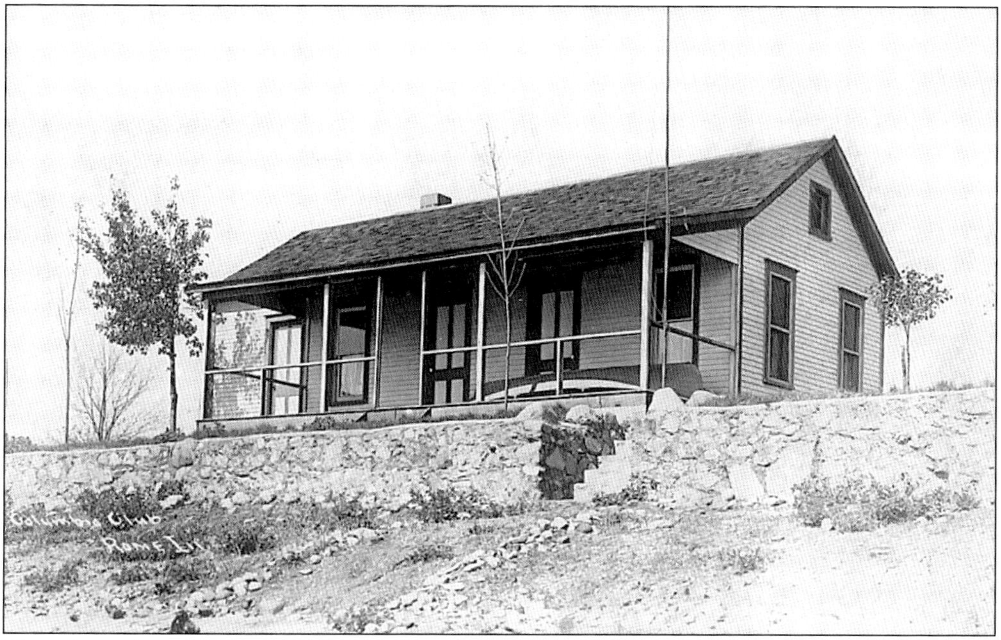

This photo depicts the Columbia Club at Rome in June of 1910.

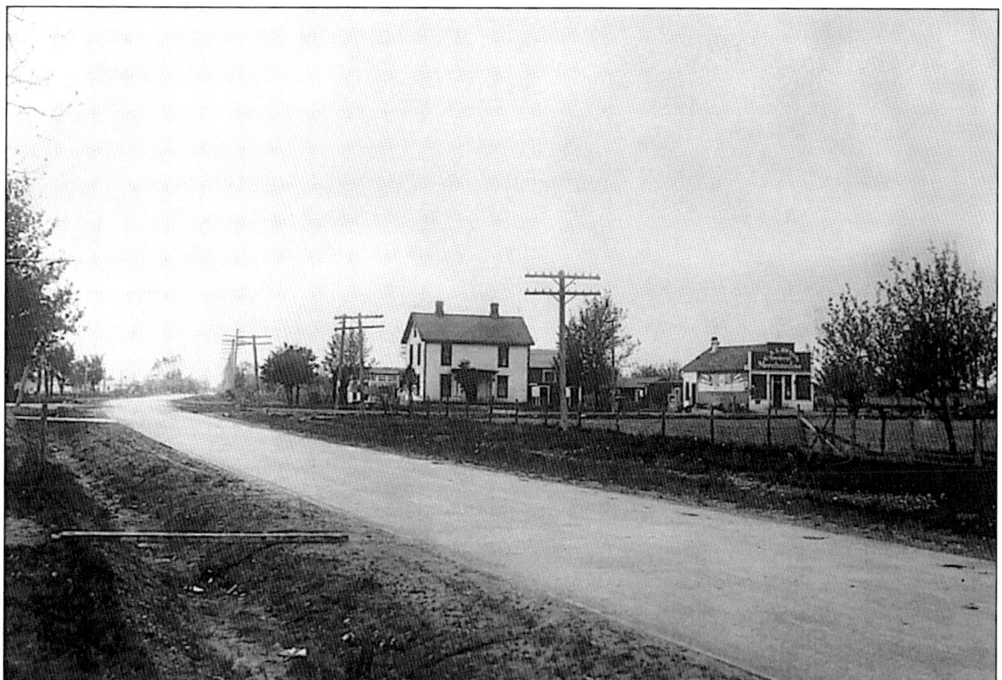

Old Route 29 and Knox in Rome, with the original Lawson's Store on the right, are pictured above. A new building was erected on the north side of Knox in 1948. The house and store were both owned by Anton Ferguson, who rented to Lawson's.

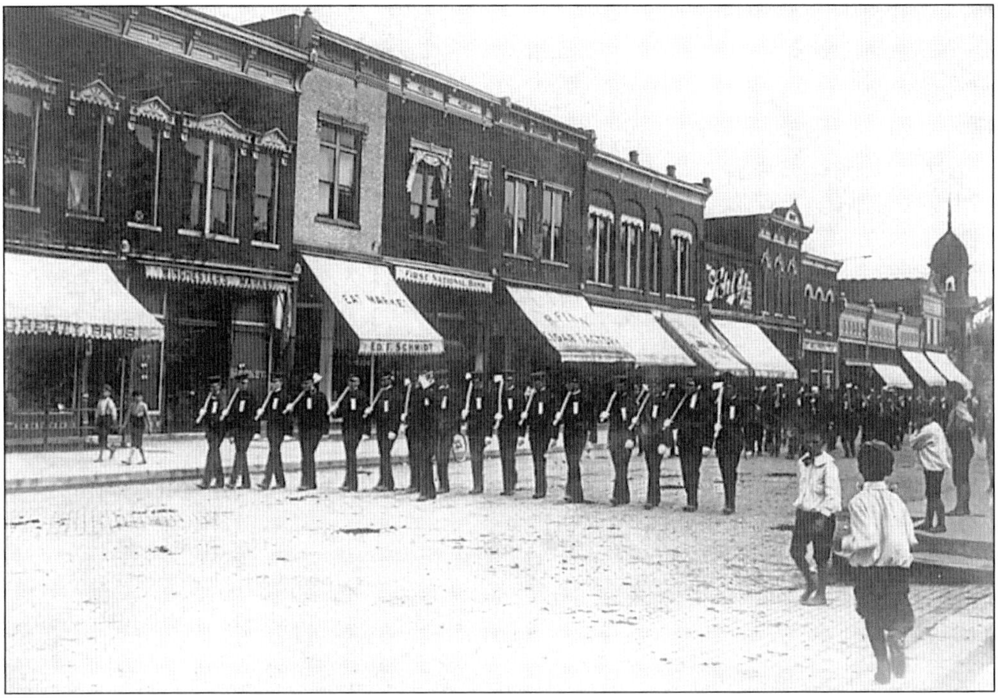

The Modern Woodmen Lodge members are pictured here in a parade up a brick Second Street. The first awning is Daugherty Brothers Saloon at 952, then Winchester Market, Ed Schmidt Meat Market, First National Bank at 944, Richard Finn Cigar Factory, the Schlitz sign on the Wolff Saloon, and the bell tower at city hall.

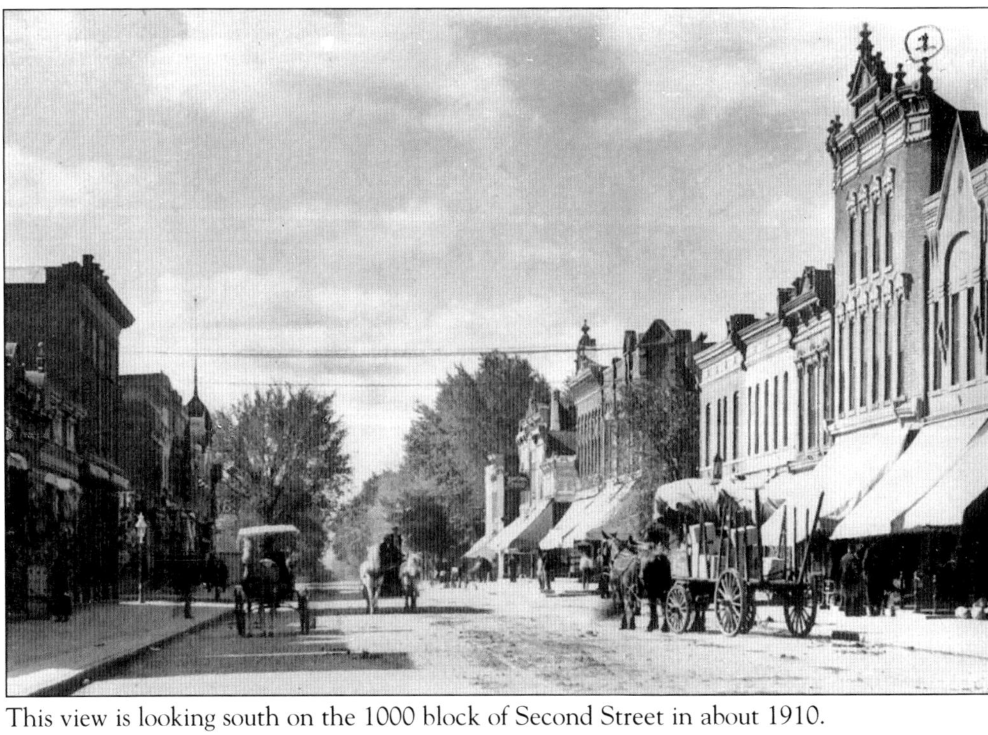

This view is looking south on the 1000 block of Second Street in about 1910.

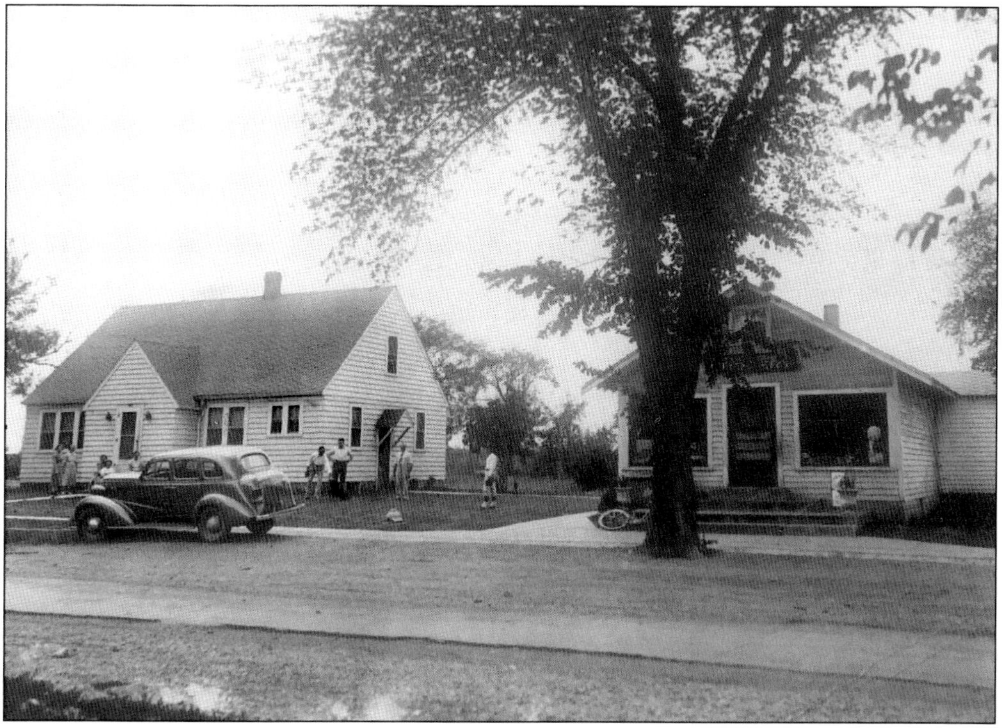

Pictured here are the Tucker family home and grocery store on Fifth Street north of Hickory Street. Tucker's was one of several small groceries that were scattered around Chillicothe.

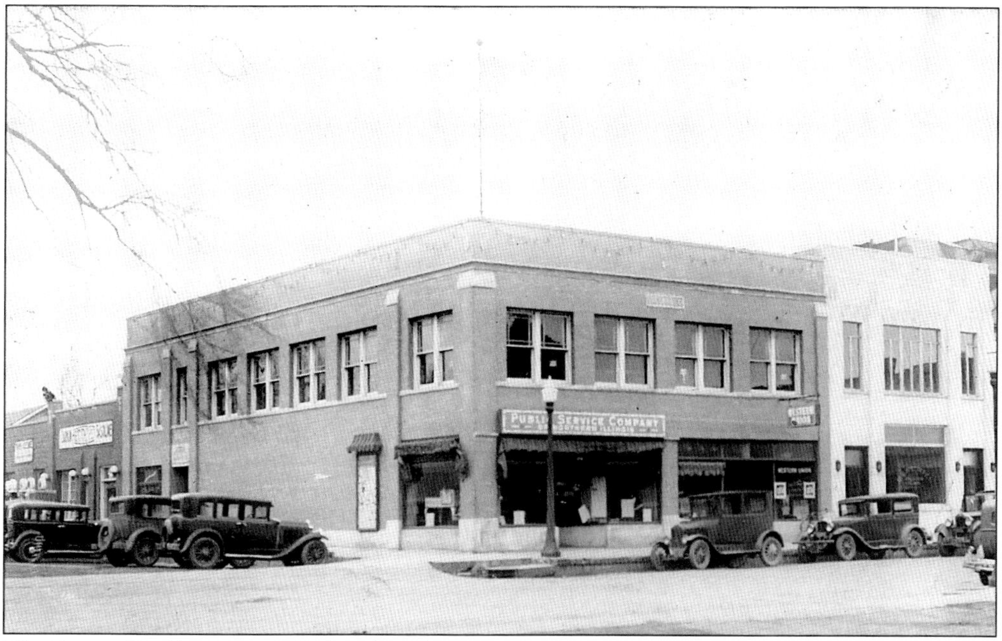

The Bacon Building at Second and Walnut Streets is pictured above. Built by Frank Bacon in 1930, it has contained many businesses throughout the years. The white building to the right was constructed by Bacon to serve as the post office, and did so until the government built another building in 1940. (Courtesy of Bernie Vonk.)

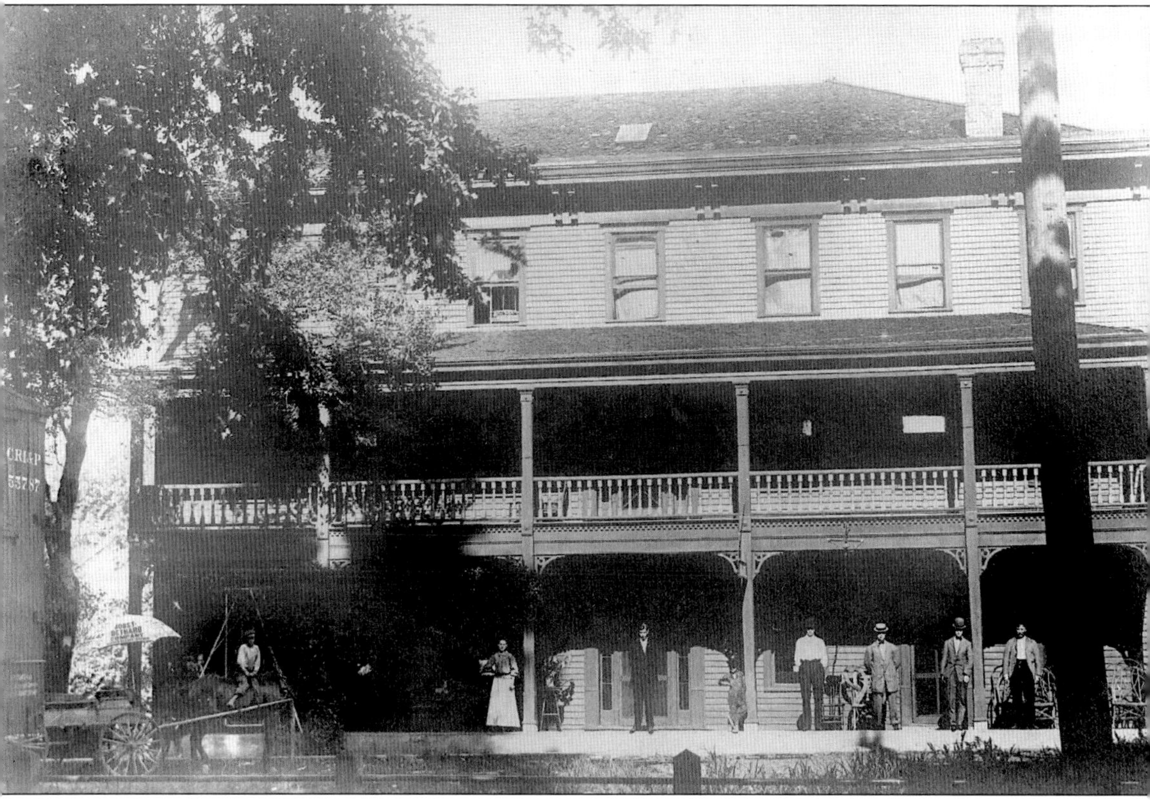

This photo depicts the Union Hotel on Third Street, south of Cedar, on August 21, 1908—Dennis McKeel was the proprietor. John Wm. McKeel is standing in the center of the photo in front of the door, and his father, Dennis McKeel, is wearing the derby and leaning against the post on the right side of the photo. The hotel was destroyed by a fire that the firemen had under control until a runaway team of horses snapped off the fire plug and left them with no water.

Two

FESTIVE GATHERINGS

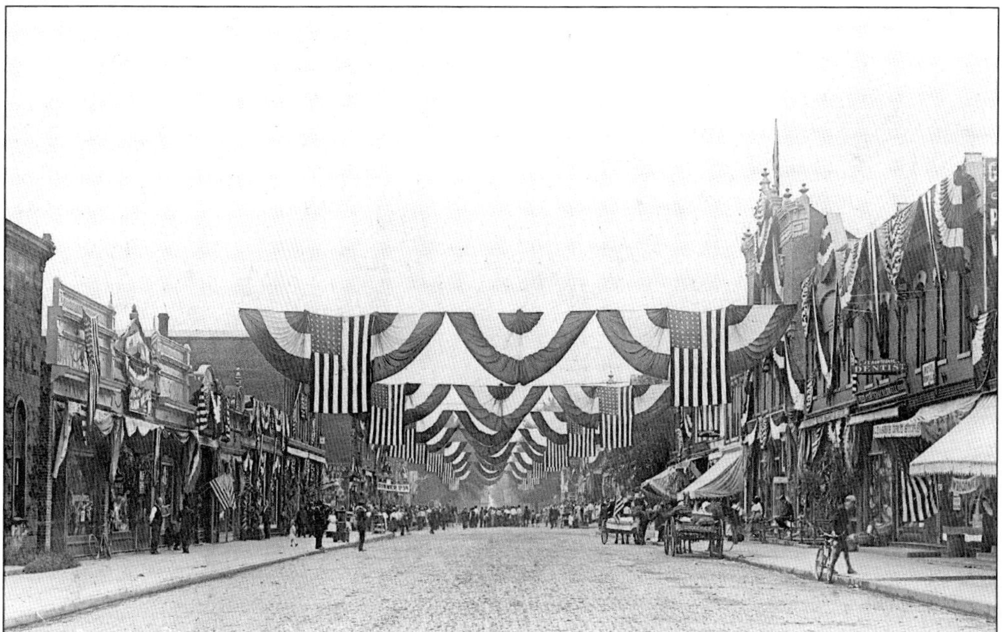

Downtown Chillicothe is pictured here about 1910, preparing for a parade. This view is looking south from the north end of Second Street. Note the absence of autos, the brick street, and the three-story Kelly Building on the right.

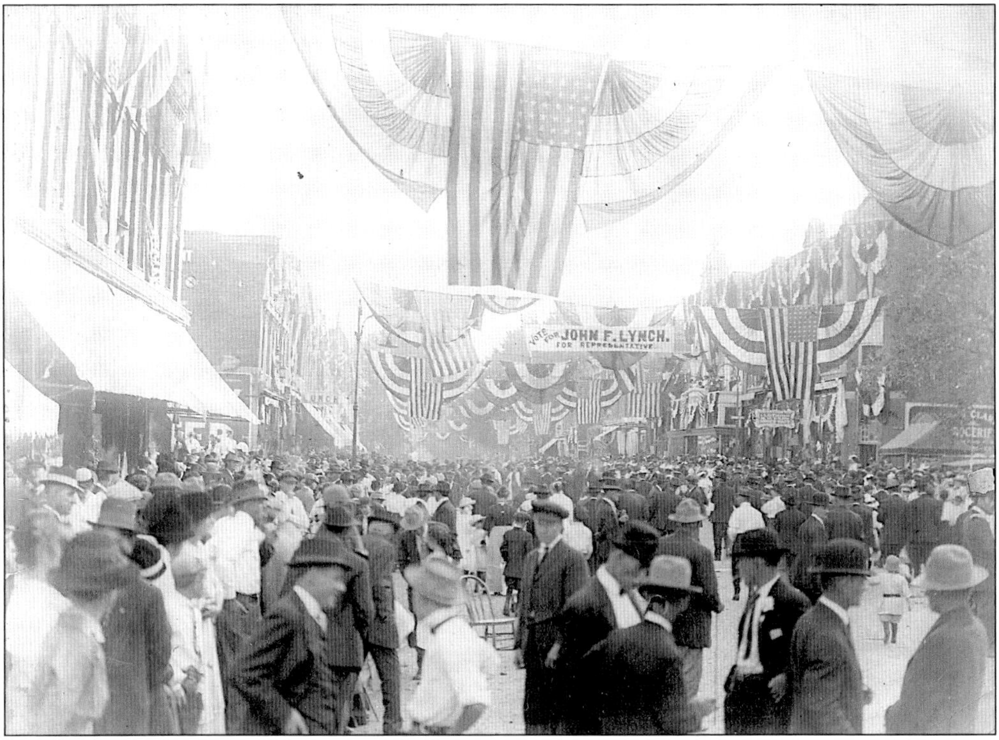

A large festival crowd is pictured here. Tom Clark was selling groceries in the building on the corner of Second and Pine Streets where Colwell and Mortag had sold dry goods.

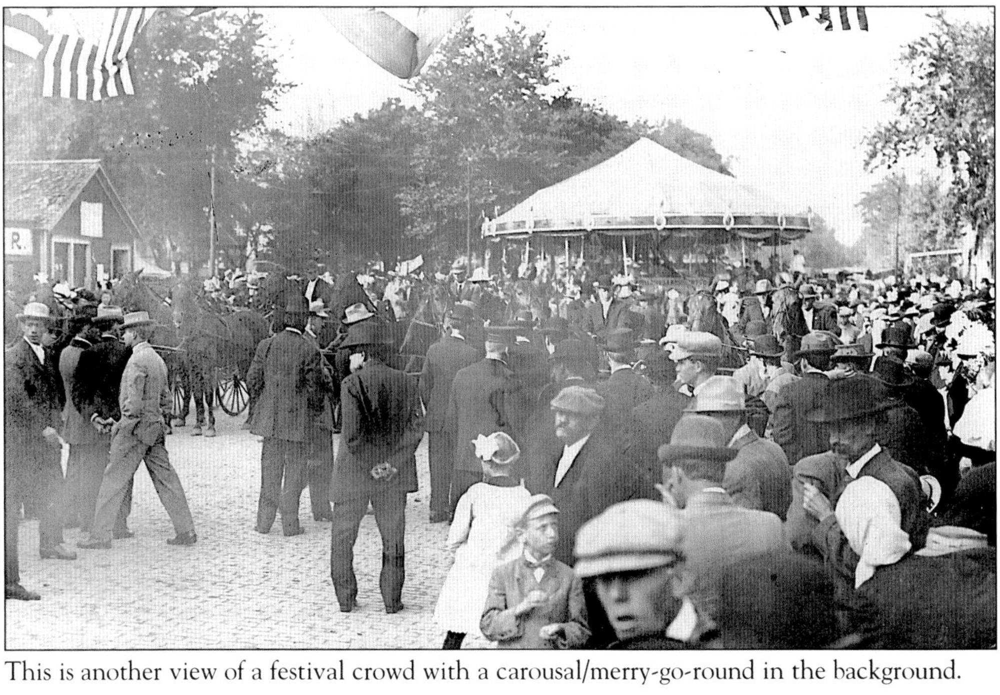

This is another view of a festival crowd with a carousal/merry-go-round in the background.

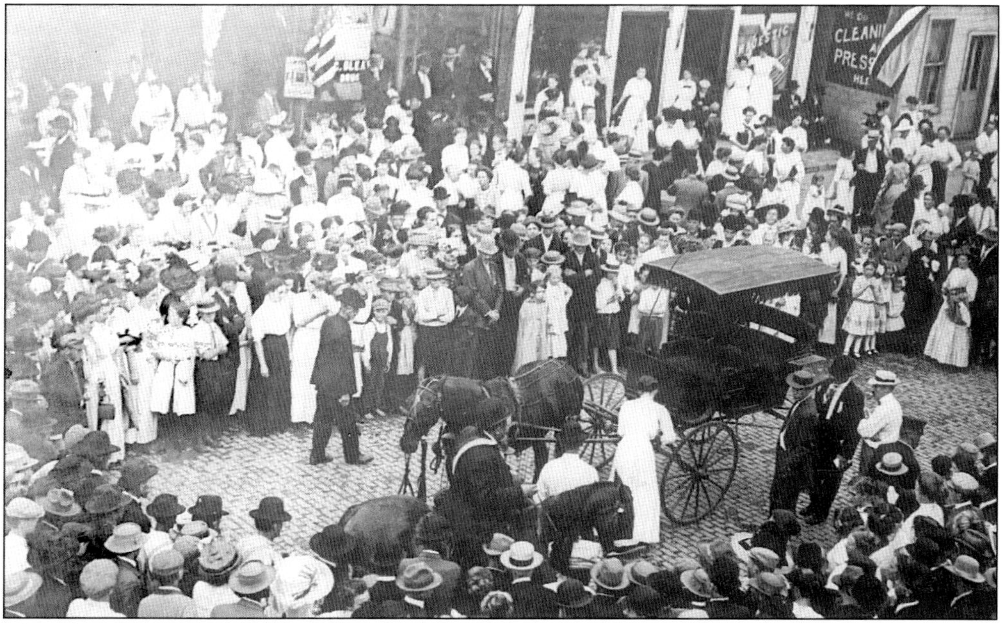

This photo depicts the September 6–7, 1911 festival. The flag in the upper center of the photo is in front of Gleason's Drugs—now the American Legion at 1043 Second Street. The next building to the right was last occupied by Andy's Barber Shop and Traub Realty, and the last building stood where Bill Devoss's barber shop was located. (Courtesy of Mary Nurse Meyer.)

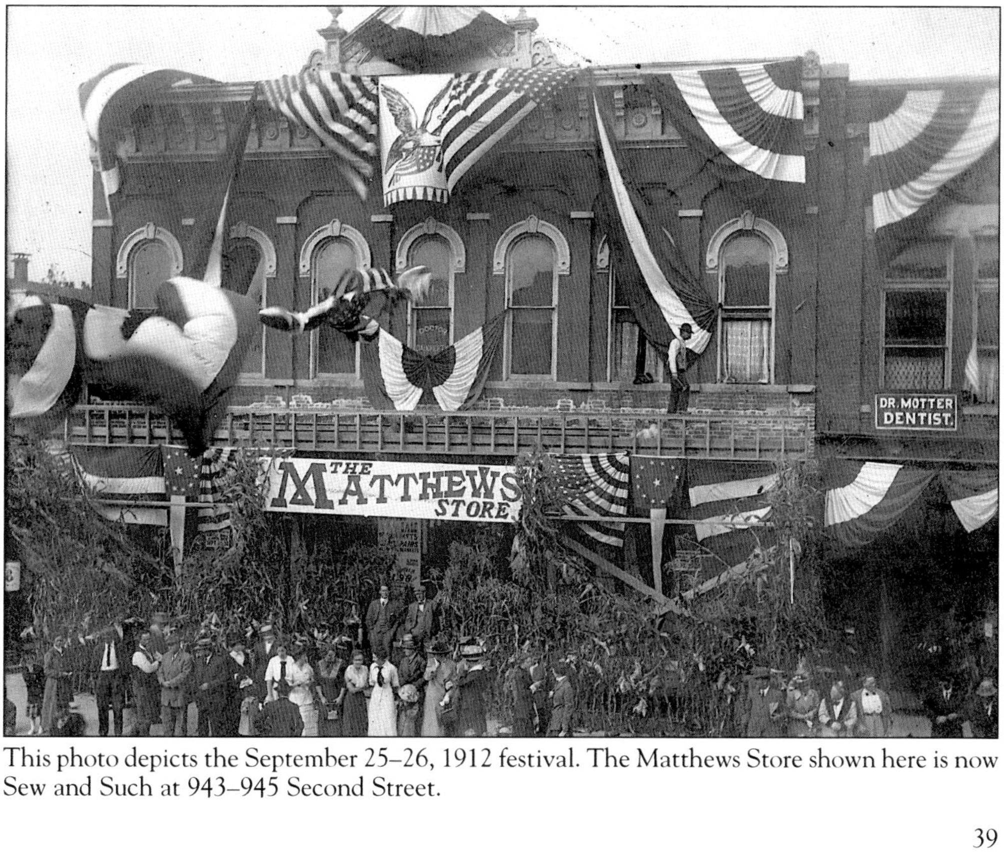

This photo depicts the September 25–26, 1912 festival. The Matthews Store shown here is now Sew and Such at 943–945 Second Street.

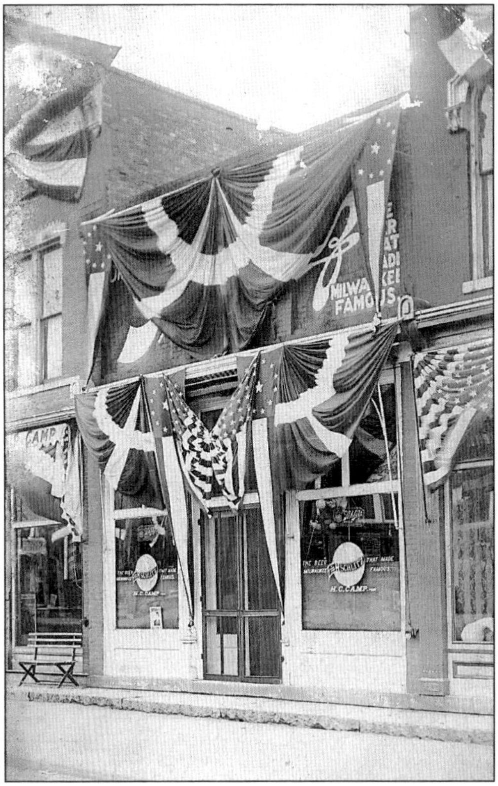

H.C. Camp tavern at 932 Second Street—now Fedora's Pizza—is pictured at left. Camp's barber shop was located to the left.

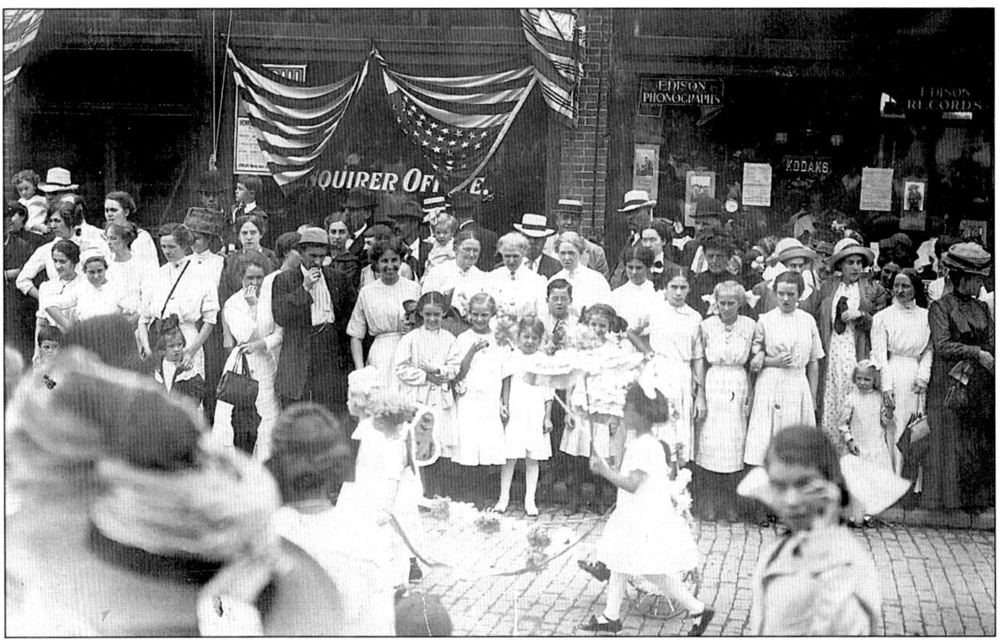

This photo depicts a festival crowd watching a children's parade. *The Chillicothe Enquirer* office was then at 1032 Second Street, and Bayles' Jewelry was at 1030 Second Street.

This baby buggy and its occupant were decorated for the 1914 Chillicothe Harvest Festival parade.

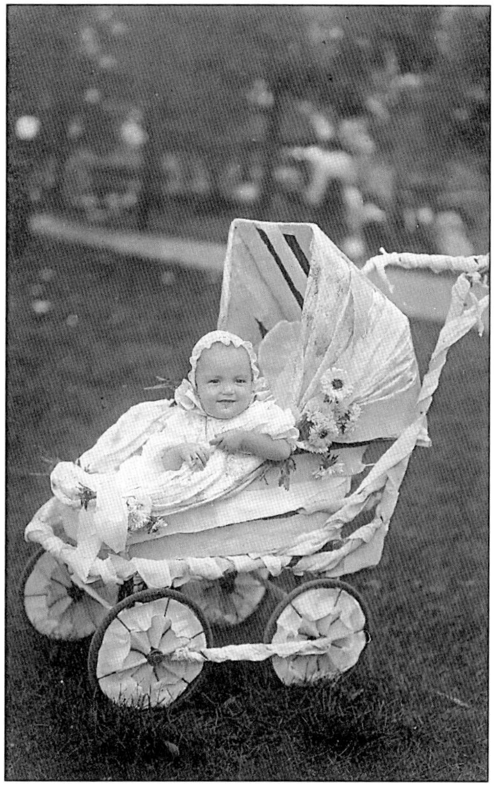

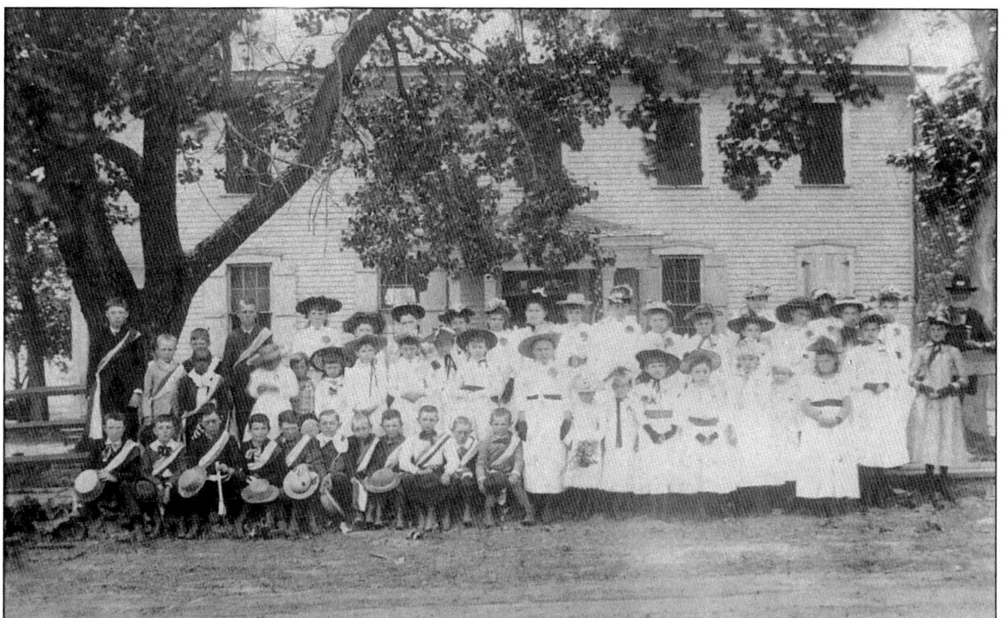

Pictured above is Lawn Ridge in Hallock Township in 1890. The boys are wearing tri-color sashes, the girls have round badges, and the elderly man at the extreme right is wearing his GAR veterans uniform. (Courtesy of Mary Nurse Meyer.)

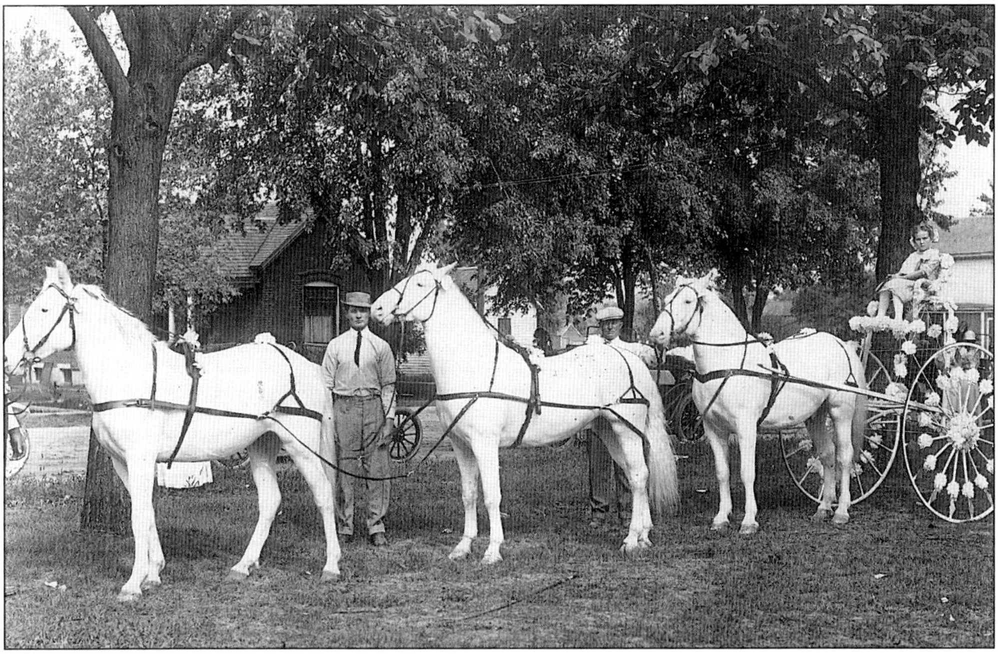

This tandem hitch of matching whites is ready for a festival parade.

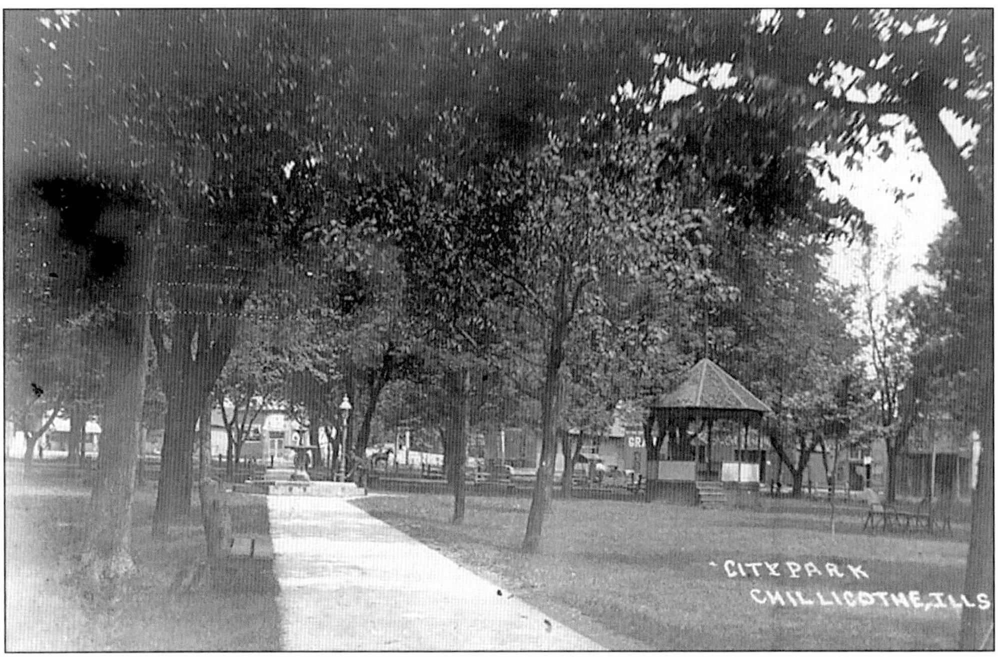

Chillicothe City Park is pictured here from the southeast corner. The sidewalk leads to the fountain and then on to the depot. To the right is the band stand, and behind it is the grain office that stood east of the depot.

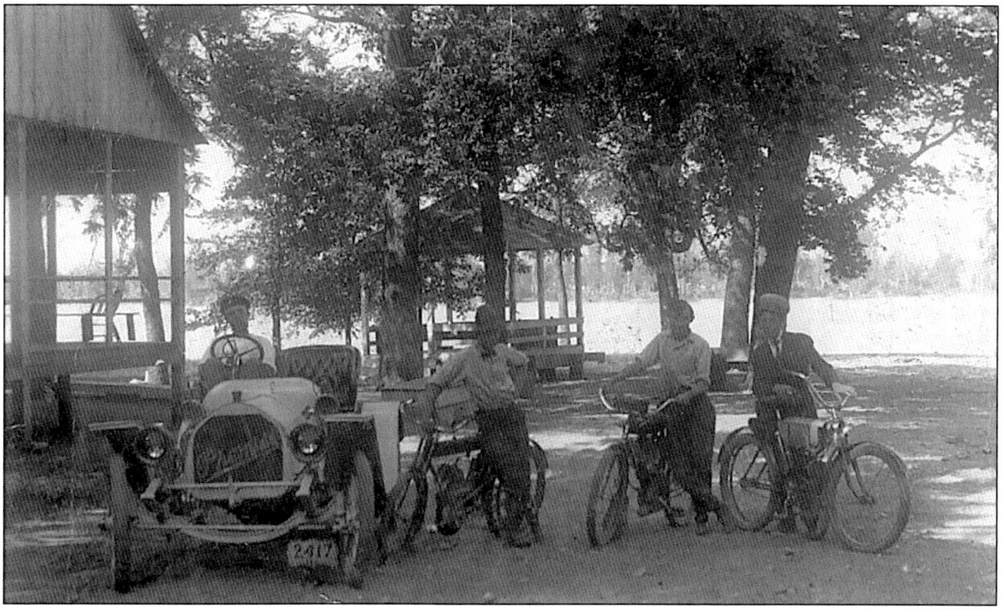

Phillip Matthews is pictured here in his Premier automobile at Columbia Park with three friends on motorcycles.

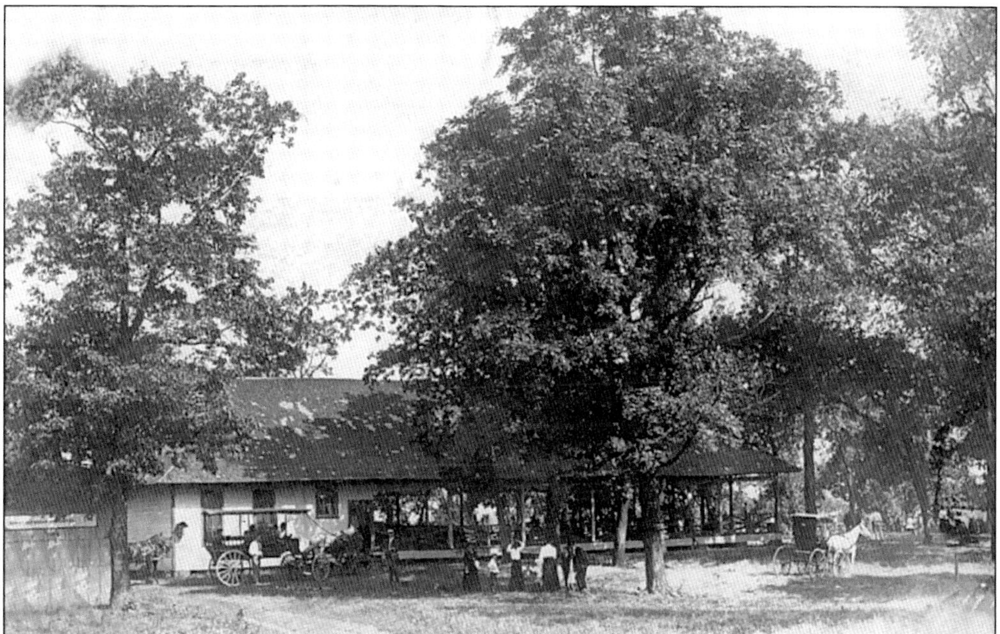

This is Columbia Park in 1903. Note the horse-drawn omnibus on the drive to the left in the photo.

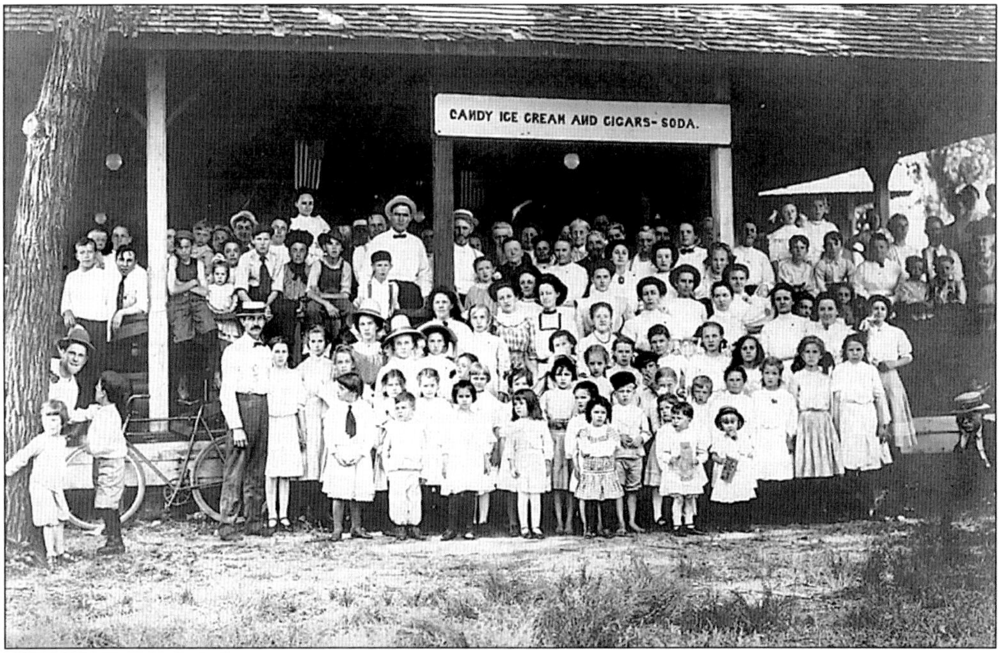

Pictured here is a group outing at Columbia Park—now Shore Acres.

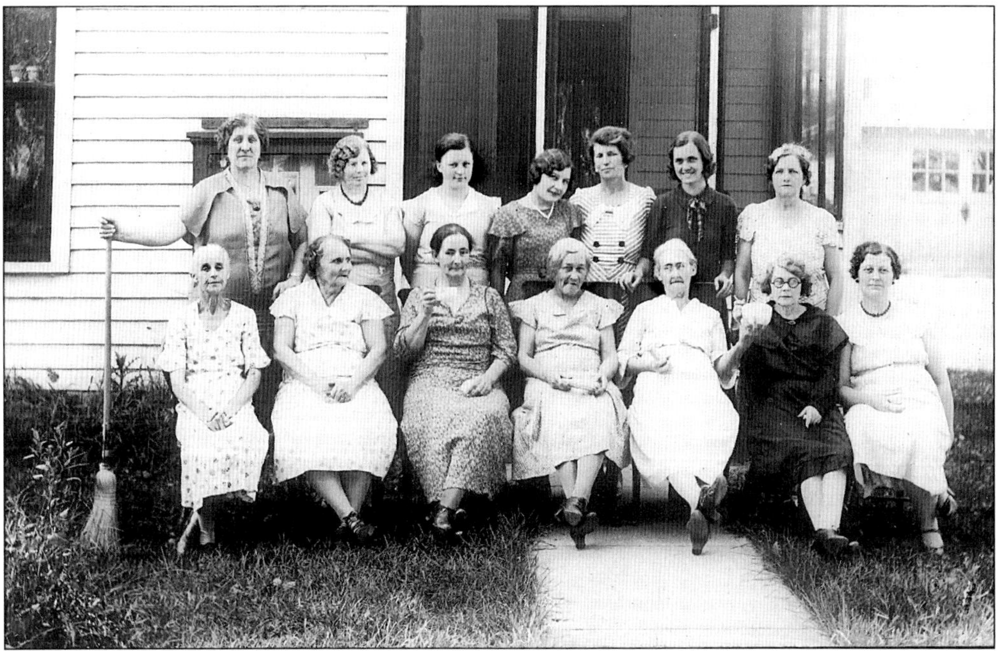

This photo depicts the Women's Society. They are, from left to right: (seated) Mrs. Clark, Mrs. McLaughlin, Mrs. Harvey, Mrs. Gurnett, Mrs. McPhail, Annie Jones, Maud Montonye; (standing) Mrs. Abbott, Mrs. Joe Beebe, Gualetta Kent, Helen Long, Mary Oakes, Jaquita Ues, Mrs. T. Goodwin. (Courtesy of Mr. and Mrs. L.E. Clark.)

Three

Area Families

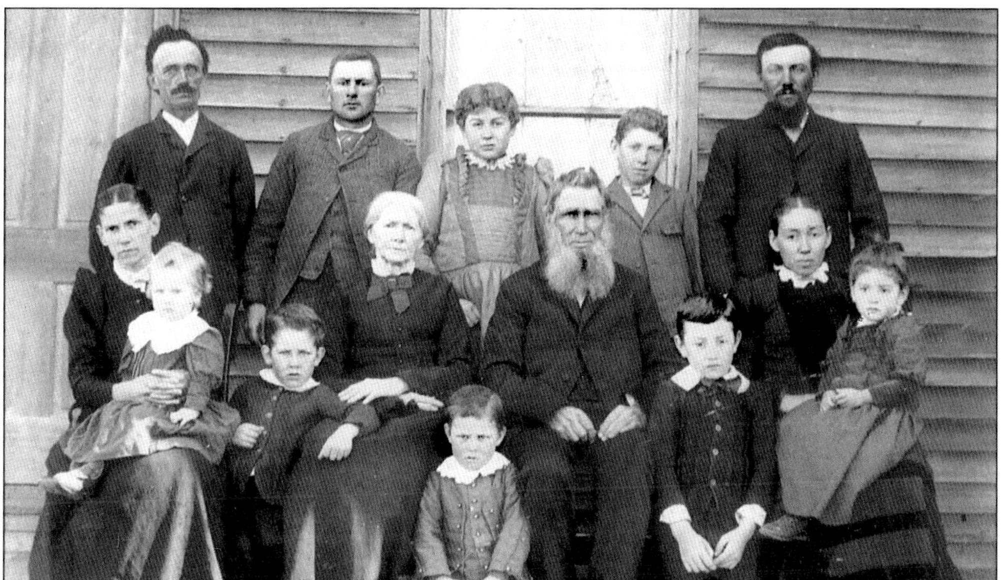

When one studies the settlement of this area, one finds that the families moved here in extended groups. There were the families of the Reeds, Sillimans, Hicks, Roots, Nurses, and Stowells, and once they arrived, they inter-married with the other families that were settling. Pictured here are: (seated) Mrs. Oscar (Alice Clark) Stowell holding Ira Stowell, Arthur Stowell, Mrs. John Clark, John Stowell, Mr. John Clark, Fred Harlin, and Mrs. Frank (Ella Clark) Harlin holding Edith Harlin; (standing) Oscar Stowell, Lew Clark, Mary Harlin (later Nurse), Alvin Harlin, Frank Harlin. (Courtesy of Mary Nurse Meyer.)

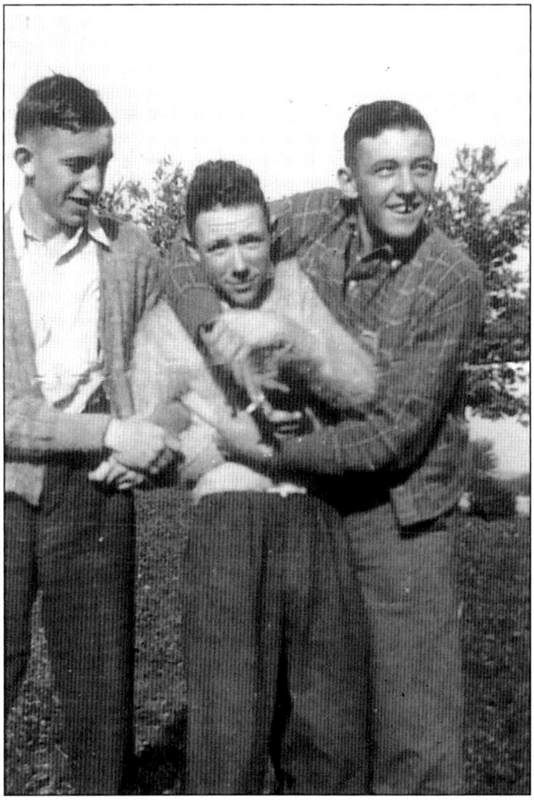

Jim Snyder, Dick Bauer, and Hank Foster are pictured here in 1937.

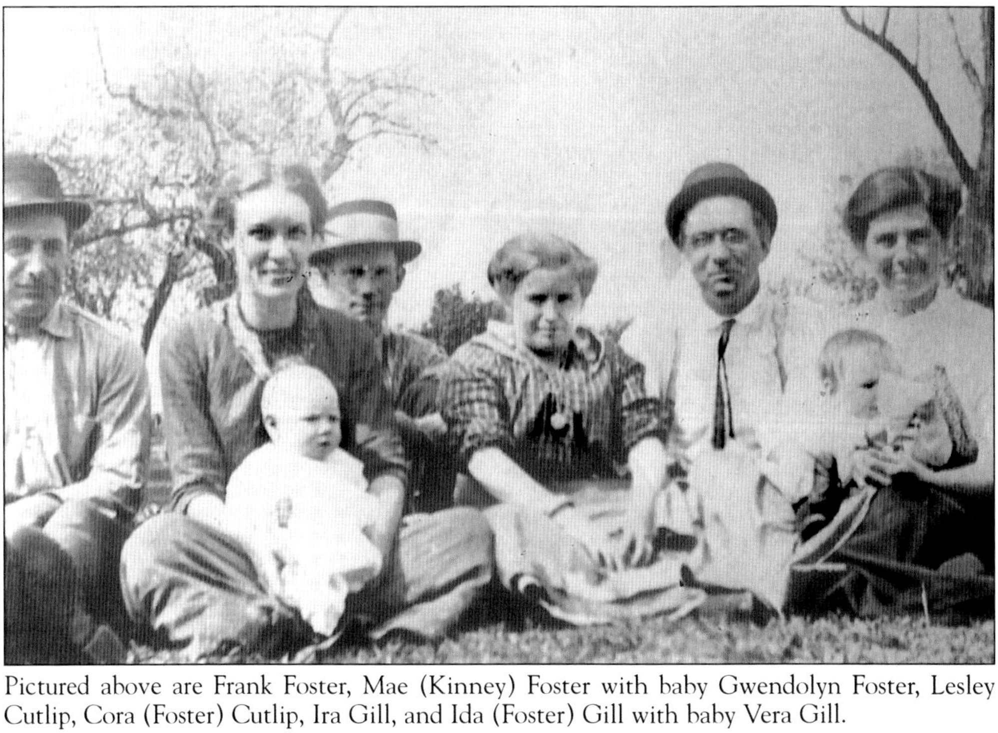

Pictured above are Frank Foster, Mae (Kinney) Foster with baby Gwendolyn Foster, Lesley Cutlip, Cora (Foster) Cutlip, Ira Gill, and Ida (Foster) Gill with baby Vera Gill.

Otto and Ida Wolske, with Inez, Mabel, and Loola are pictured here.

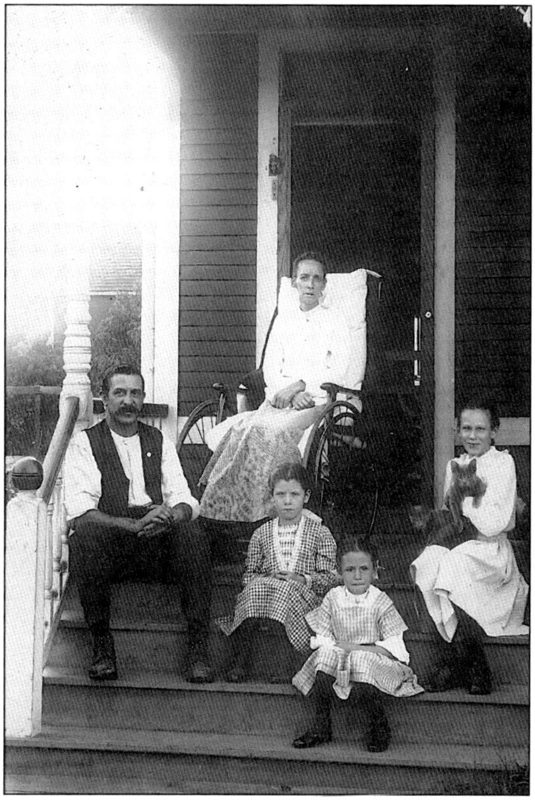

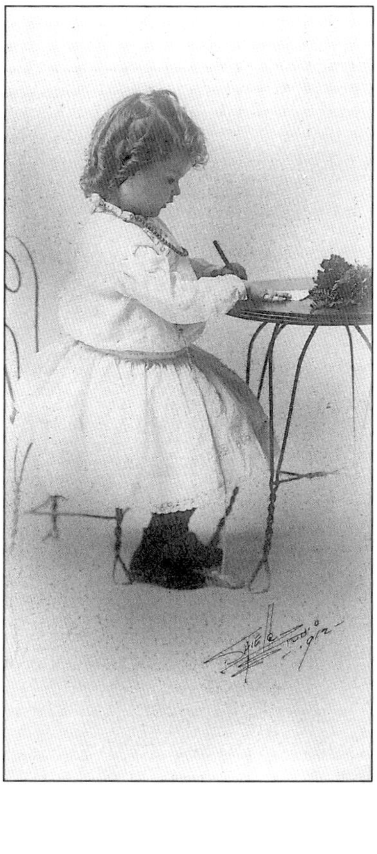

Ruth Sturm practices her new skill of writing at a child-sized ice cream parlor-style table and chair in this photo.

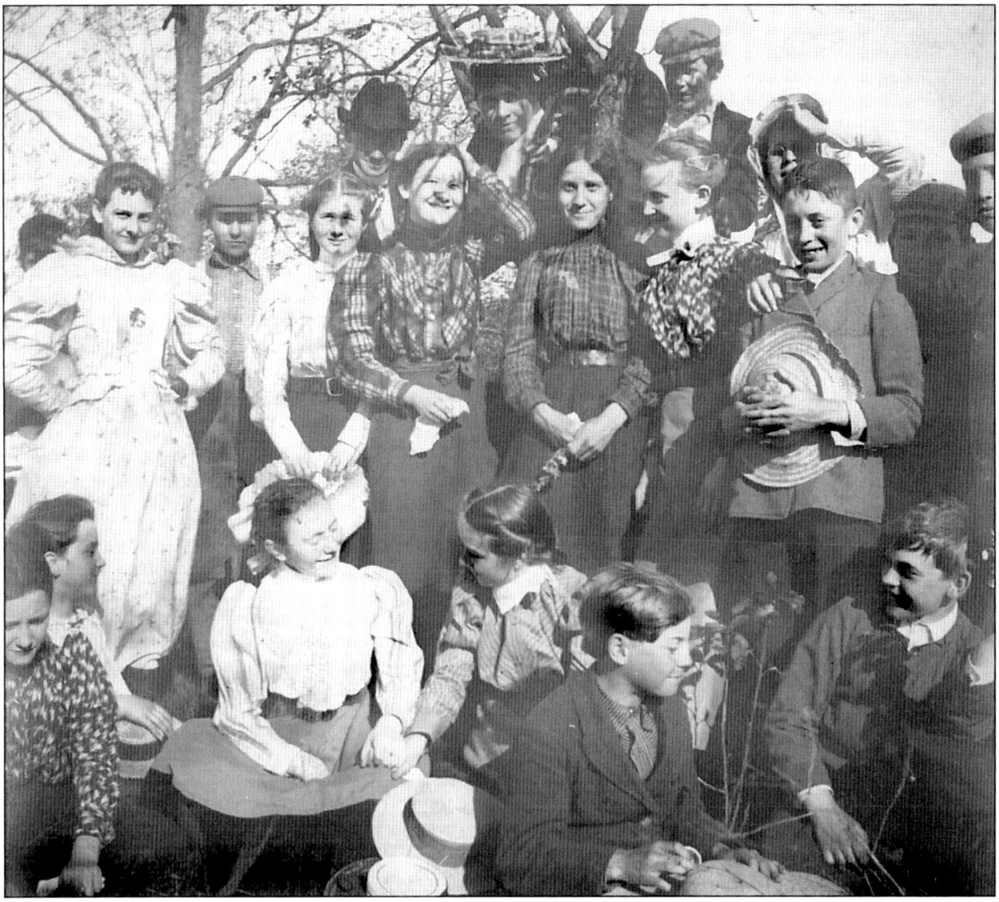

Pictured here are Gerald Trimble, Harry Bailey, Frank Kilroy, Charlie Christman, Ollie Epley, Alfred Hawkins, Anne Caldwell, Edna Hunter, Ida Taylor, Mabel Merrill, Stella Van Dusen, Arthur Burns, George Brewer, John O'Dowd, Willie Piper, Joe Gullett, Edith Littell, Ruby Stevenson, Nina Edminster, and Laura Drillon.

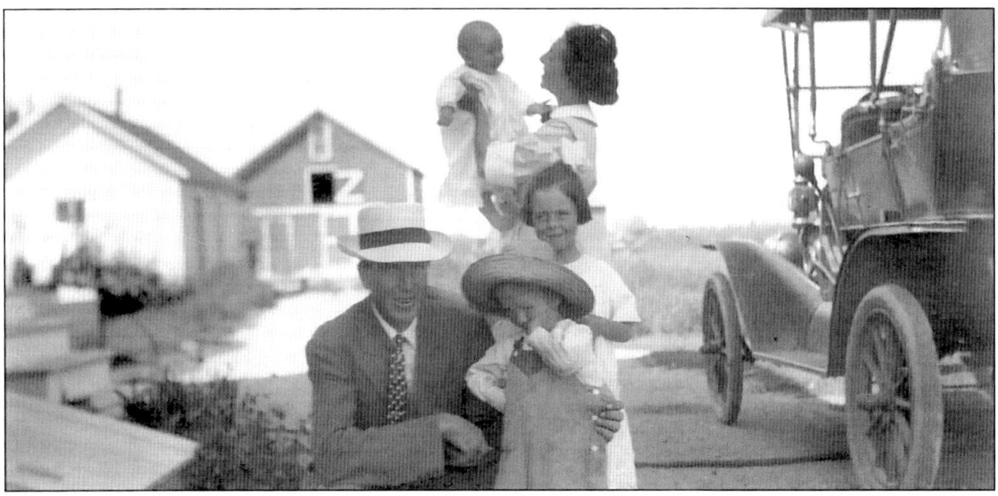

The Bliss family is ready to leave in this photo. (Courtesy of the Bliss family.)

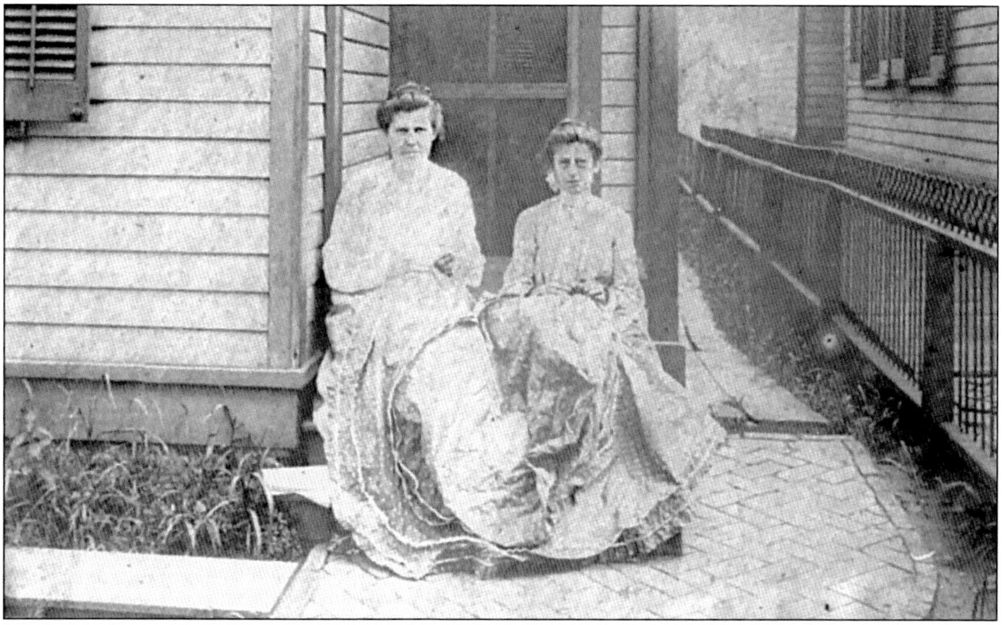

Pictured above is Elva Gray on the left—the mother of John, Wallace "Wally," Alfred "Tote," Harley, and Judy. In 1917, the Grays bought the hotel at Second and Cedar Streets and sold it in 1922.

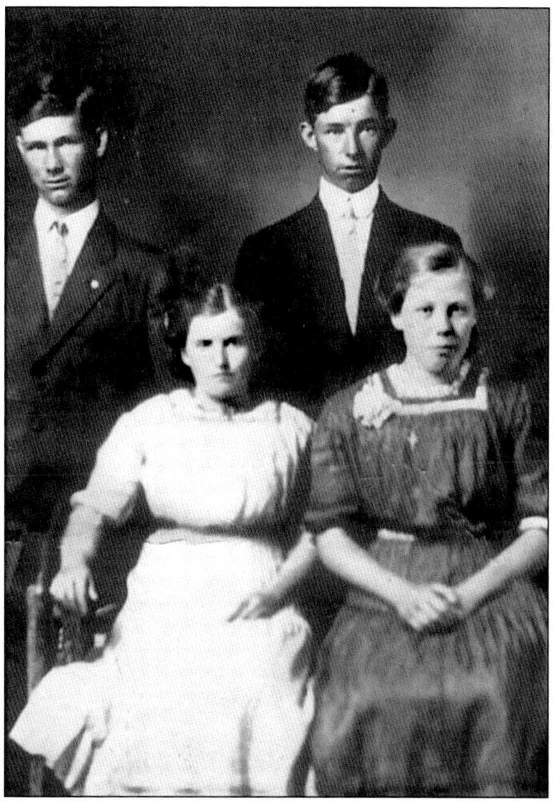

Lesley Cutlip, Joseph Fogg, Cora (Foster) Cutlip, and Lena (Foster) Fogg are pictured here.

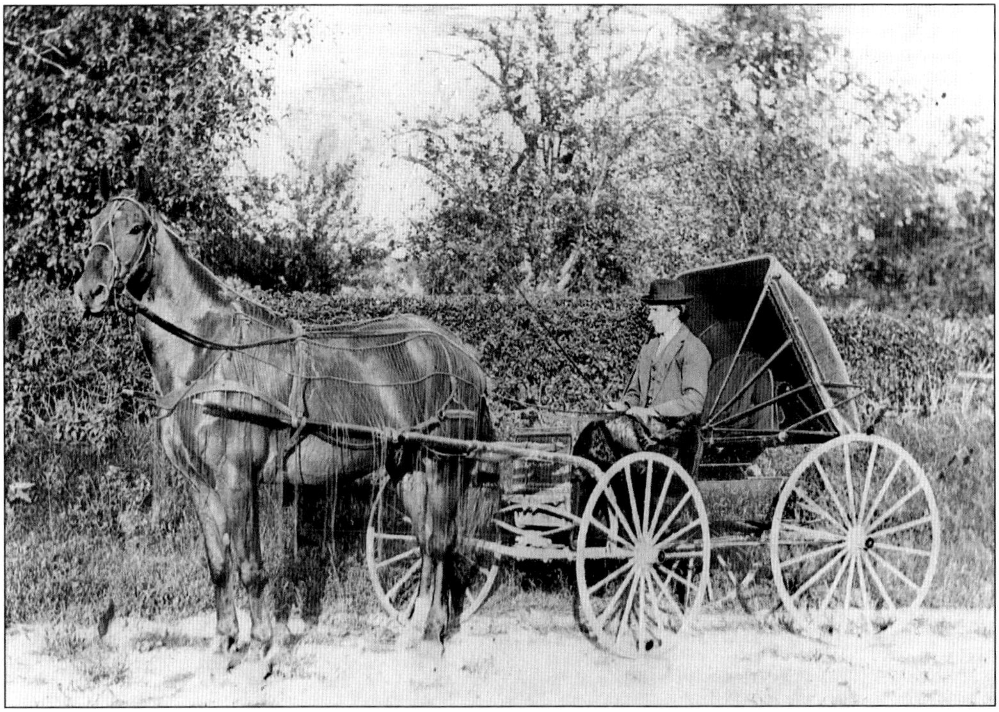

Ready to go! Alvin Harlin, uncle of Rupert H. Nurse of Blue Ridge, Hallock Township is pictured here. (Courtesy of Mary Nurse Meyer.)

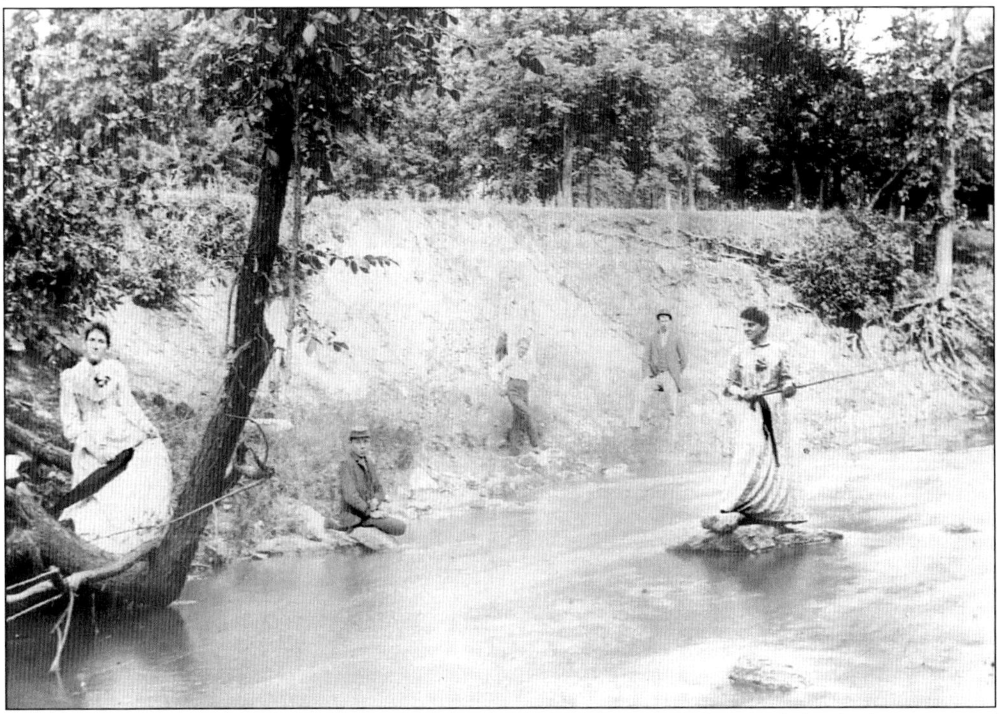

This photo depicts a summer outing with Elbert Nurse sitting on the creek bank. (Courtesy of Mary Nurse Meyer.)

Pictured here is Henry H. Nurse (1843–1922), son of Isaiah Nurse (1815–1894), and grandson of Roswell Nurse (1787–1863). Henry was a veteran of the 86th Illinois Volunteer Infantry. (Courtesy of Mary Nurse Meyer.)

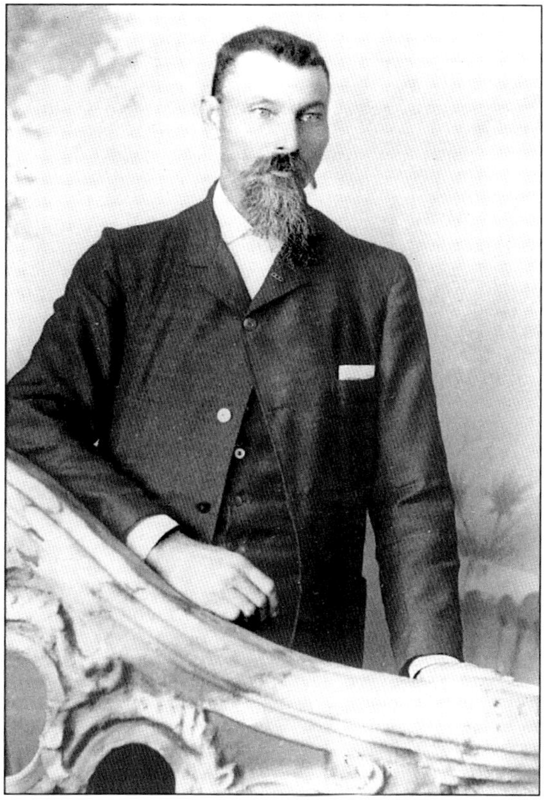

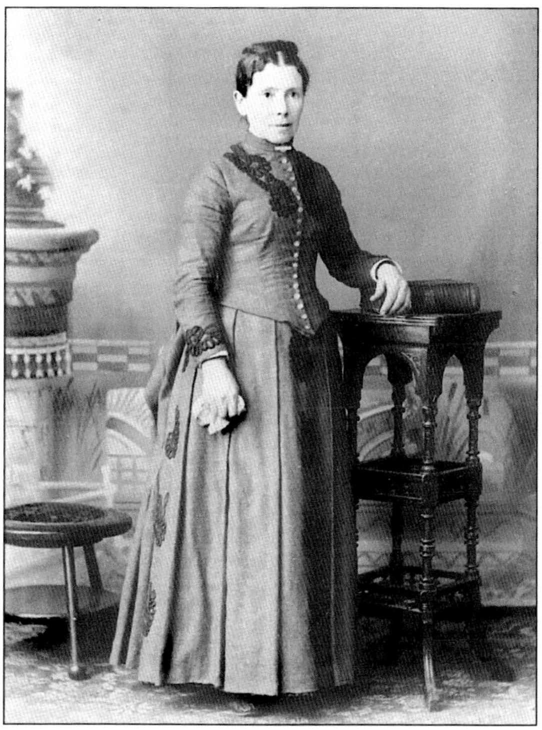

Lucinda Stevens Nurse is pictured here. (Courtesy of Mary Nurse Meyer.)

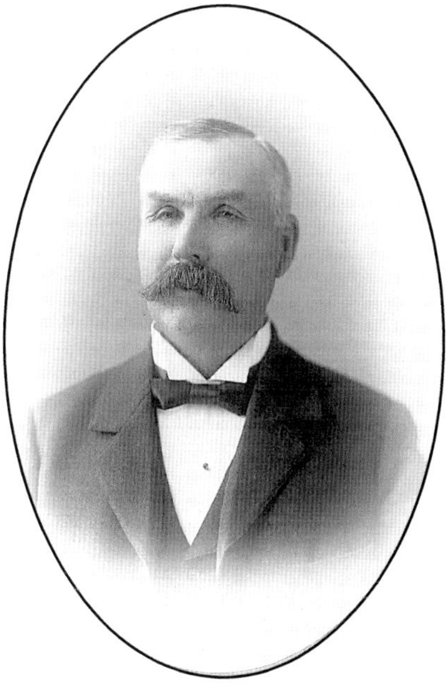

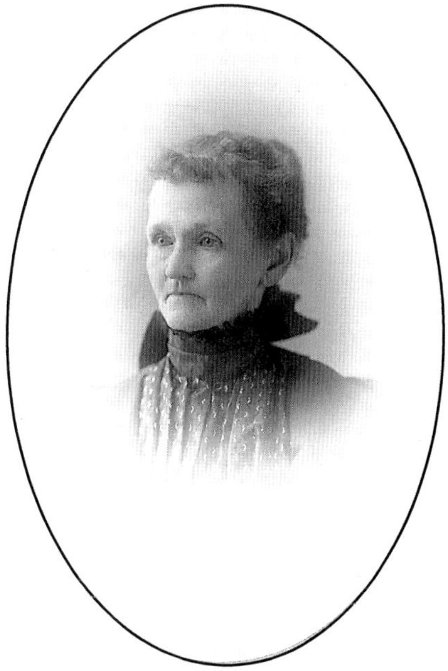

Pictured at left is William Root (1843–1913), son of Erastus Root (1805–1896), and grandson of Jeriel Root. Pictured at right is Mary Anne Caldwell Root (1841–1913) who married William Root on September 12, 1866.

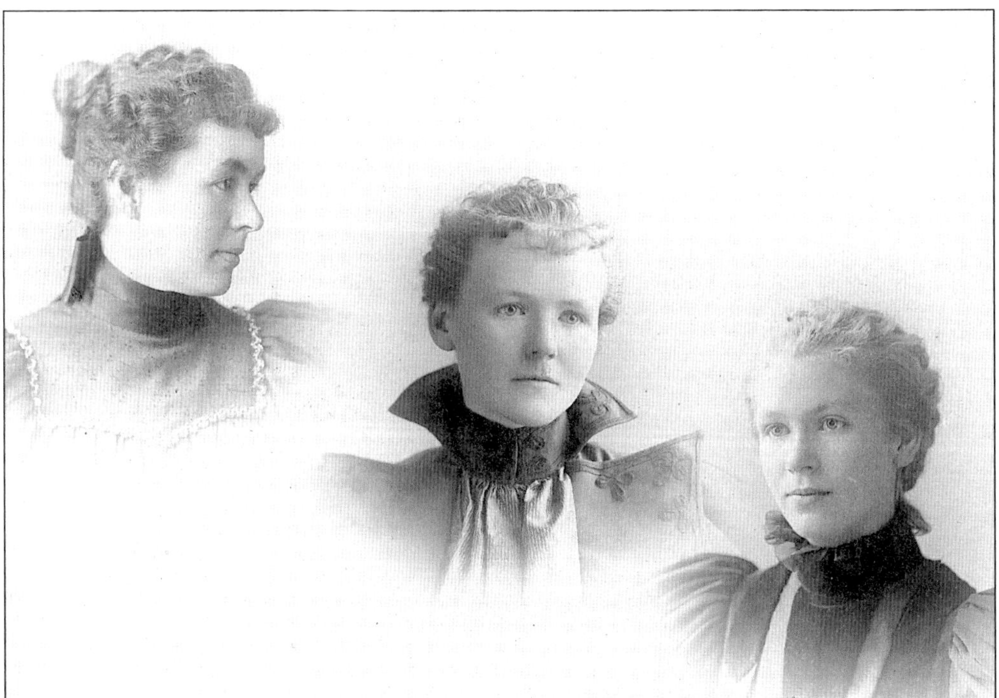

Nell, Jess, and Alice Root are pictured here.

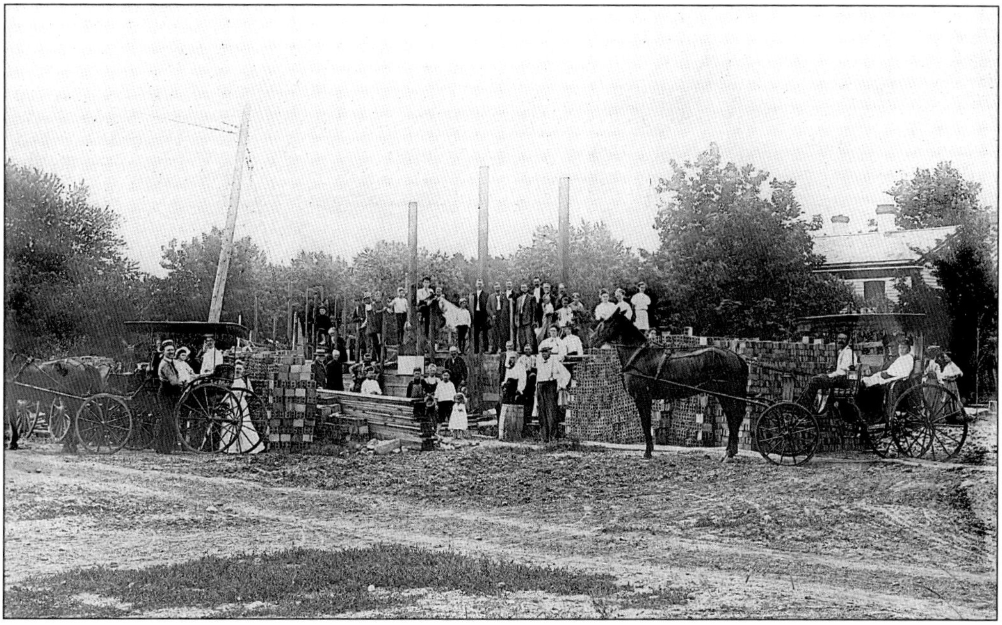

In this photo, note the piles of brick and lumber on the building site.

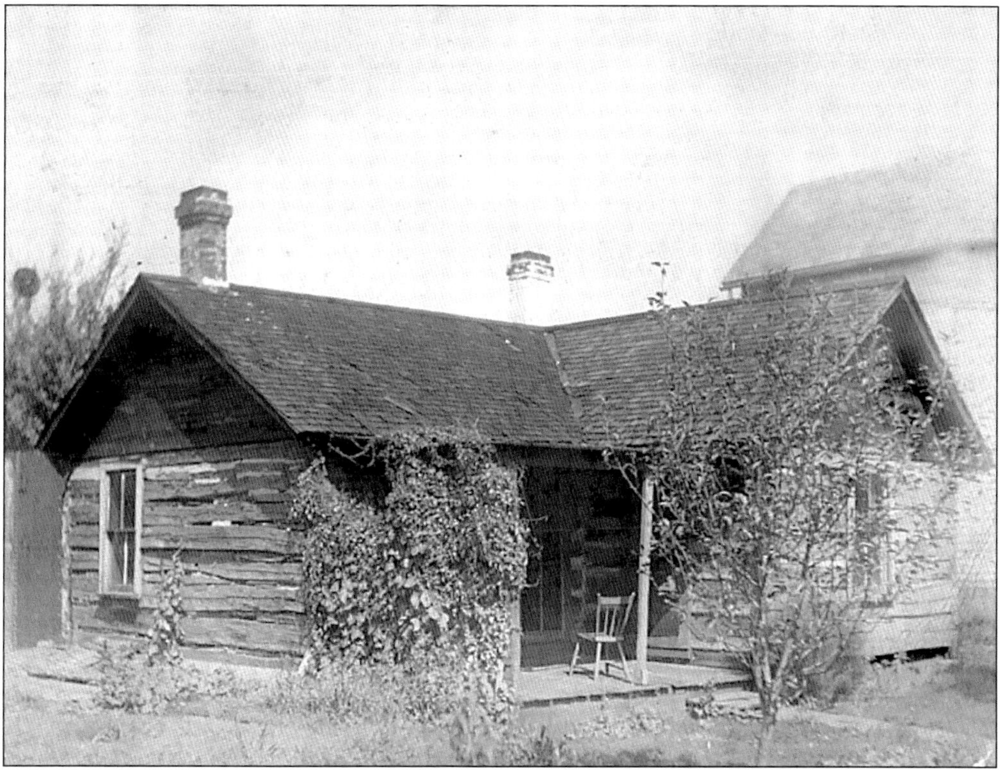

This log cabin was built by Charles Brewer in 1892, and was later covered with siding—it is located in the 1500 block of Second Street. Eva Milessa Brewer Snyder was born here on September 30, 1896.

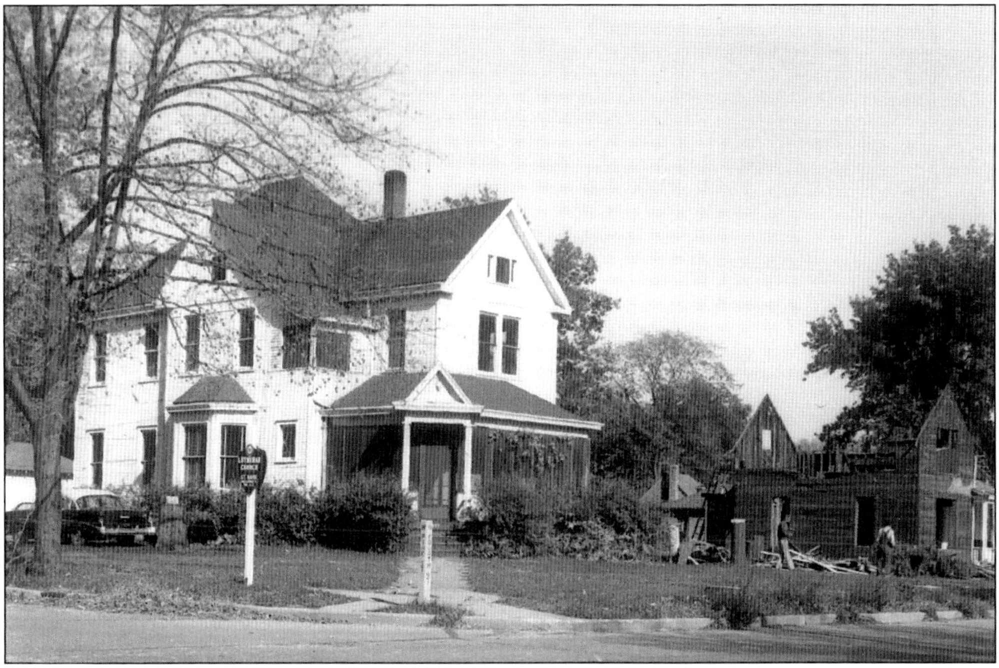

This house—the former Dr. Kelly house—stood on the northwest corner of Fourth and Pine Streets until it was demolished to build the People's S&L new building. The structure being destroyed in the background was the Dr. Kinsella house.

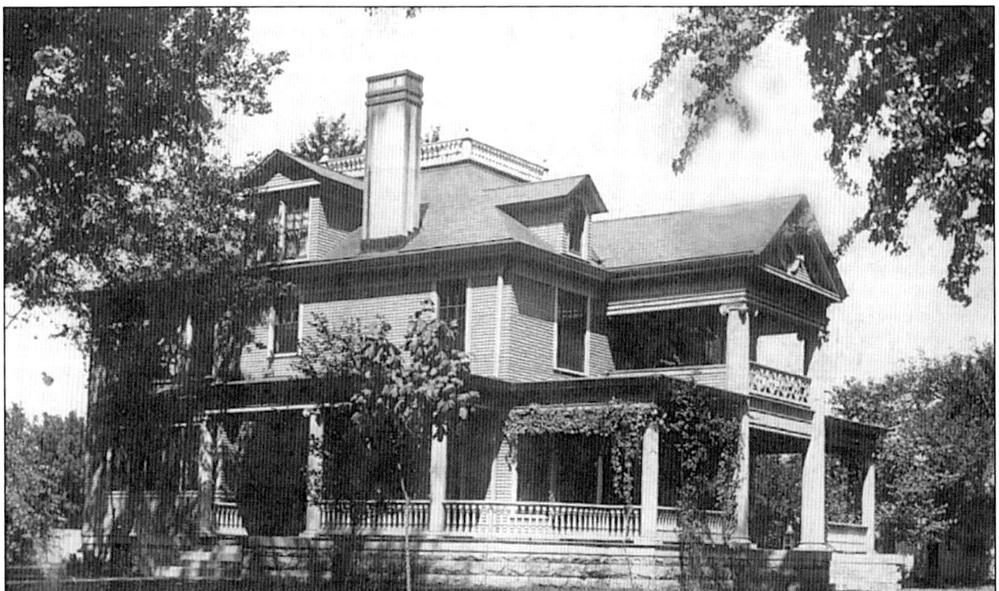

The Sydney Wood home is pictured here. Gene Weber bought this house at Fourth and Chestnut Streets from Darb Woodruff.

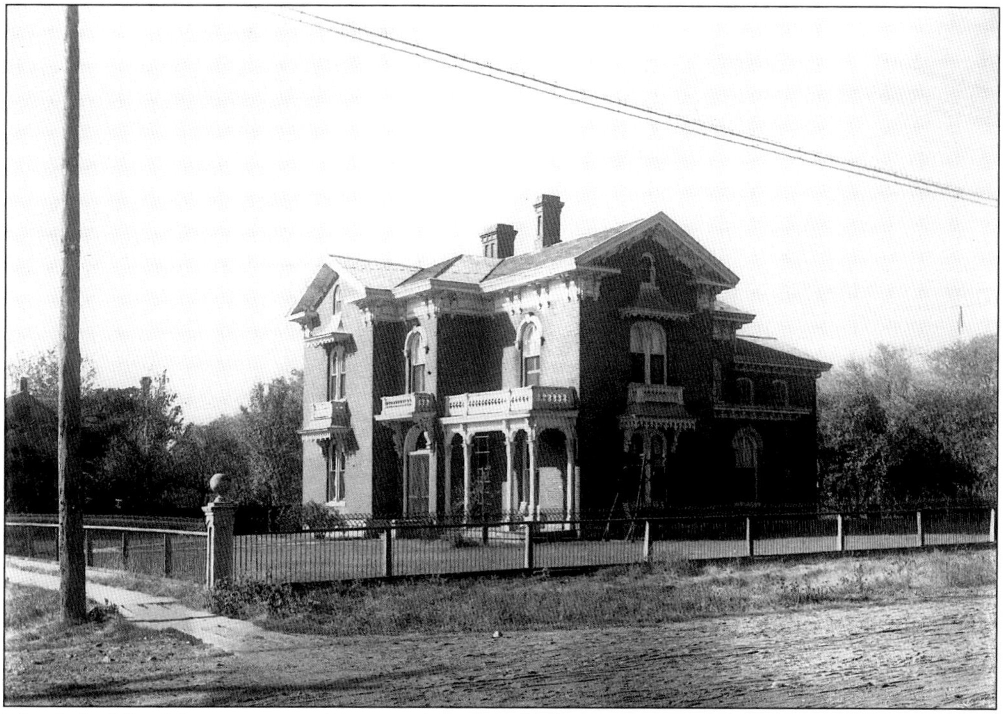

The L.A. Wood house pictured here at Third and Elm Streets is also shown in the 1873 Atlas of Peoria County.

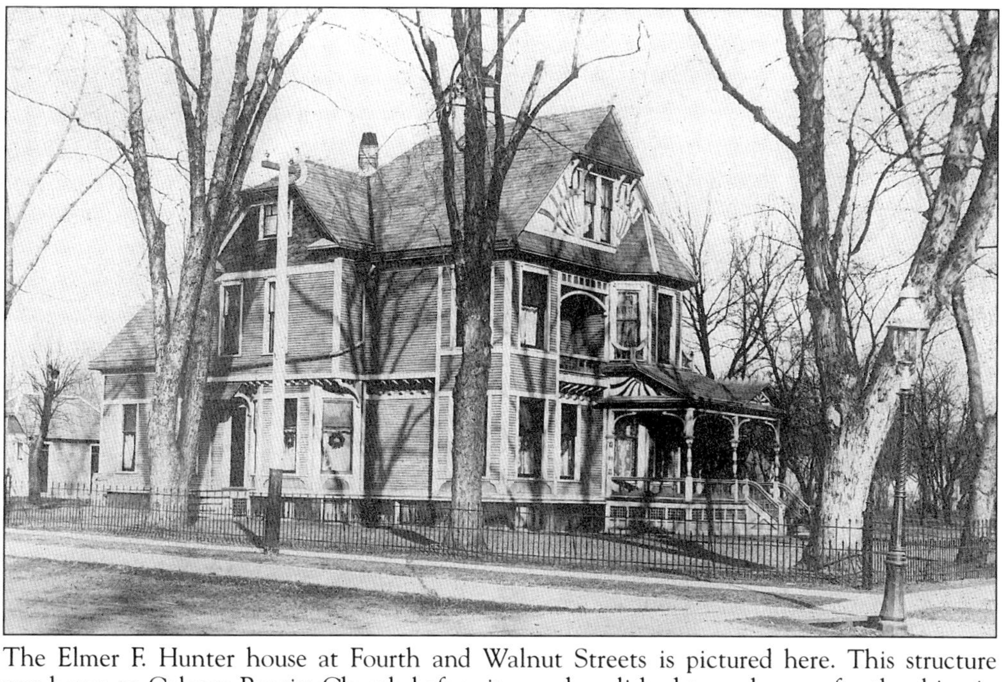

The Elmer F. Hunter house at Fourth and Walnut Streets is pictured here. This structure was home to Calvary Baptist Church before it was demolished to make way for the drive-in auto bank.

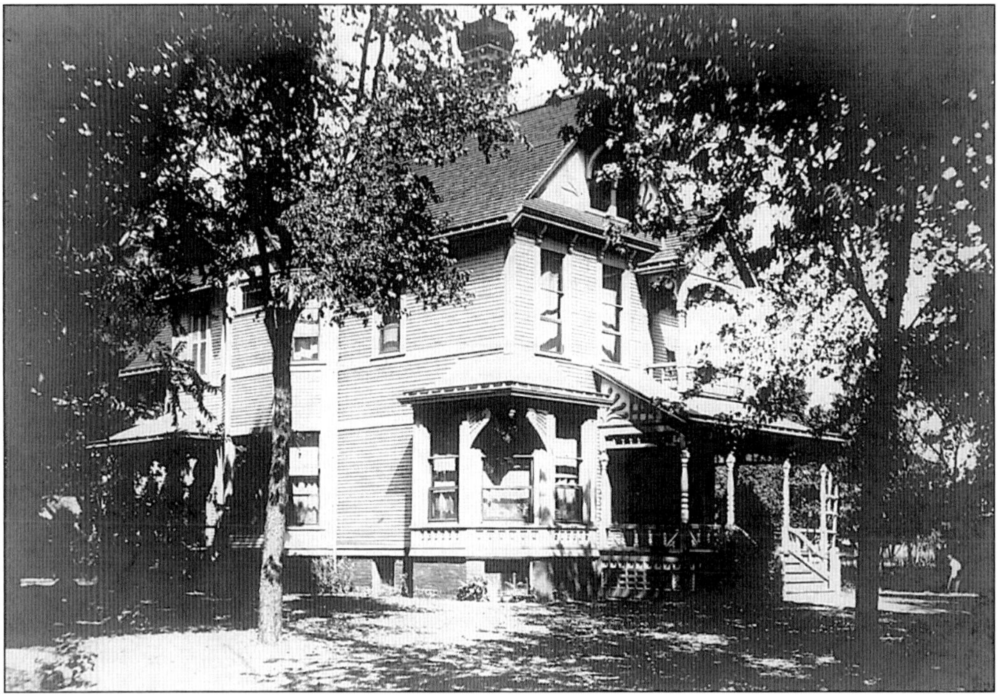

This is the George McWhorter house—now Bennie Razo's—at Fifth and Walnut Streets as photographed for the October 16, 1908, *Chillicothe Bulletin*.

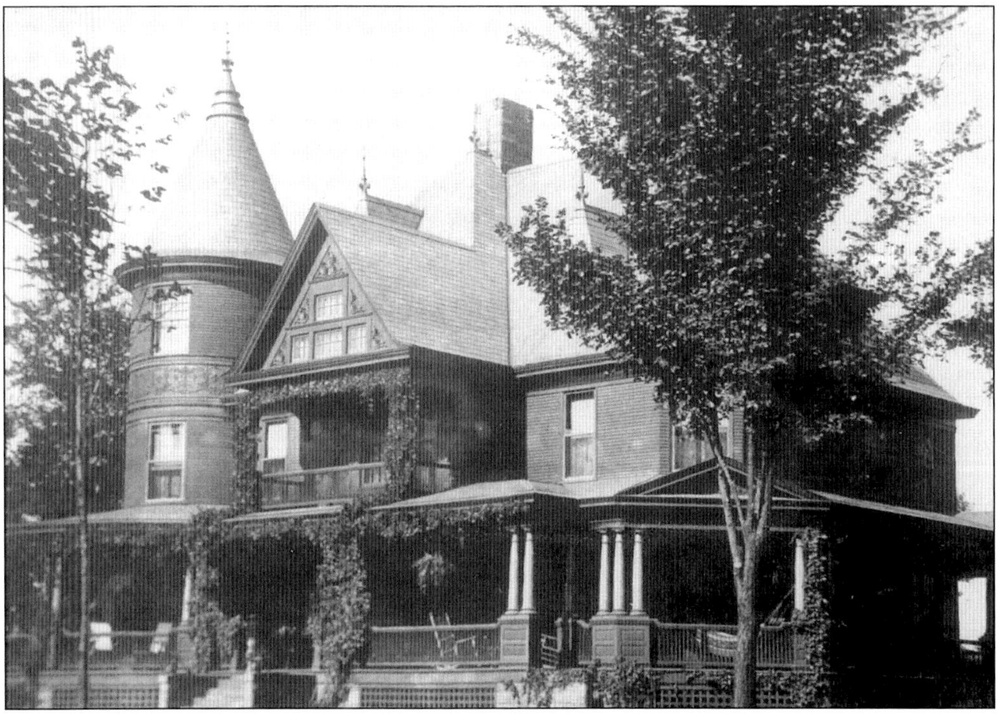

The William Mead house—now Wareco—is pictured here in 1938 as it stood at Fourth and Hickory Streets.

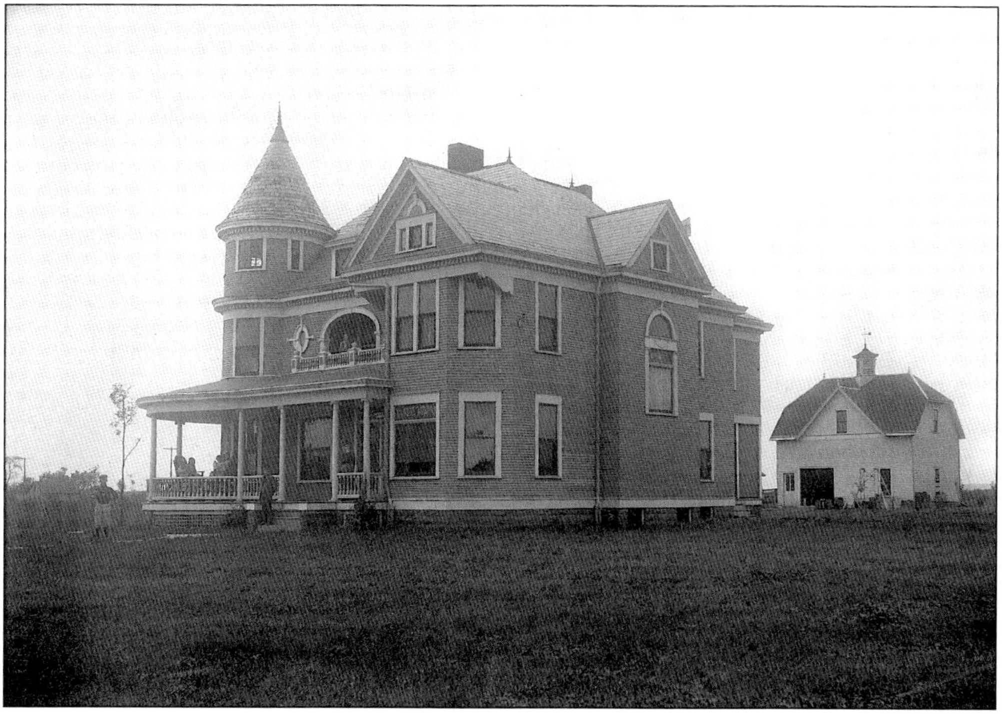

The Zinser house at Santa Fe and Walnut Streets was destroyed by fire.

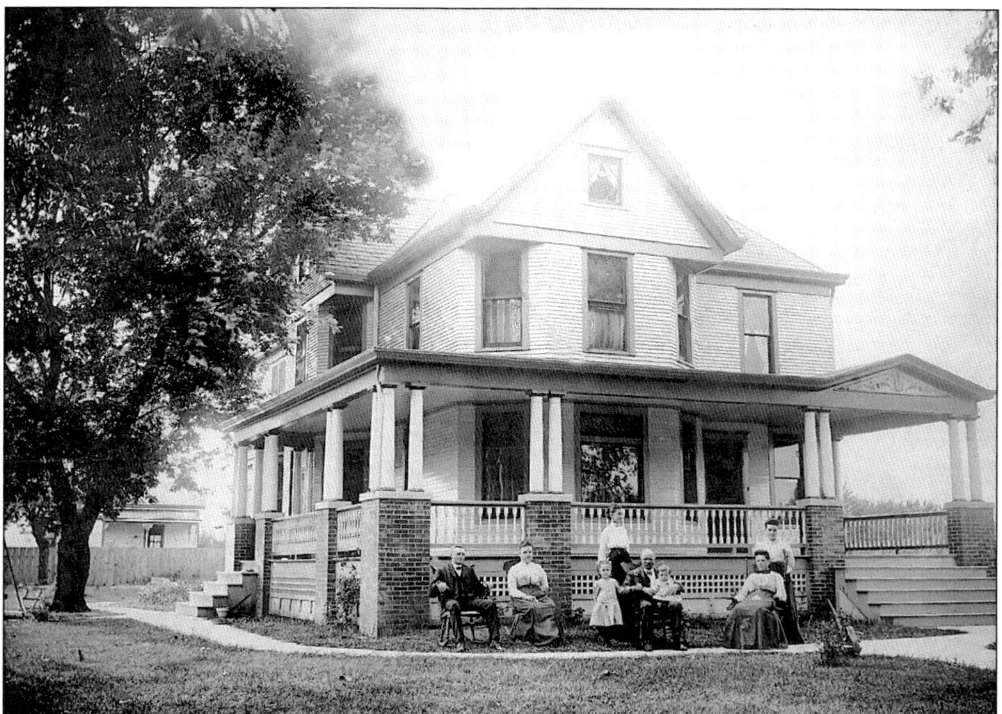

Pictured here is the Ed Mattice house and family at Sixth and Walnut Streets.

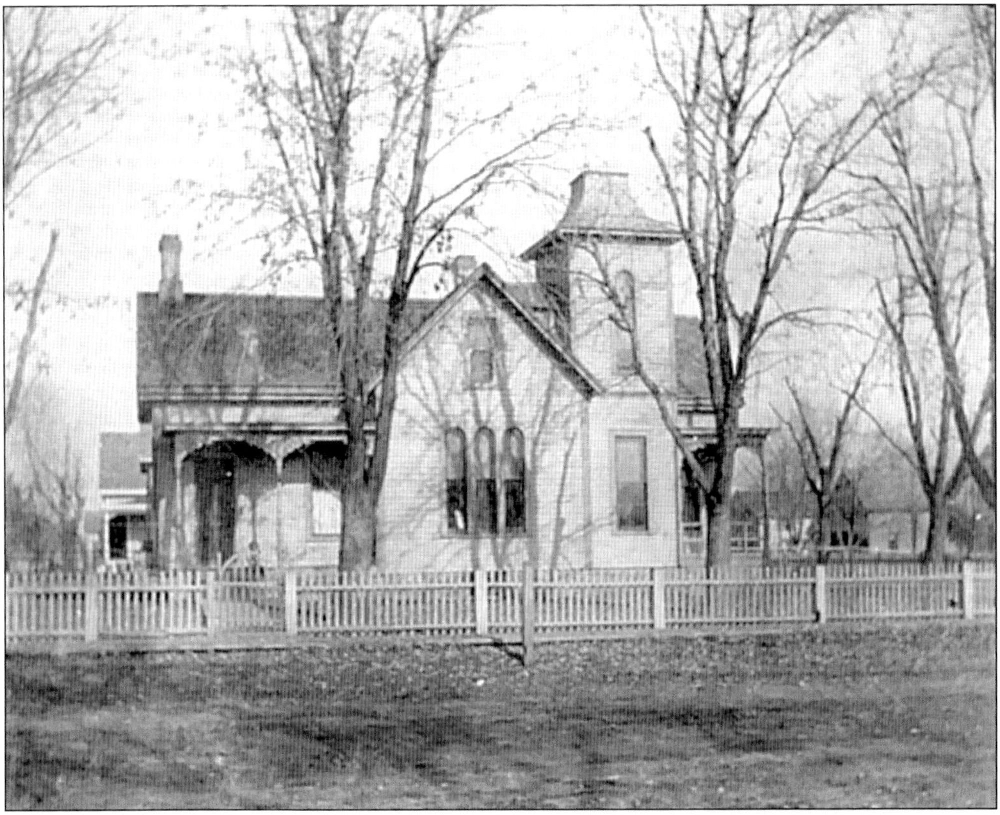

The Bill Ratliff house is pictured here in 1905 at Fourth and Beech Streets—now the location of Pizza Hut.

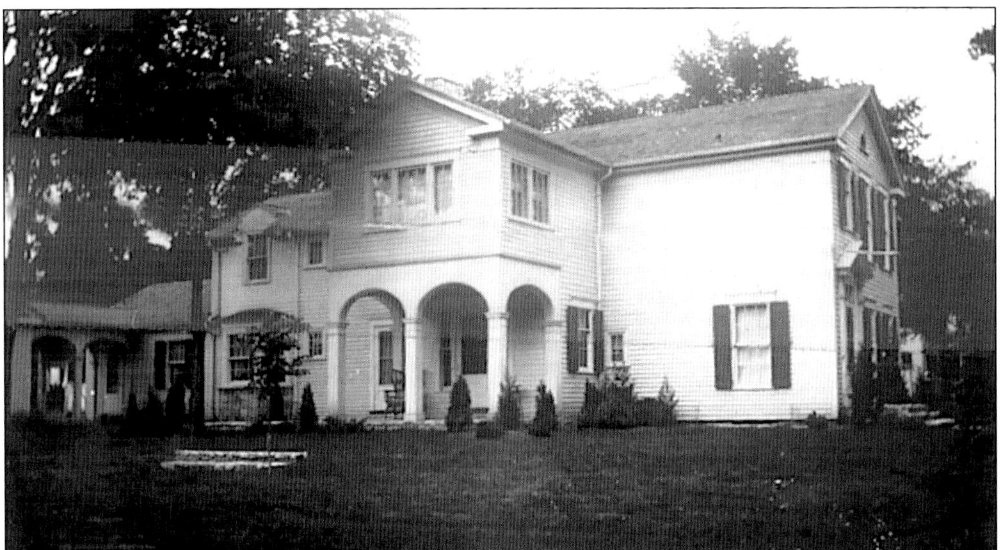

The Russell Hunter house pictured above was moved from Fourth and Pine Streets to Santa Fe and Sunnyside Streets by Rick and Marti Hinck.

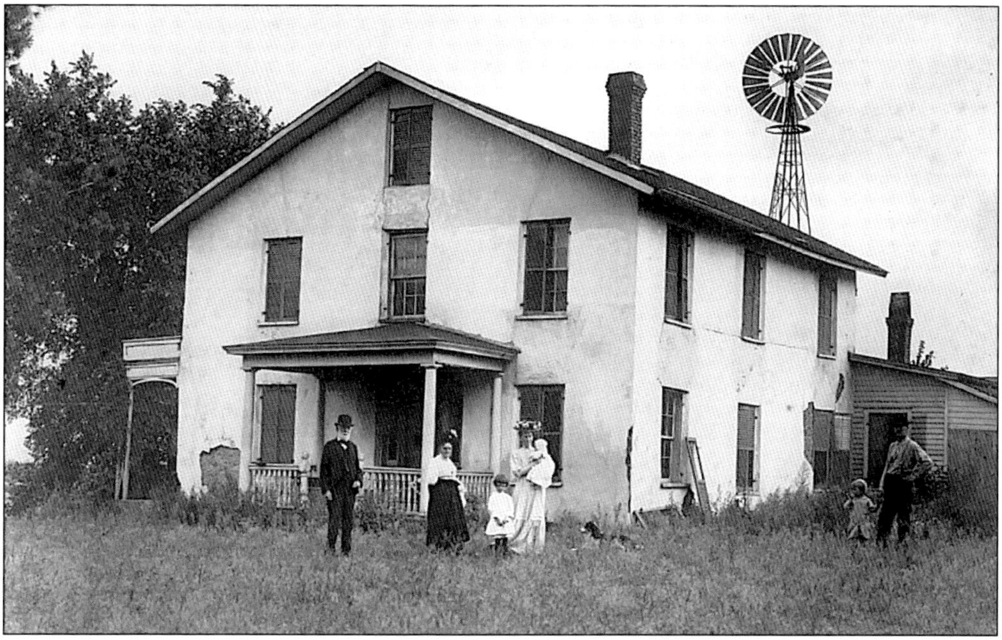

The first stucco house in the area was built in 1856 across from Blarney Castle, west of the tracks in Rome. It was torn down in 1909.

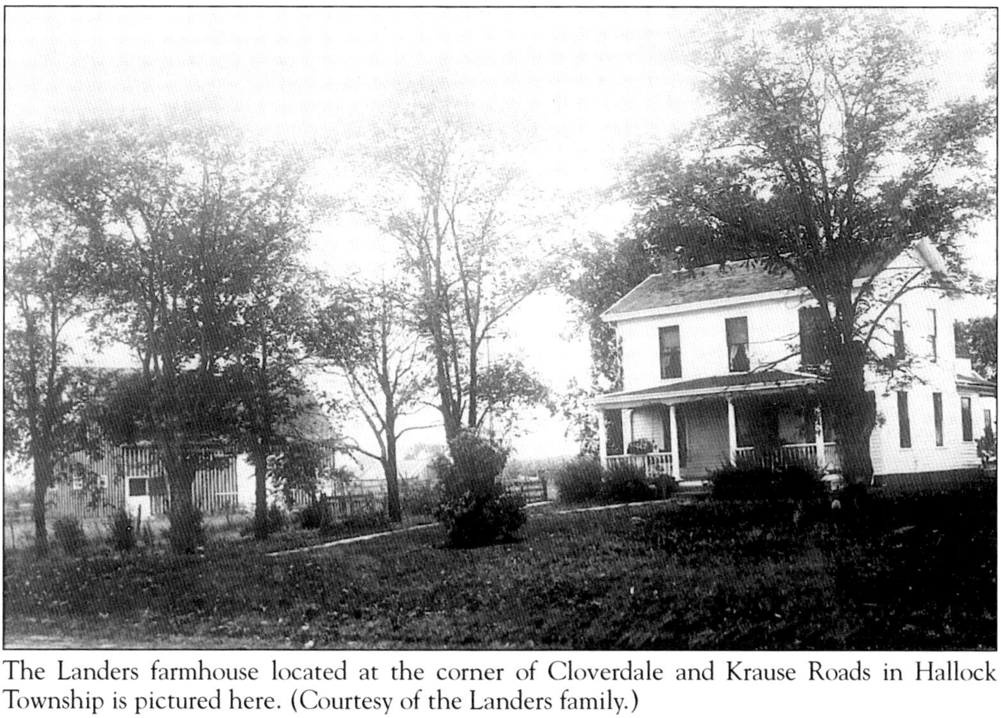

The Landers farmhouse located at the corner of Cloverdale and Krause Roads in Hallock Township is pictured here. (Courtesy of the Landers family.)

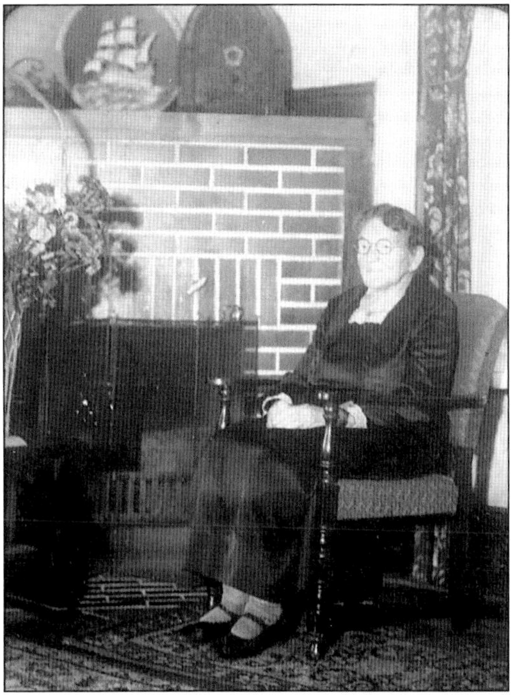

Bridget Humphrey Landers was photographed here in 1885. (Courtesy of the Landers family.)

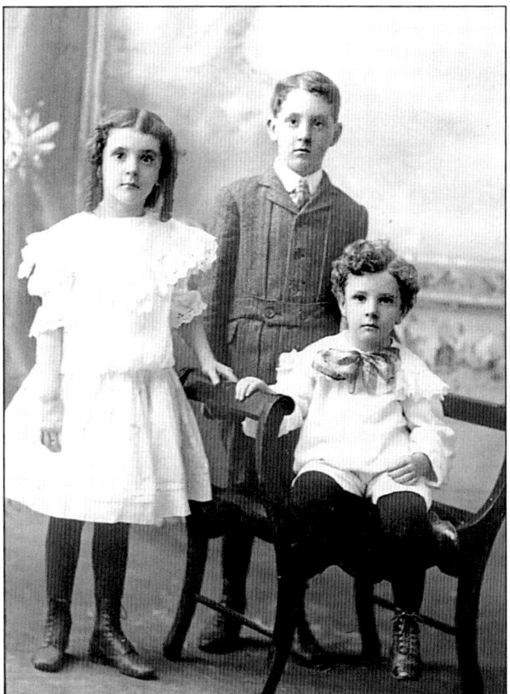

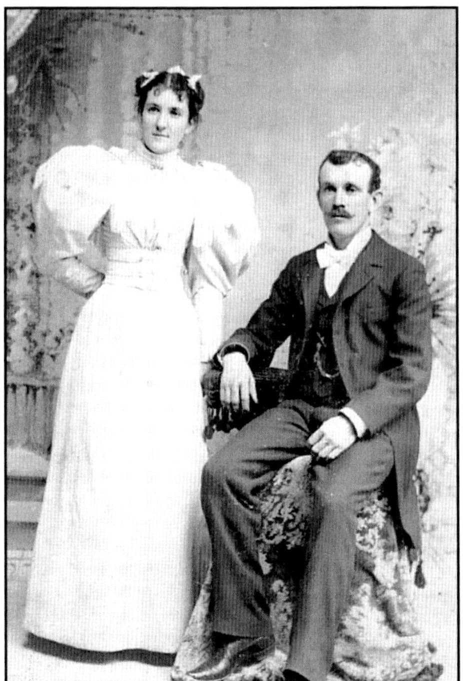

Pictured at left are Ethel Landers—born 1899, Henry Landers—born 1897, and Raymond Landers—born 1900. On the right is a wedding photograph of Martha Bauer and John Landers taken in the spring of 1896. (Courtesy of the Landers family.)

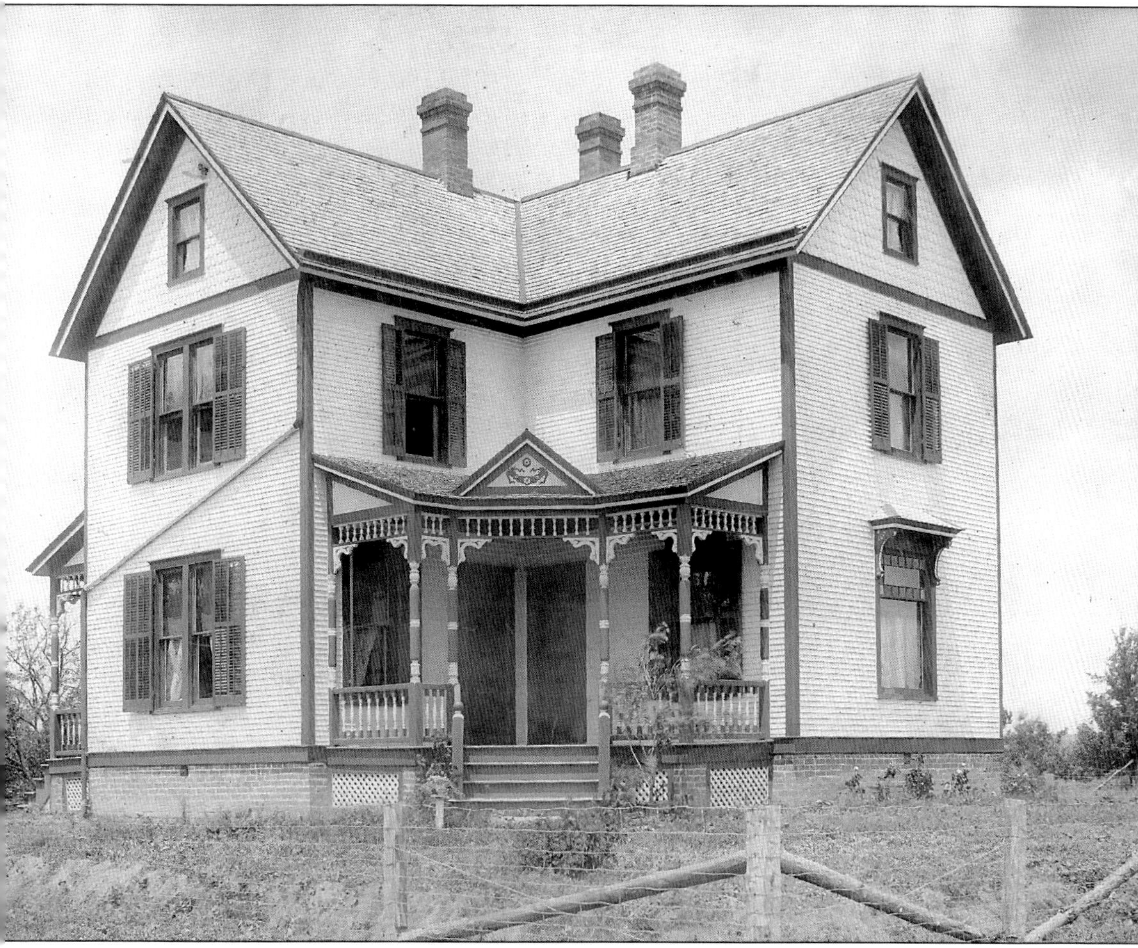

This photo depicts the Robert Bruce Dickison home in 1915. This house was on the south side of Neal Road about .25 miles west of Galena Road in Medina Township. (Courtesy of Doris M. Dickison.)

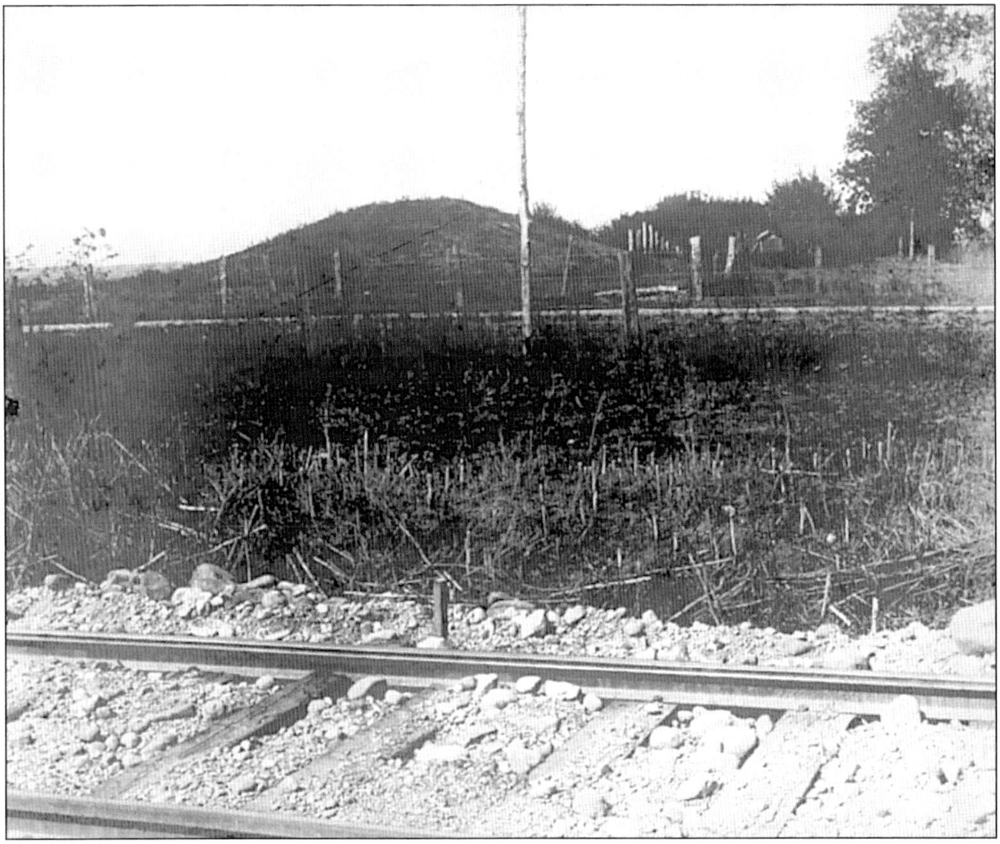

Pictured here is the Hopewell burial mound, located on what was the J.B. Dickison farm—now Caterpillar—in about 1914. This mound was removed in 1940 when Route 29 was improved. Information on the artifacts is available from the Illinois State Museum. (Courtesy of Doris M. Dickison.)

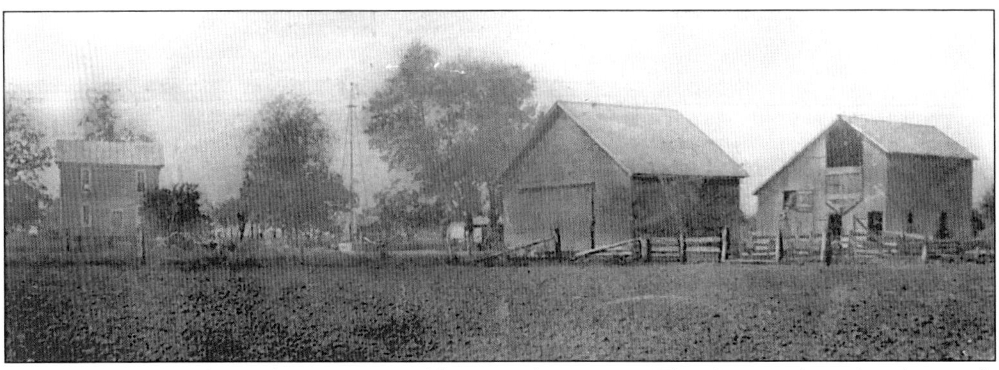

The Edward R. Dickison farm is pictured here in about 1914. This farm is about 2 miles north of Mossville in Medina Township. (Courtesy of Doris M. Dickison.)

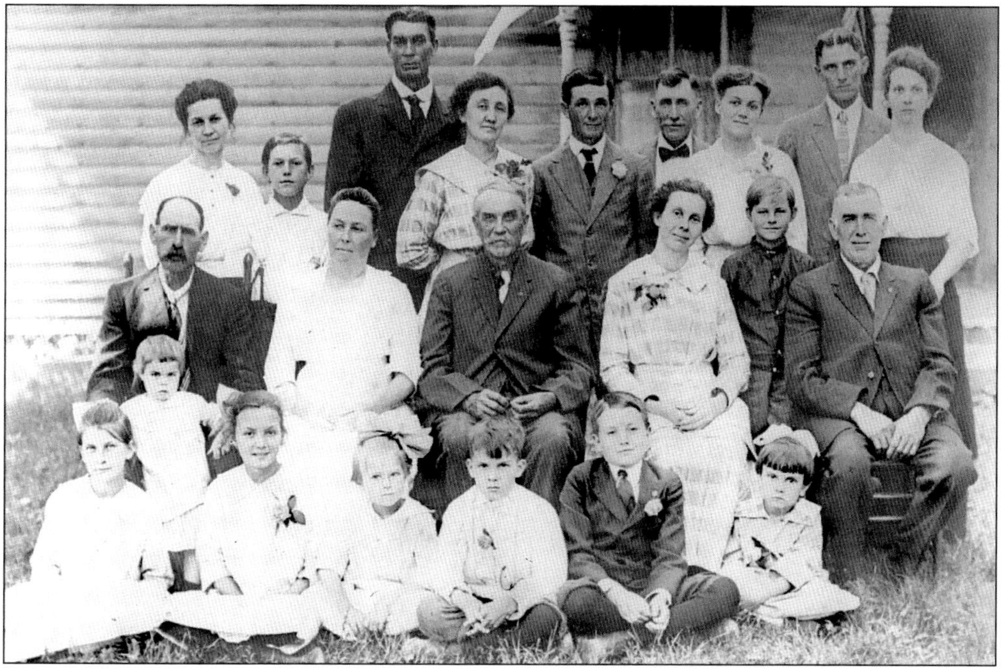

The Krotz family is pictured here in 1916. They are: (back) Dollie Miller, Maurice Miller, Fred Krotz, Ella Krotz, Max Williams, Mike McDonald, Lillian Williams, Rose Williams, Minnie Williams; (middle row) Lou Neuman, Tillie Neuman, Baltzer Bixler Krotz, Mima Burns, Freeman Miller, Adam Burns; (front) Florence Miller, Inez Williams, Hazel Williams, Maxine Williams, Ernie Williams, Russell Valentine, and Lola Williams. (Courtesy of Mary Nurse Meyer.)

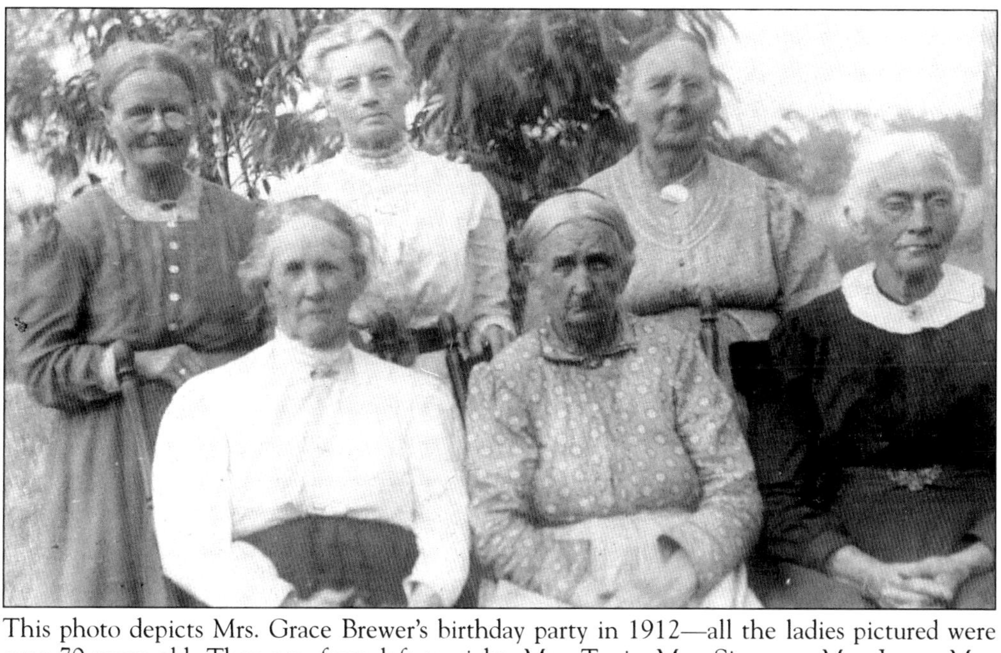

This photo depicts Mrs. Grace Brewer's birthday party in 1912—all the ladies pictured were over 70 years old. They are, from left to right: Mrs. Tunis, Mrs. Simpson, Mrs. Jones, Mrs. Brewer, Mrs. Winchester, and Mrs. Staab. (Courtesy of Hank Foster.)

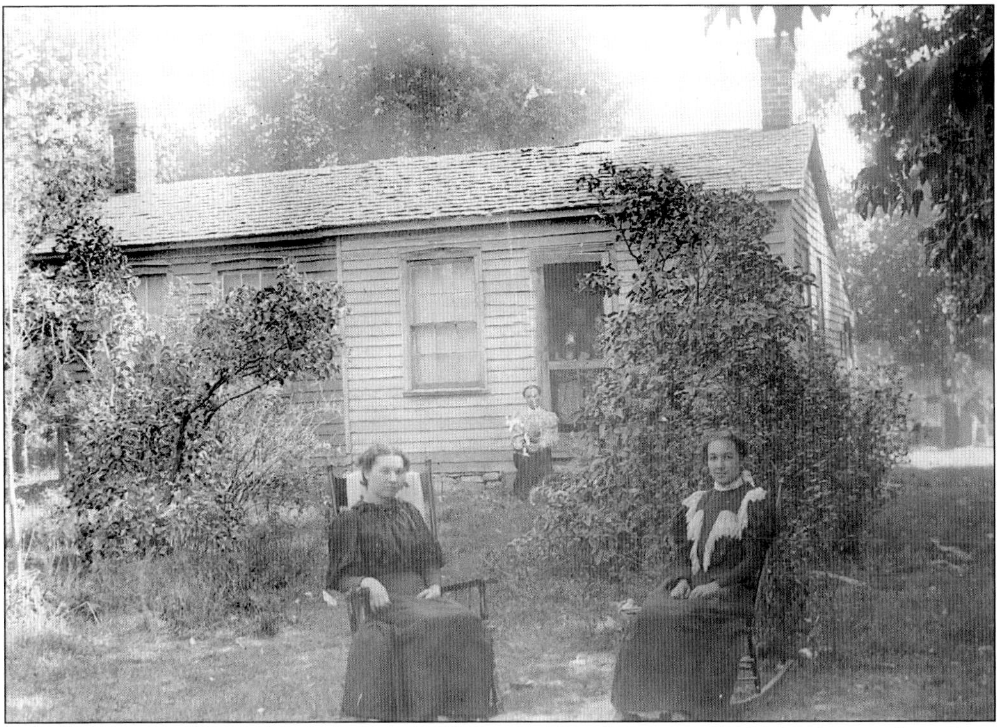

Dollie Krotz and Mae Stowell are pictured here with Tillie Krotz in the background, at their homeplace north of Northampton in the late 1890s. (Courtesy of Mary Nurse Meyer.)

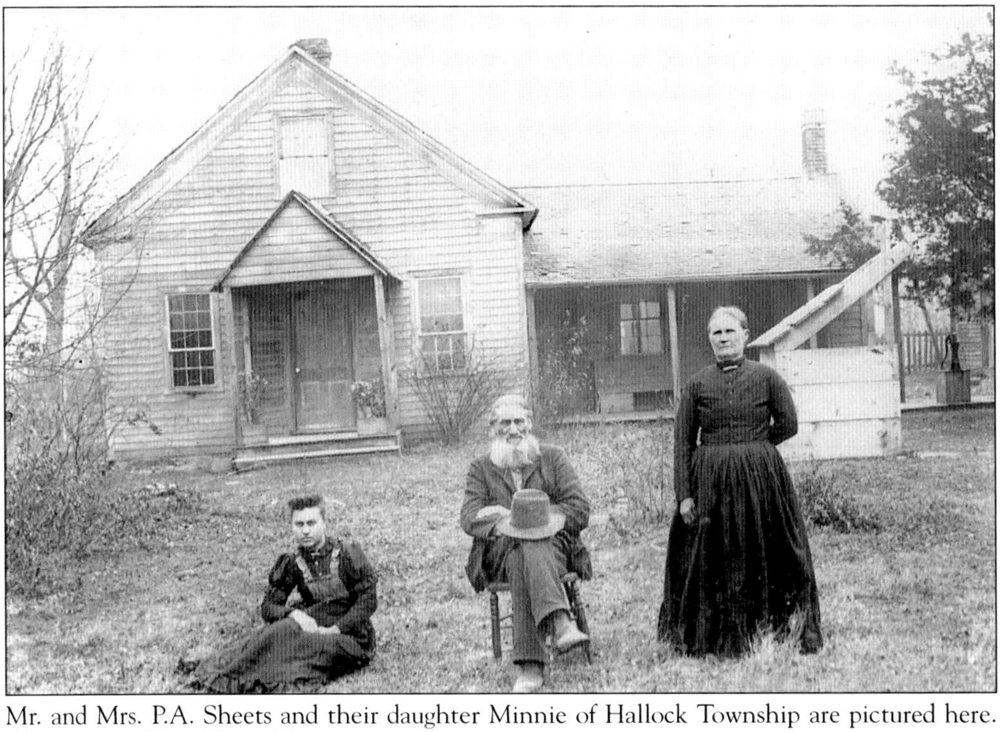

Mr. and Mrs. P.A. Sheets and their daughter Minnie of Hallock Township are pictured here. (Courtesy of Mary Nurse Meyer.)

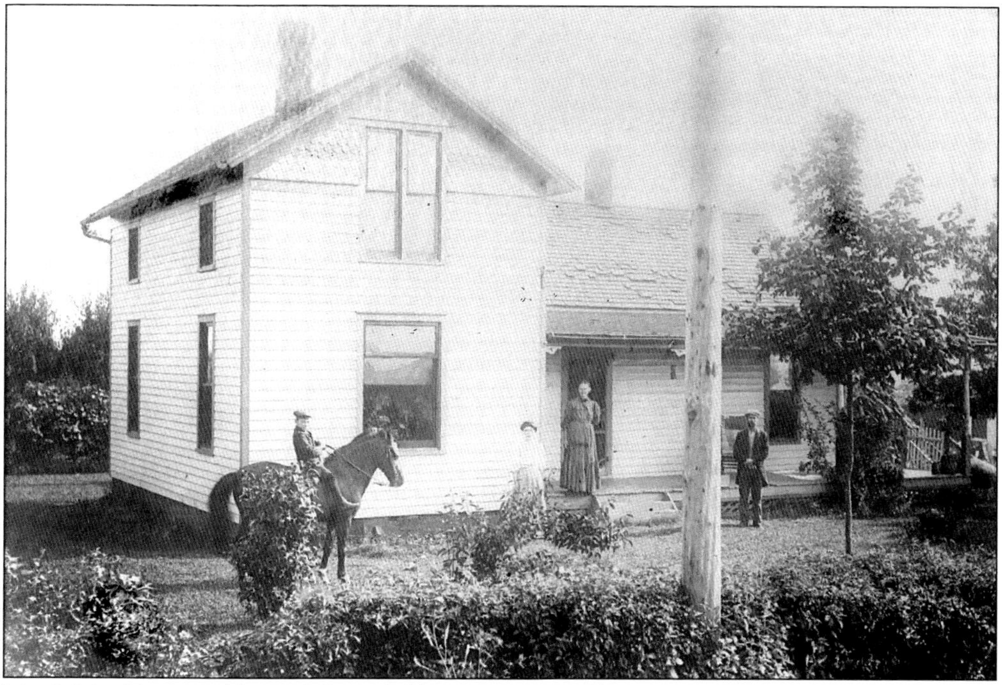

Mr. & Mrs. Erwin Calder and their children are pictured here in front of their Blue Ridge home in about 1905. This was later known as the Webber or Duckworth place. (Courtesy of Mary Nurse Meyer.)

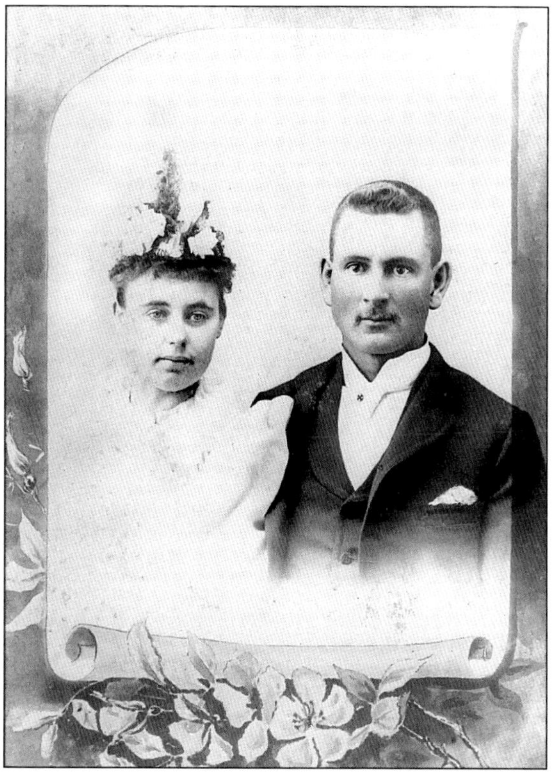

Lew and Stella Clark are pictured here. Lew was a photographer in the Chillicothe area, and Stella was related to the Stowells of Blue Ridge, Hallock Township. (Courtesy of Mary Nurse Meyer.)

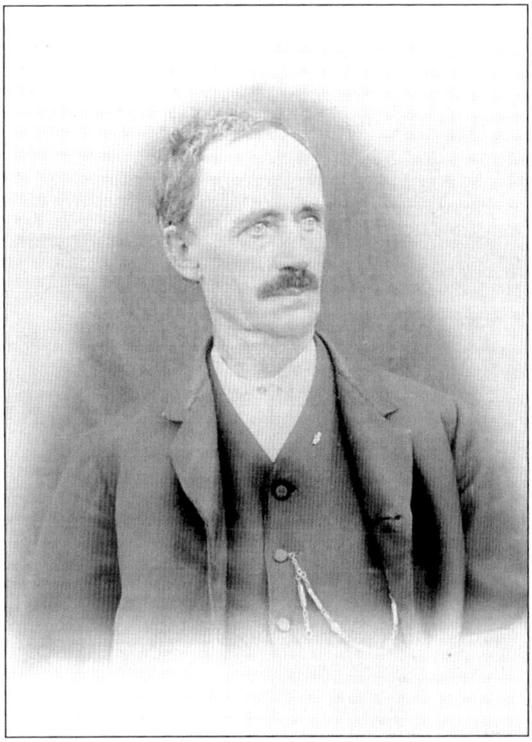

Oscar D. Stowell of Blue Ridge, Hallock Township is pictured here. (Courtesy of Mary Nurse Meyer.)

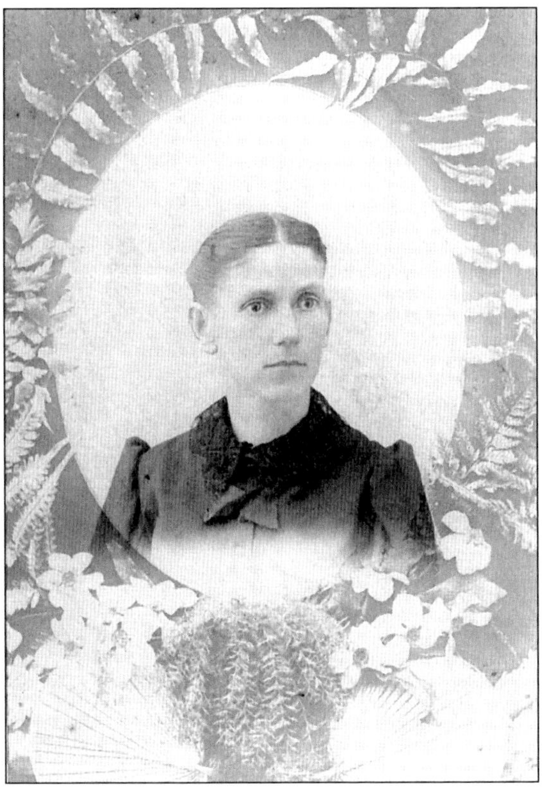

This is Alice Clark Stowell. (Courtesy of Mary Nurse Meyer.)

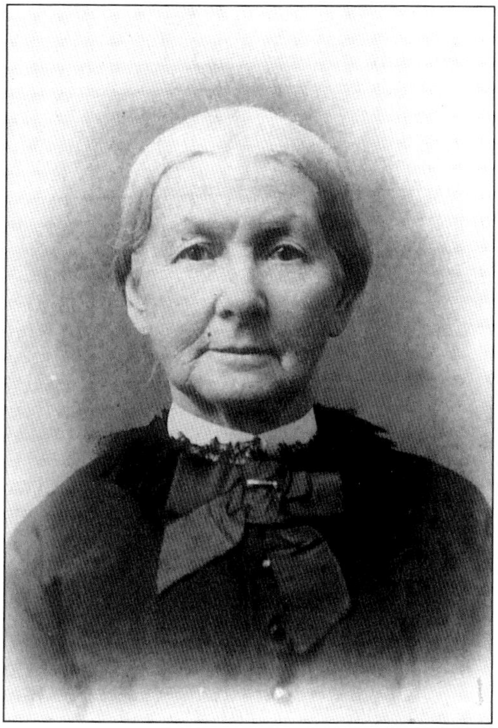
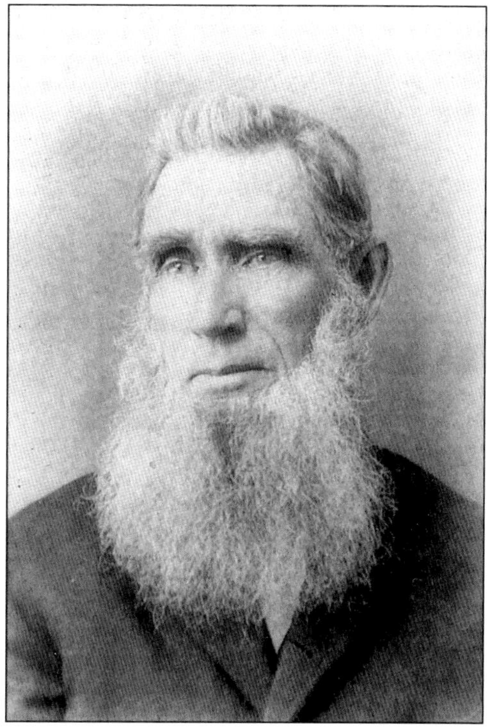

Electa Clark is pictured at left, and John Clark is pictured at right. (Courtesy of Mary Nurse Meyer.)

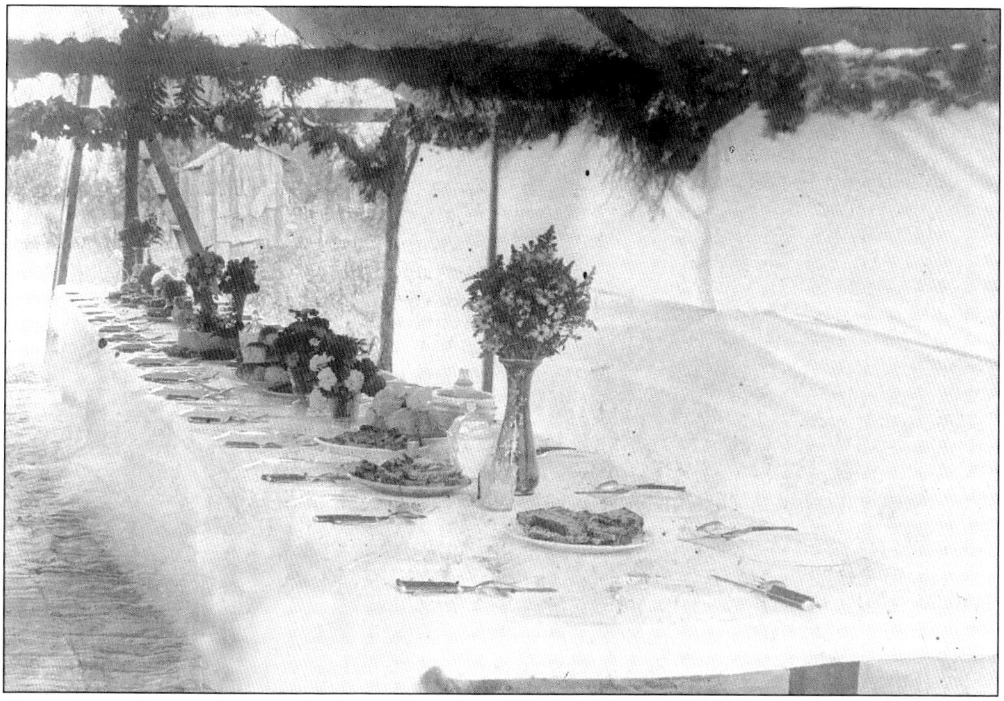

This photo depicts John and Electa Clark's golden wedding celebration in October of 1901. (Courtesy of Mary Nurse Meyer.)

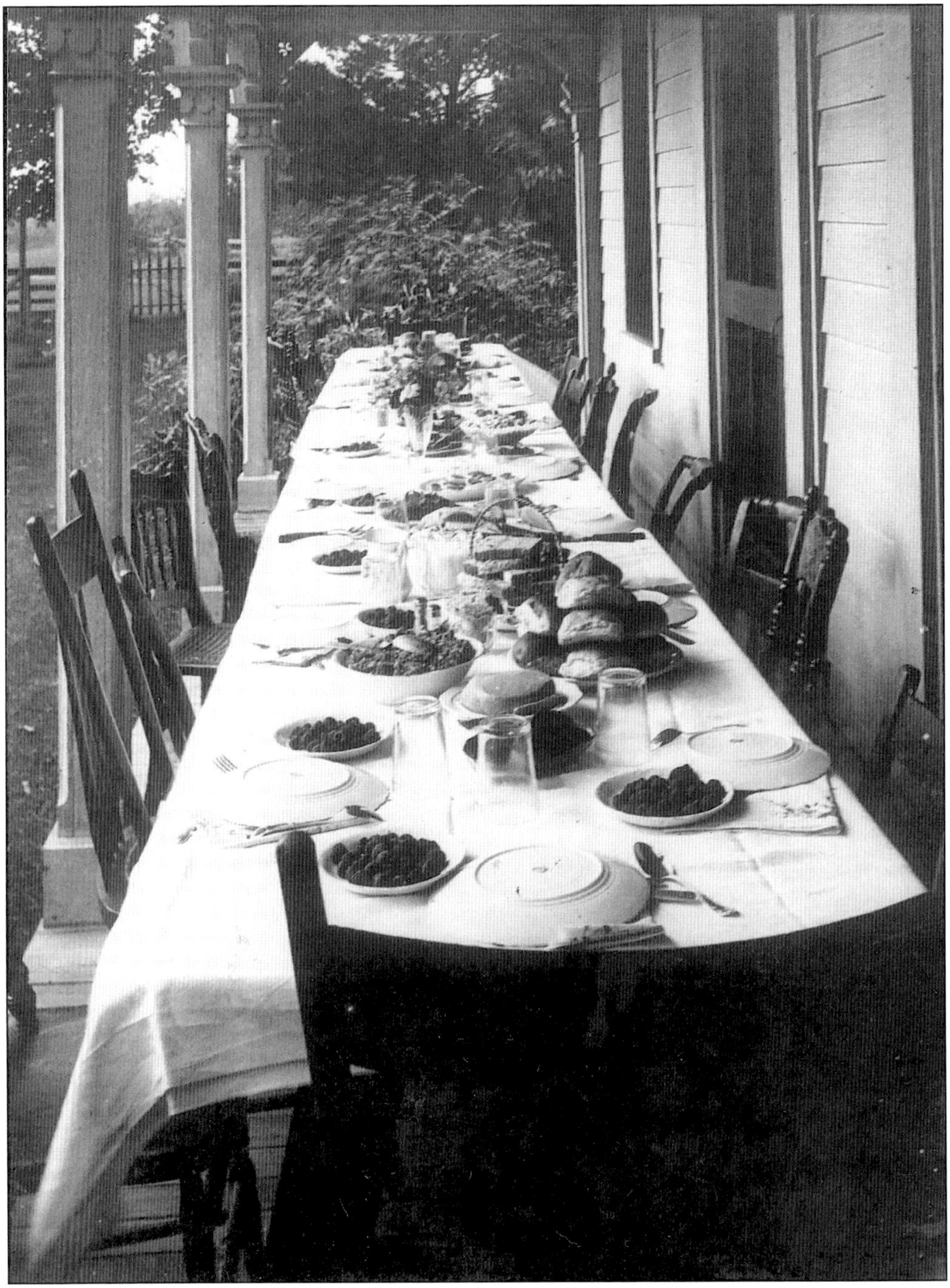

The dinner table at Elbert Nurse's is set here for the Fourth of July, 1906. (Courtesy of Mary Nurse Meyer.)

Nell and Merry Justice are pictured here on July 4, 1925. This house is on the southeast corner of Second and Ash Streets. (Courtesy of Hank Foster.)

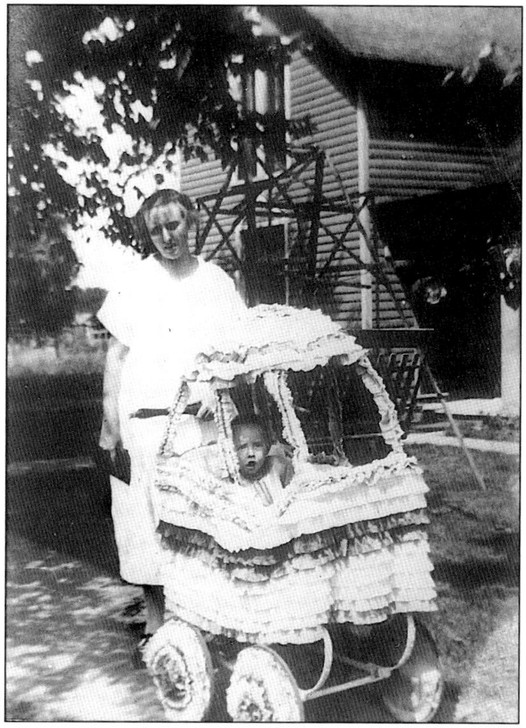

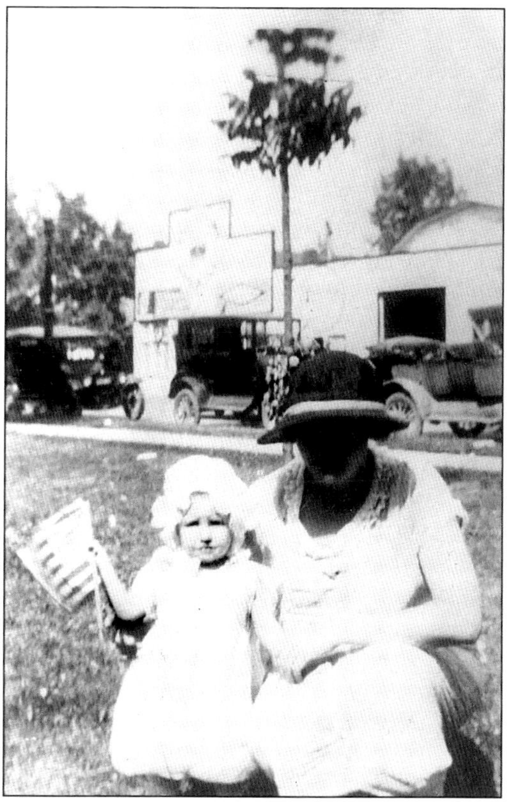

Nell and Merry Justice are pictured in City Park on July 4, 1925. The buildings in the background are now John's Autobody and the post office parking lot. (Courtesy of Hank Foster.)

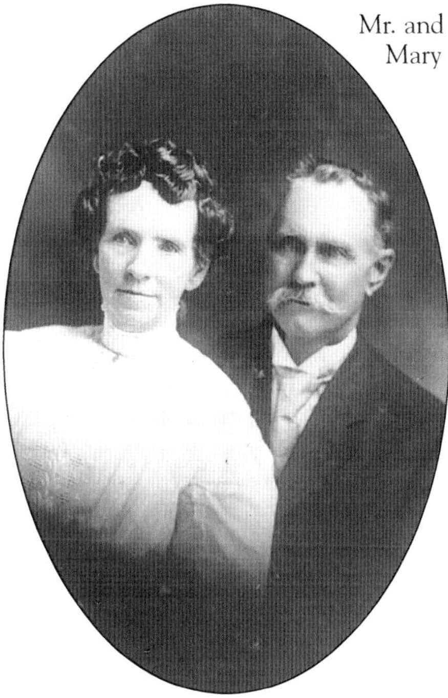

Mr. and Mrs. Newell Nurse are pictured here. (Courtesy of Mary Nurse Meyer.)

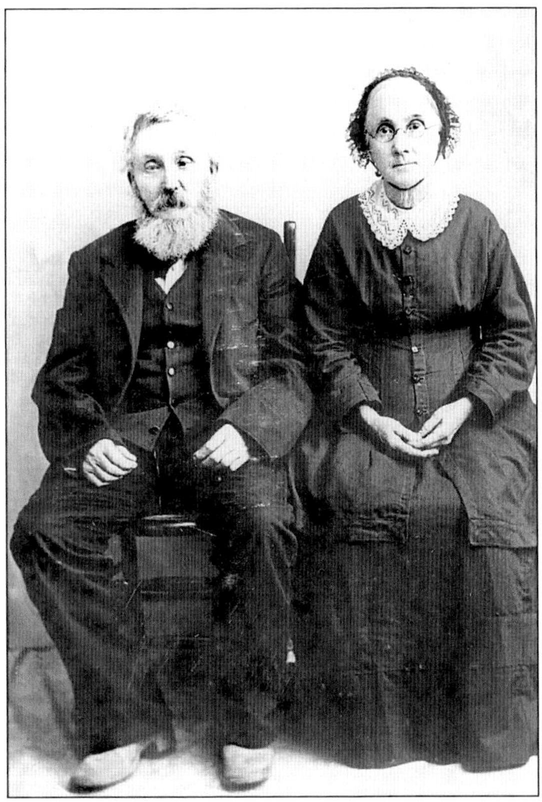

Pictured here are Thomas and Phebe Stevens, parents of Lucinda Stevens Nurse—the wife of Henry Nurse. (Courtesy of Mary Nurse Meyer.)

Henry and Irene Moulter Hickock are pictured here. (Courtesy of Mary Nurse Meyer.)

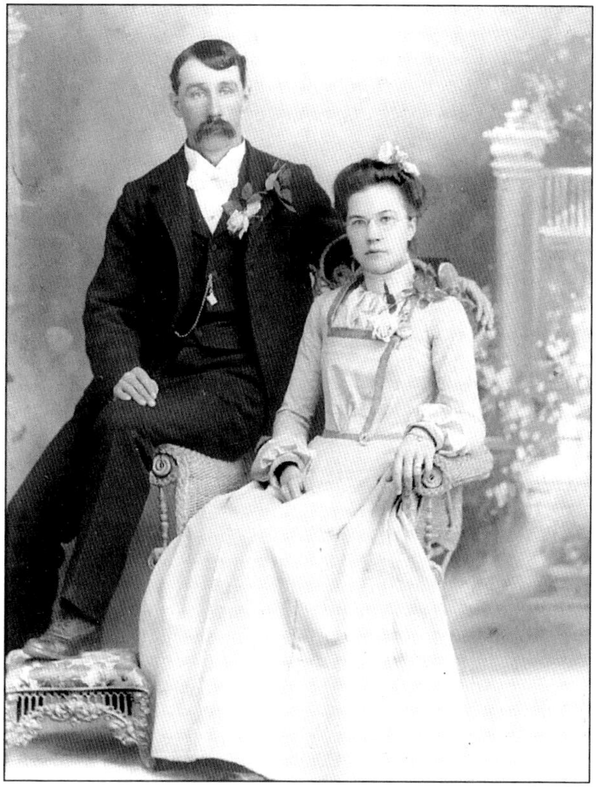

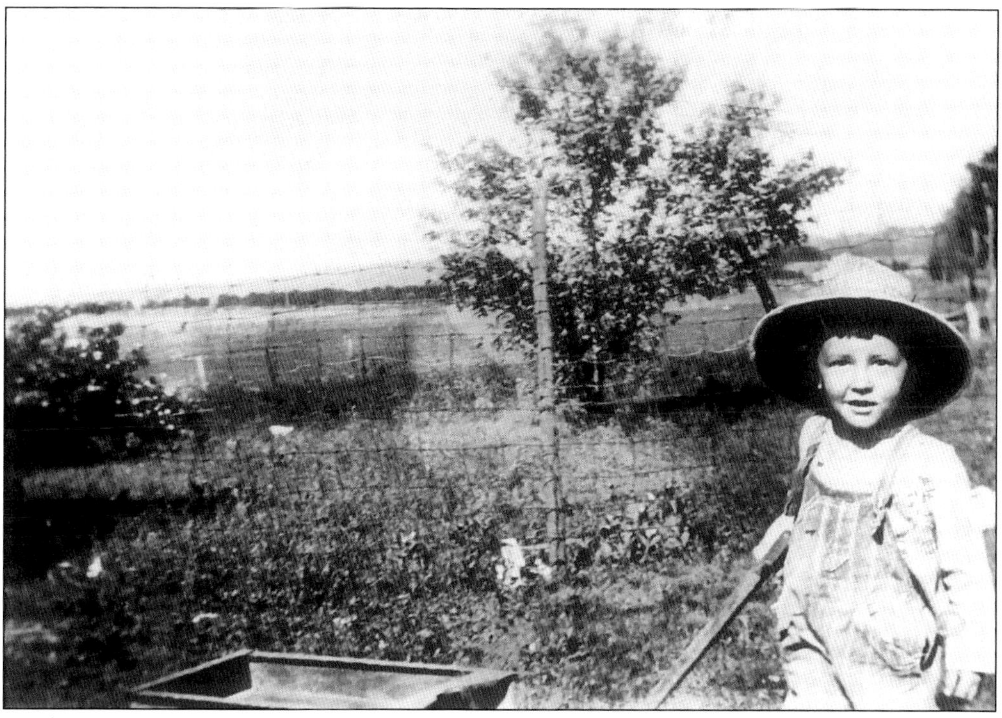

Hank Foster is pictured here in 1925 at the age of six. (Courtesy of Hank Foster.)

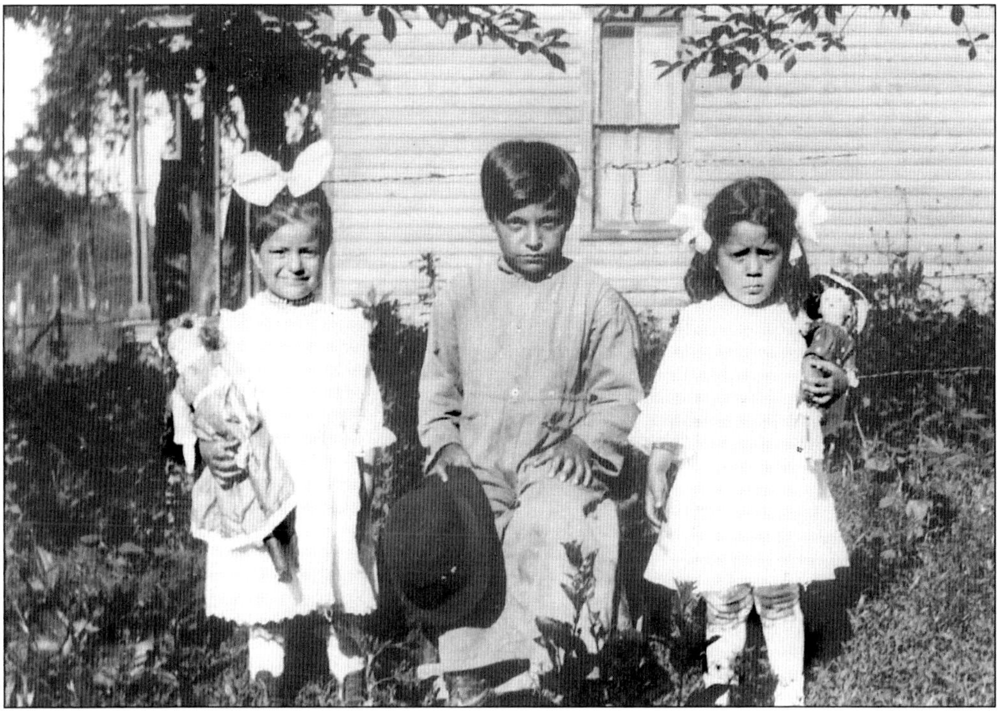

Pictured here, from left to right, are: Catherine Huerta, Frank Huerta, and Carmen Razo. (Courtesy of Carmen Herron.)

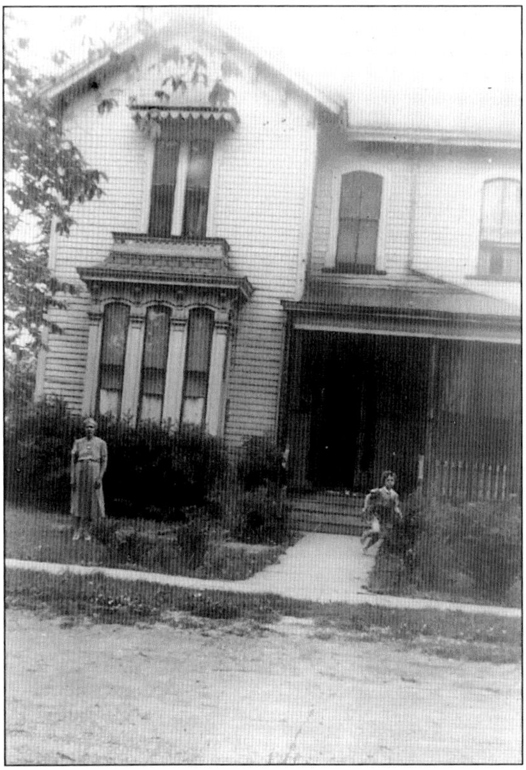

Ruperta Razo is pictured here in front of her house, "the old Winchester House," at 105 Benedict Street. (Courtesy of David Herron.)

Pictured here, from left to right, are: Ruperta Razo, Carmen Razo Herron, and Natividad Razo. (Courtesy of Carmen Herron.)

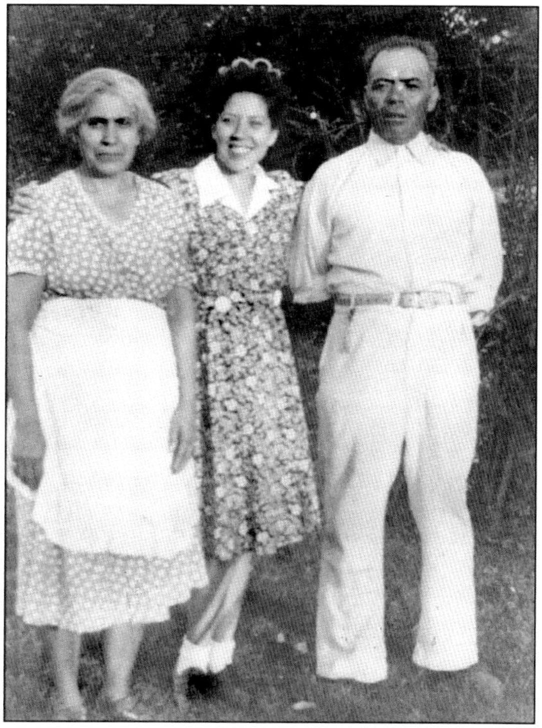

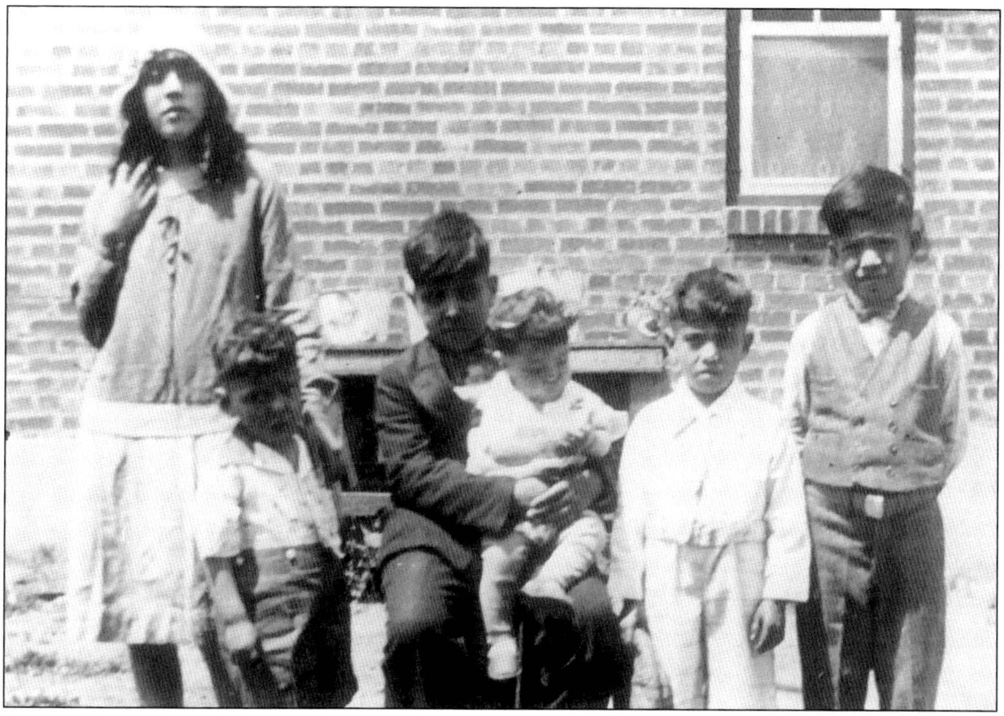

Pictured here, from left to right, are: Carmen, Richard, Sal, David, John, and Frank Razo in about 1930. (Courtesy of David Herron.)

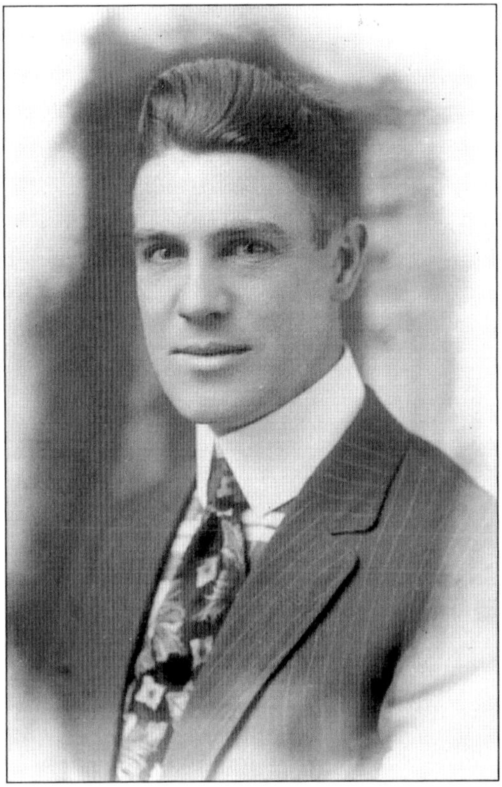

Harry Nelson is pictured at left.

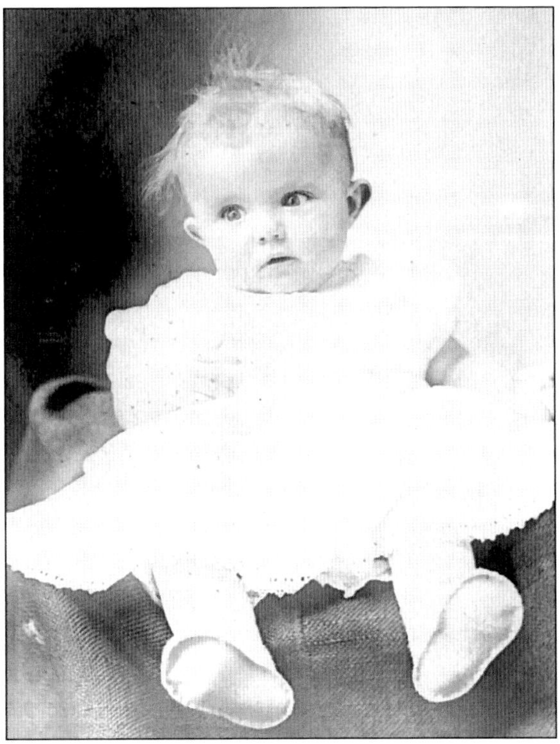

June Nelson Stiers, daughter of Harry Nelson, is pictured here.

Four

CHURCHES AND SCHOOLS

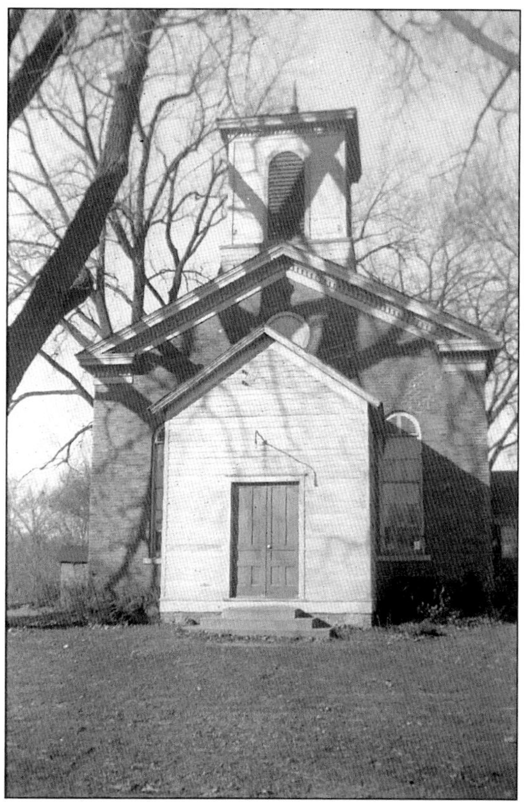

This is a 1940 view of Mossville Methodist Church from the east. This building now houses a bed-and-breakfast on Mossville Road. (Courtesy of Mr. and Mrs. Glen Hannah.)

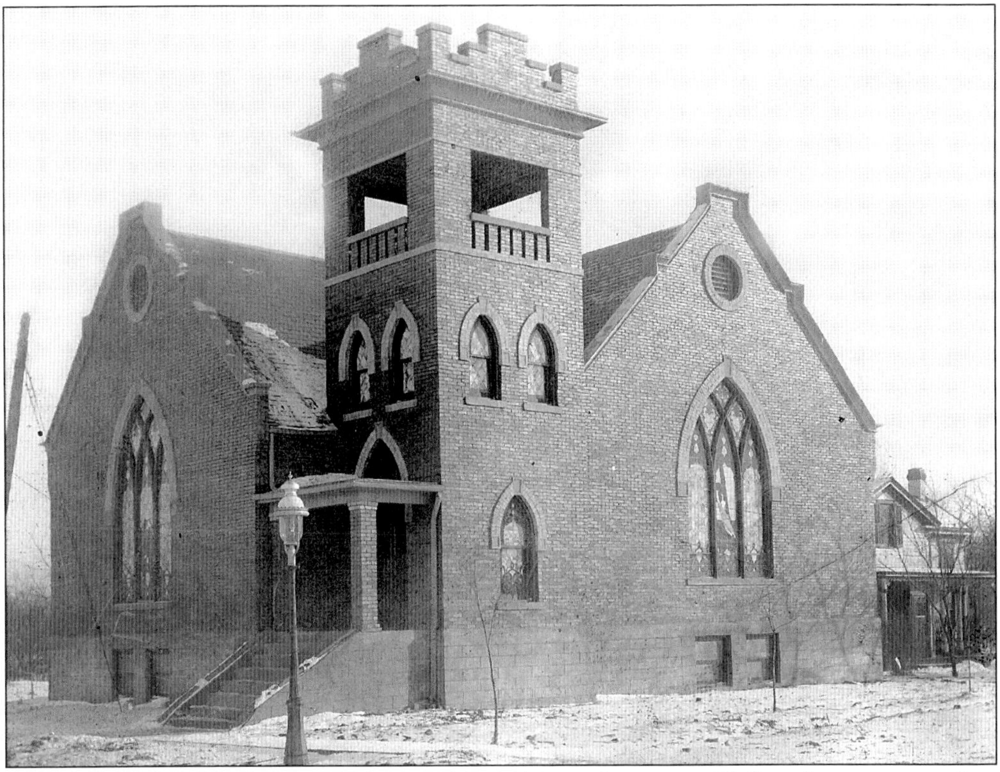

First Baptist Church at Seventh (Santa Fe) and Pine Streets in Chillicothe was erected in 1907. It is shown here before the remodeling and addition. This was the third building owned by First Baptist.

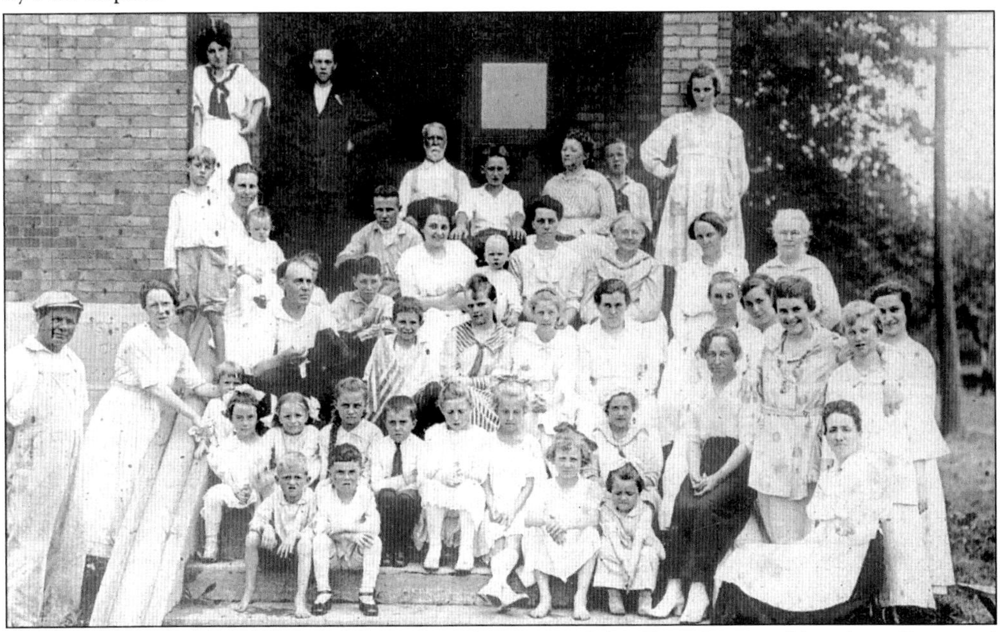

Pictured here is a Sunday School class on the steps of the First Baptist Church at Pine and Santa Fe Streets in Chillicothe. (Courtesy of Elsie Stoecker.)

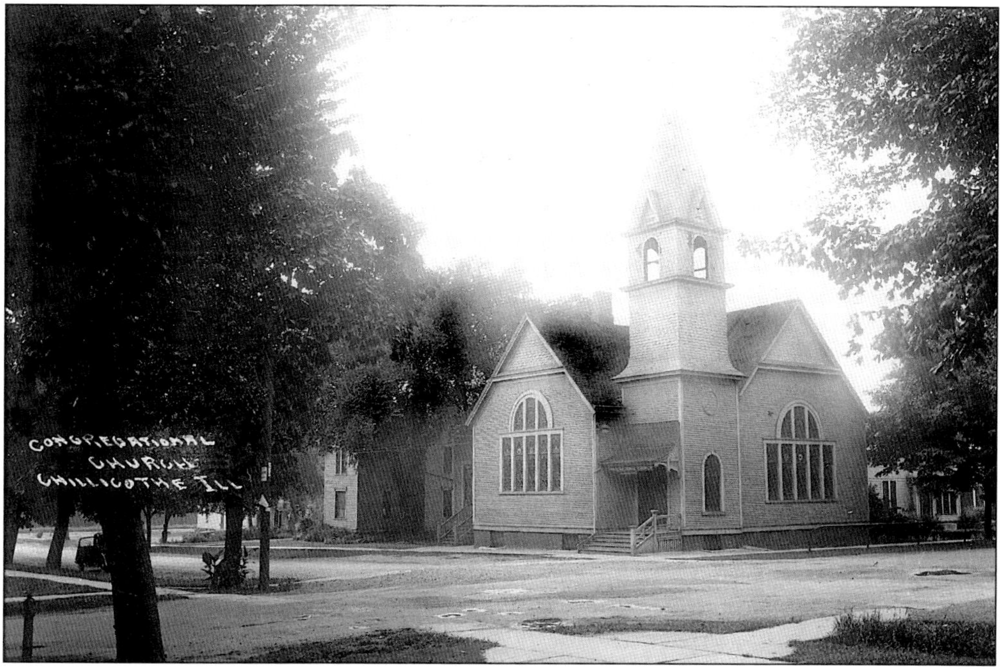

Plymouth Congregational Church at Fourth and Pine Streets was completed in August of 1893.

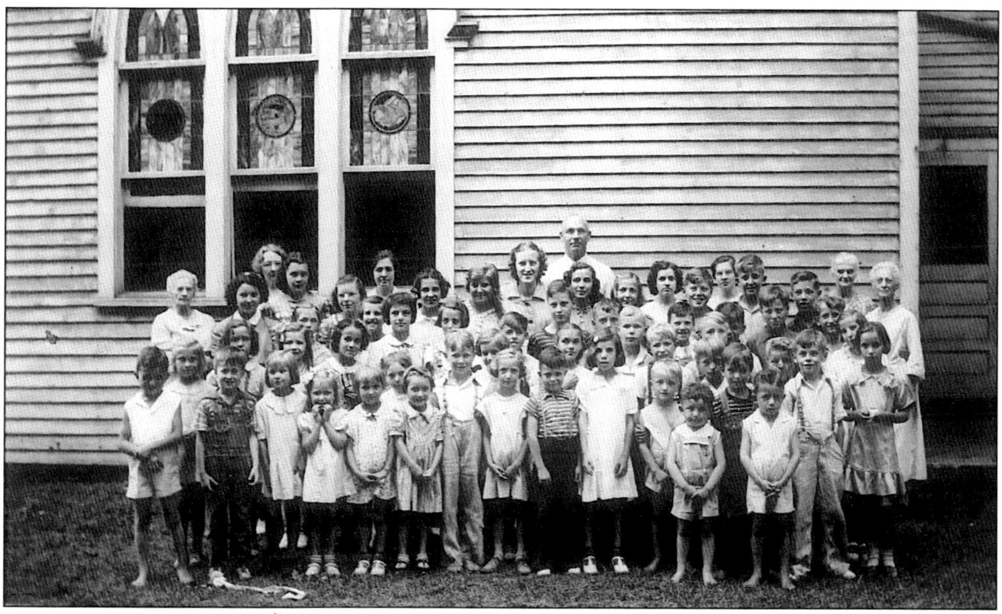

The Congregational Sunday School is pictured here.

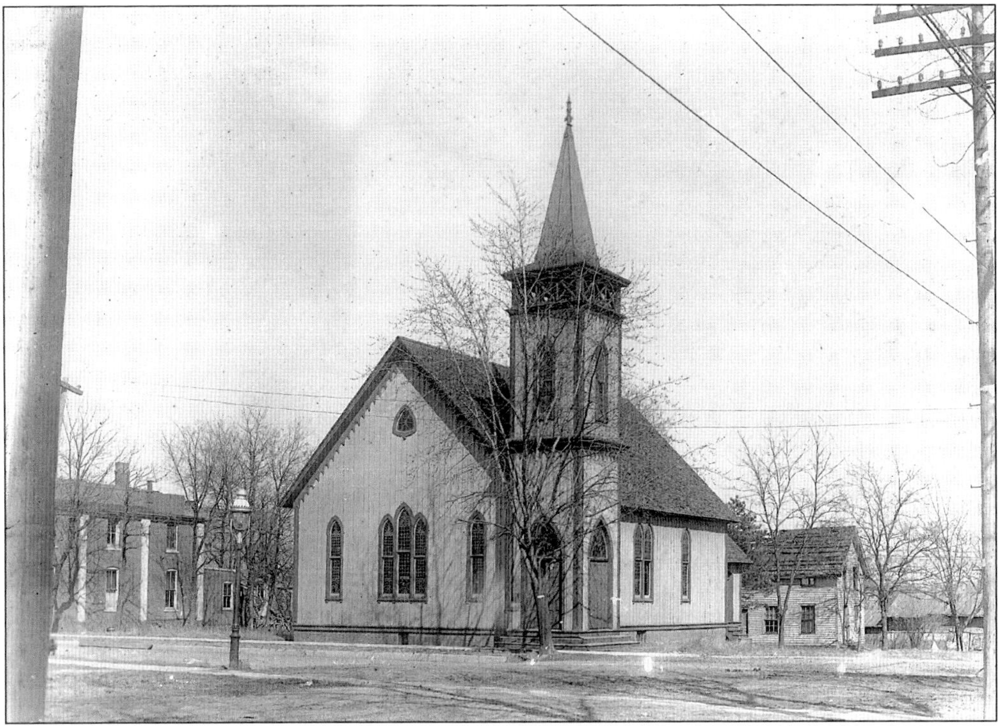

This photo is identified as the old Episcopal Church on the northeast corner of Second and Elm Streets. In 1874, the St. John's Protestant Episcopal Church at Third and Walnut Streets voted to affiliate with the Reformed Episcopal Church at Second and Elm Streets. The brick building to the left would have been the Weber Building.

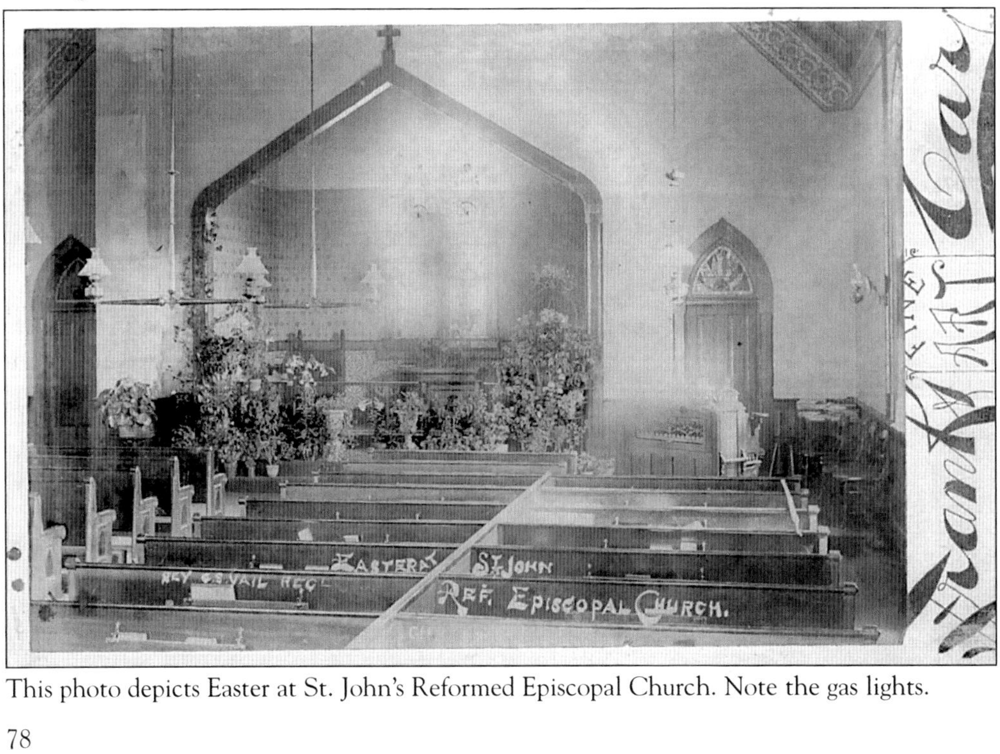

This photo depicts Easter at St. John's Reformed Episcopal Church. Note the gas lights.

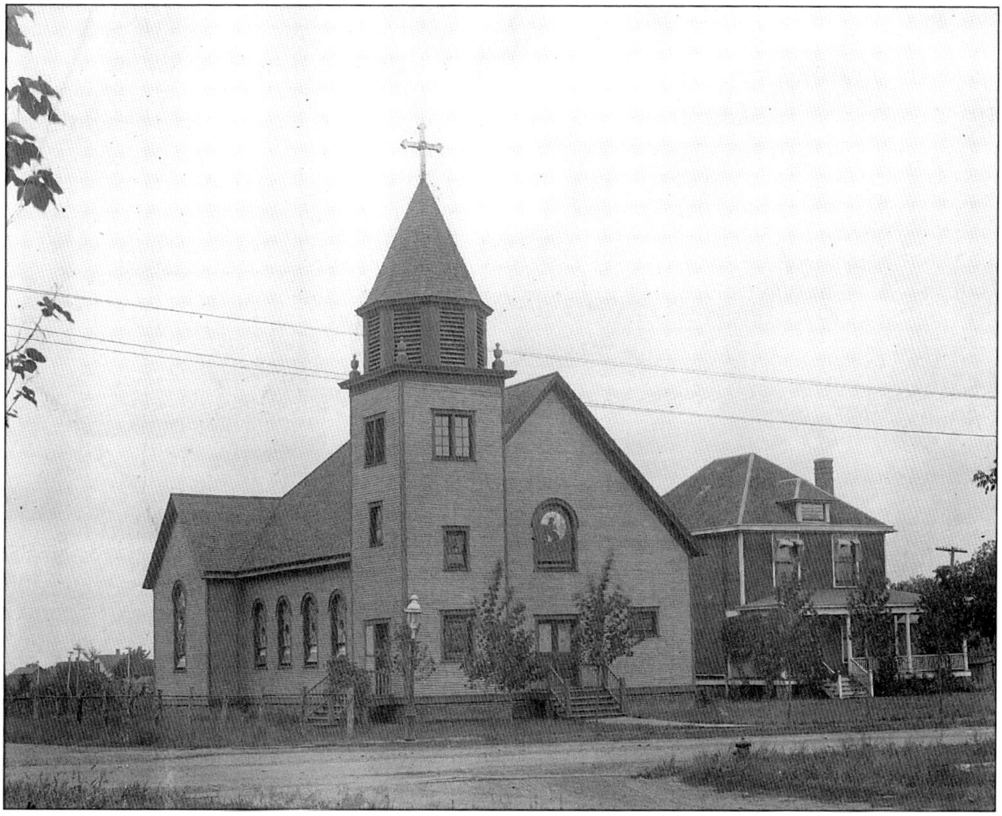

The first St. Edward's Catholic Church and Rectory at Sixth and Pine Streets is pictured here. Construction began on the church in 1900.

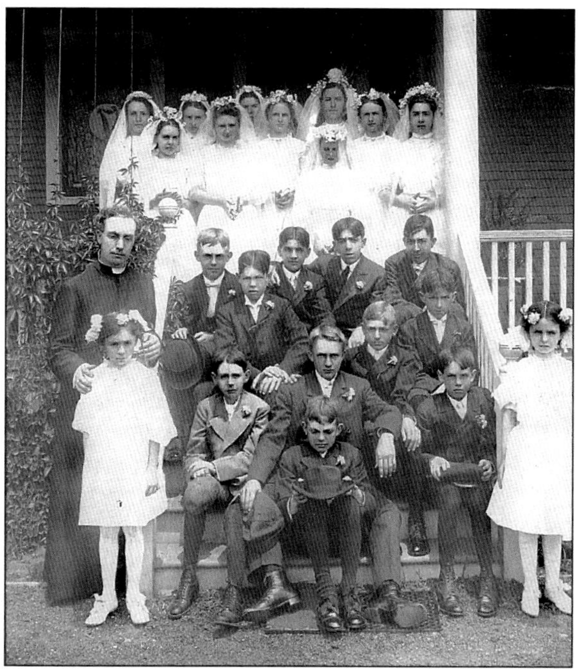

A confirmation class at St. Edward's is pictured here in about 1907. Note the high-top shoes and knee pants the smaller boys are wearing. Apparently, the boy on the far right sitting next to the standing girl in front is Fred Kelly. Rudy Kelly is the boy in the middle of the back row of boys—his hair is parted in the middle.

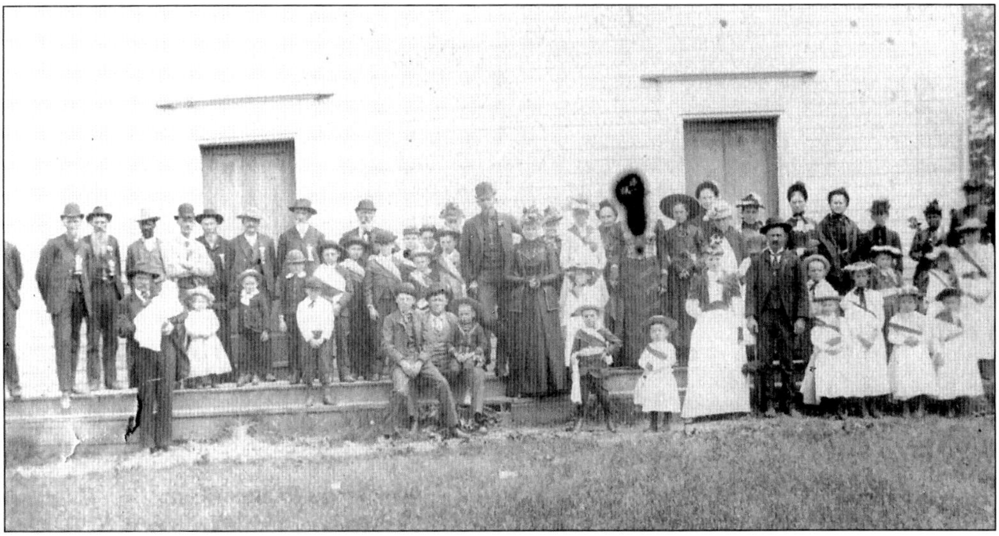

This photo depicts Decoration Day 1891 at the Old Blue Ridge Methodist Church. (Courtesy of Mary Nurse Meyer.)

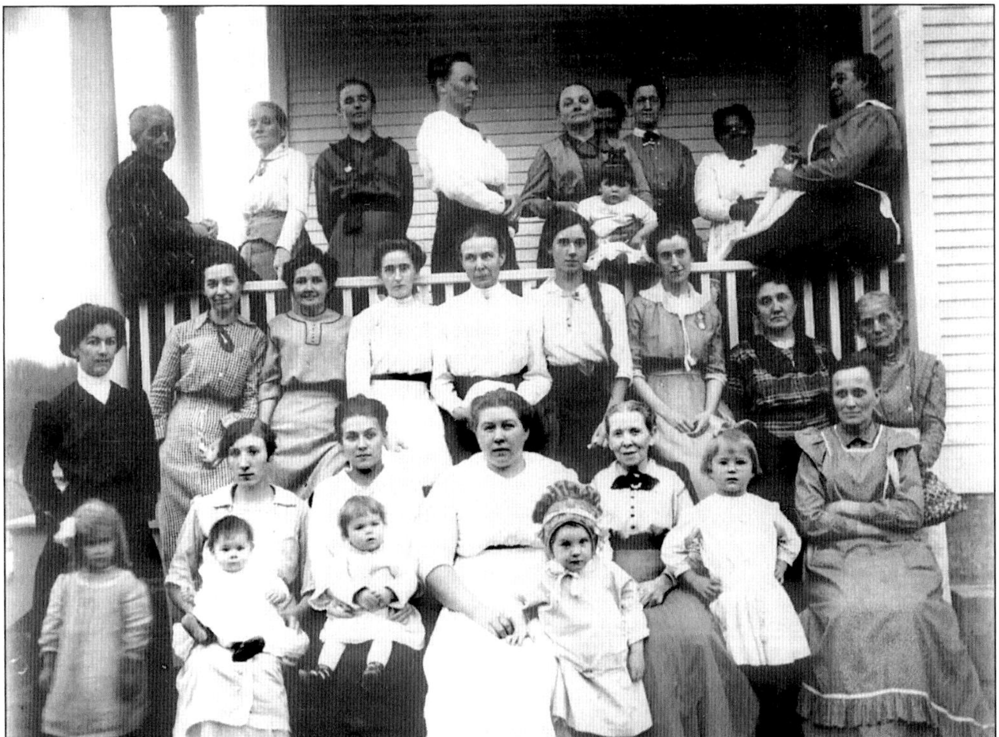

Blue Ridge Ladies Aid is pictured here at the Sheets' place. They are: (on porch) Ellen Marshall, Rose Reed, Stella Clark, Tilli Neuman, Lucy Kendall holding Jessie McQuilkin, Mildred McQuilkin hidden behind, Clara Stowell in back, Jennie Fields, Nellie Colwell; (middle) Maude Stowell and Ruth, Dollie Miller, Myrtle Harlin, Edna Stowell, Ella Krotz, Alice Stowell; (front) Mrs. Cecil Rusk and baby, Lillian Williams and Inez, Mary Nurse and Edith, Lucinda Nurse, Maxine Williams, and Emma Sheets. (Courtesy of Mary Nurse Meyer.)

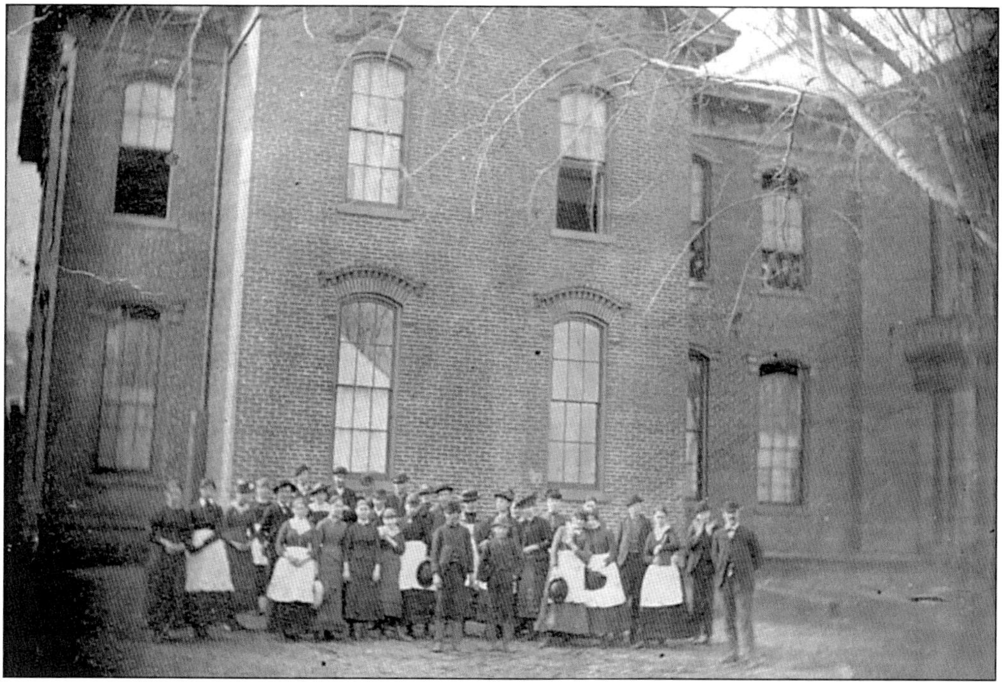

The Chillicothe Public School on the west side of Fourth Street between Elm and Walnut Streets is pictured here. Built after the 1855 Free School Law, the original four-room building had a four-room addition in 1870 and burned in 1891.

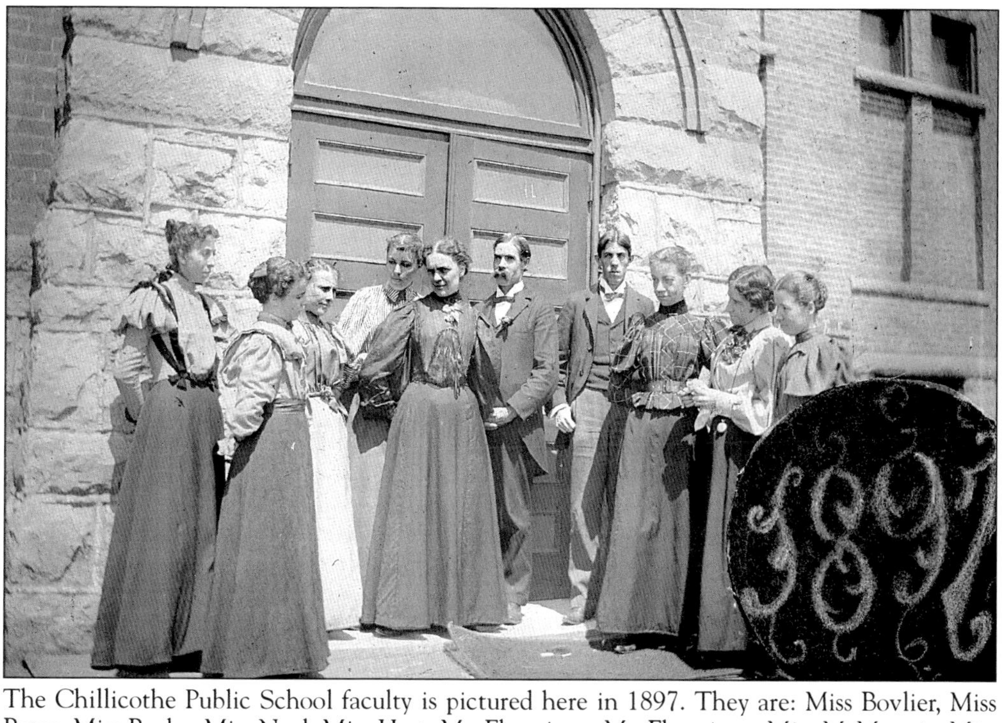

The Chillicothe Public School faculty is pictured here in 1897. They are: Miss Bovlier, Miss Bates, Miss Beebe, Miss Neal, Miss Hart, Mr. Flannigan, Mr. Flannigan, Miss McMurtrie, Miss Weatherwax, and Miss Caldwell.

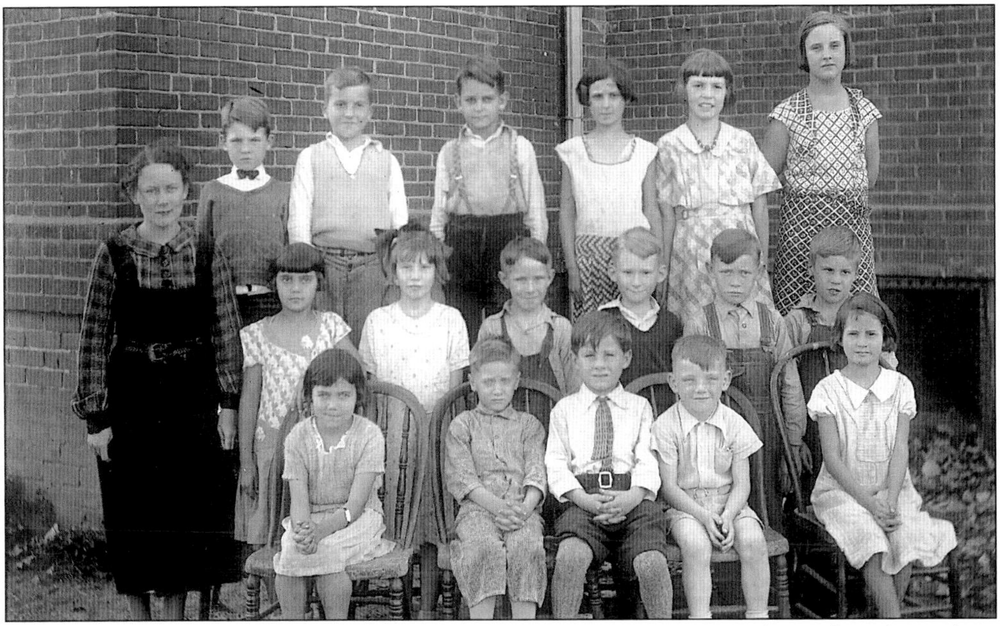

Pictured here are the lower grades of Mossville School in 1934. They are: (seated) Lyal Hendryx, Paul Baker, Paul Neal, Jake Gilmore, Marjorie Daily; (standing) teacher Cetha Walkington, Gloria Hendryx, Patsy Harker, Jay King, Sealy, Kenneth Hendryx, Walter Harker; (back) Ralph Wilson, John Forbes, Bill Adams, Edith Daily, Margaret Feuchter, and Betty Salter. (Courtesy of Mr. and Mrs. Glen Hannah.)

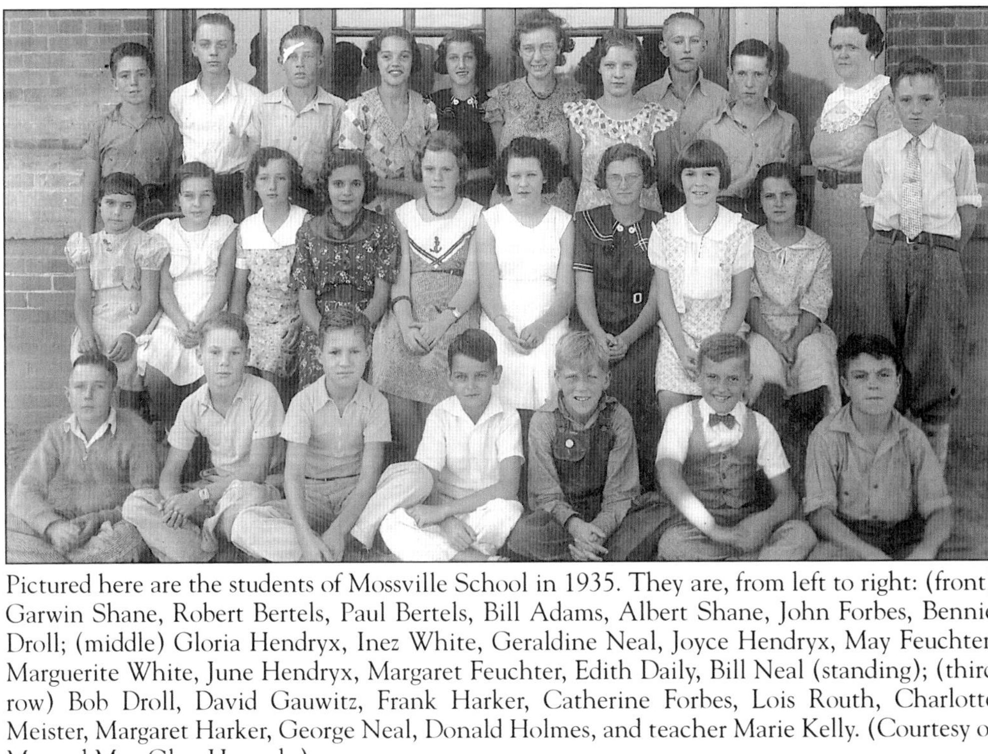

Pictured here are the students of Mossville School in 1935. They are, from left to right: (front) Garwin Shane, Robert Bertels, Paul Bertels, Bill Adams, Albert Shane, John Forbes, Bennie Droll; (middle) Gloria Hendryx, Inez White, Geraldine Neal, Joyce Hendryx, May Feuchter, Marguerite White, June Hendryx, Margaret Feuchter, Edith Daily, Bill Neal (standing); (third row) Bob Droll, David Gauwitz, Frank Harker, Catherine Forbes, Lois Routh, Charlotte Meister, Margaret Harker, George Neal, Donald Holmes, and teacher Marie Kelly. (Courtesy of Mr. and Mrs. Glen Hannah.)

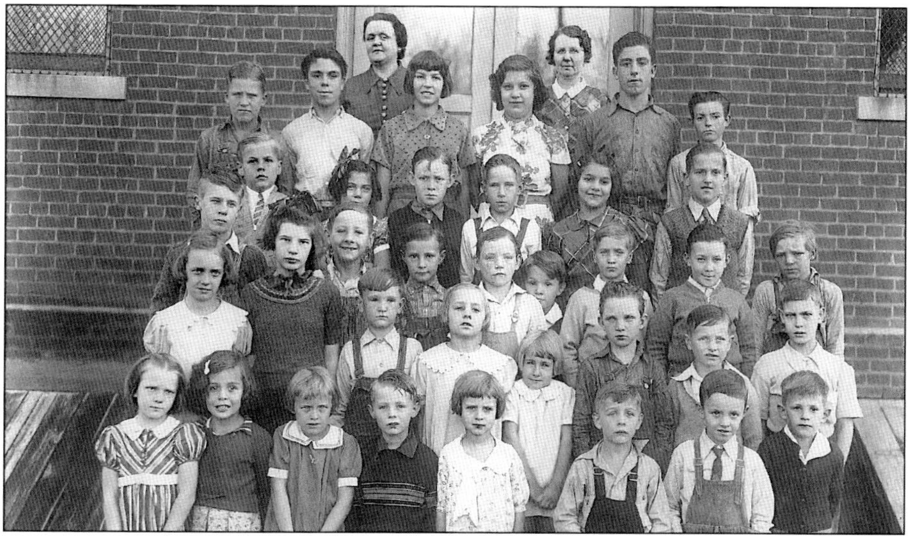

Mossville School students are pictured here in 1937. They are: (front) Shirley Martin, Doris Dickison, Shirley Laurence, Charles Burns, unidentified, Kenny Dickison, Paul Dickison, unidentified; (second row) ? Dickison, Patsy Harker, unidentified, ? Dickison, Darlene Bugg, Eddie Foster, unidentified, unidentified; (third row) Walter Harker, Paul Neal, Gene Krause, Jake Gilmore, unidentified, Paul Baker, Robert Clark, Louis Weaver; (fourth row) Bob Brown, Lyal Hendryx, Kenneth Hendryx, Jay King, Gloria Hendryx, John Forbes; (fifth row) Albert Shane, Bennie Droll, Margaret Feuchter, Margaret Harker, Bob Droll, Roy Weaver; (teachers) Marie Kelly—upper four grades, and Marie Taylor—lower four grades. (Courtesy of Mr. and Mrs. Glen Hannah.)

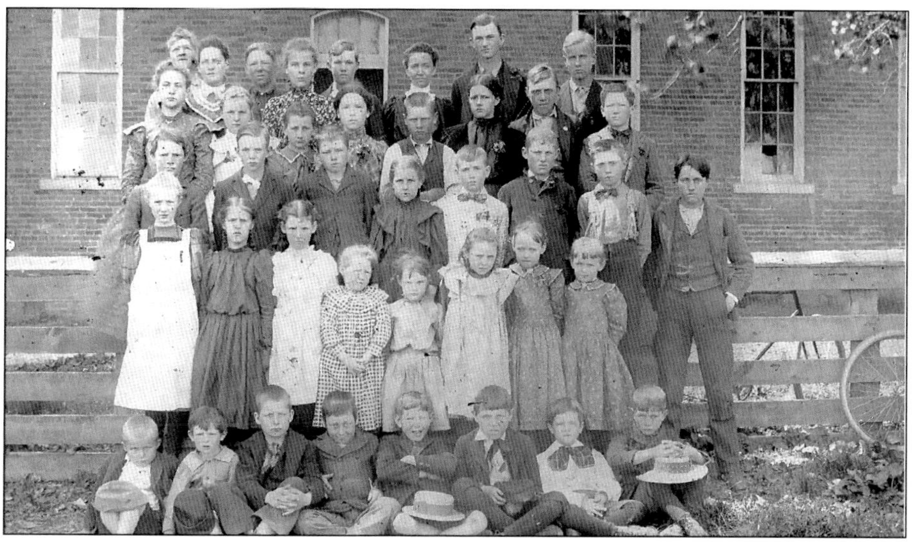

Pictured here are Mossville School students on May 23, 1899. They are: (rear row) Albert Francis, Allie Goodwin, Victor Thorne, Bessie Martin, Walt Thorne, Miss Norwood, Bud Thorne, Guy McFarland, Bertha Kriete, ? Evans, Nellie Clark, Debbie Thorne, Albert Hayes, May Clark, Wesley Rhoades, Frank Thorne, Guy Shaw, Joe Thorne, Willie Challacombe, Ethel Clark, Clarence Robins, Maurice Holmes, Bob Droll, Ed Hayes, Nellie Thorne, Ella Hayes, Grace Shaw, Mabel Thorne, Ruby Shaw, Ruth Thorne, Mabel Krete, Anne Kriete, Clarence Thorne, Charlie Nash, Eddie Thorne, Bradford Rhoades, Charlie Holmes, and Eddie Clark.

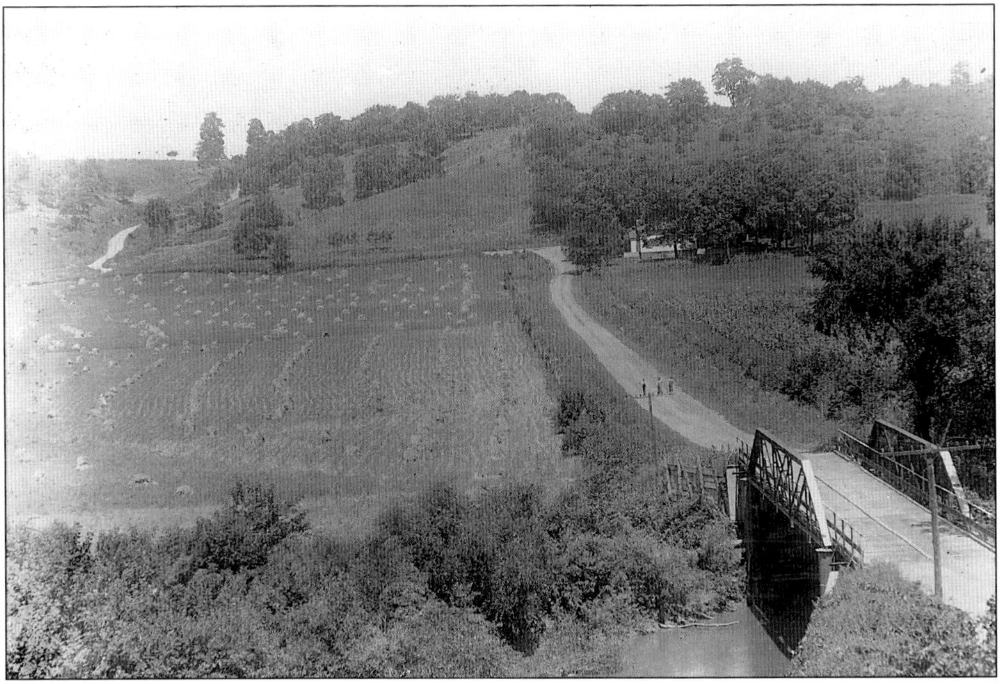

This photo depicts a view near Chillicothe in August of 1924. Pictured here is Benedict Road north of the Santa Fe depot with the old bridge across Senachwine Creek, Senachwine/Shepard School is in the background to the right of the road, shocks of grain are visible to the left, and three boys in overalls are walking toward the bridge.

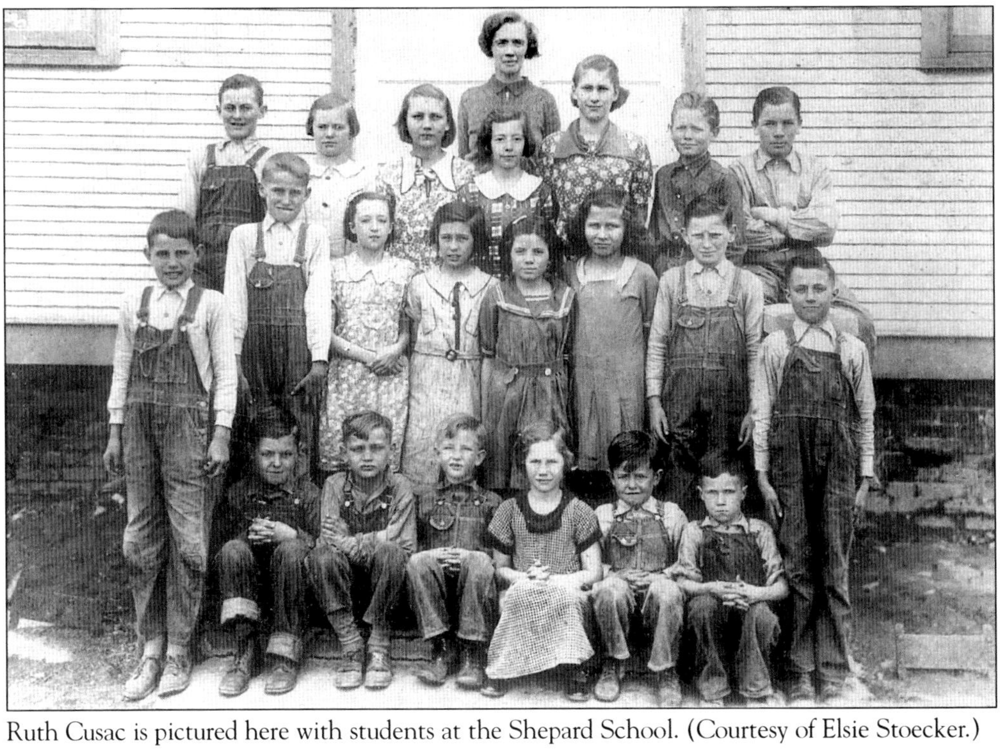

Ruth Cusac is pictured here with students at the Shepard School. (Courtesy of Elsie Stoecker.)

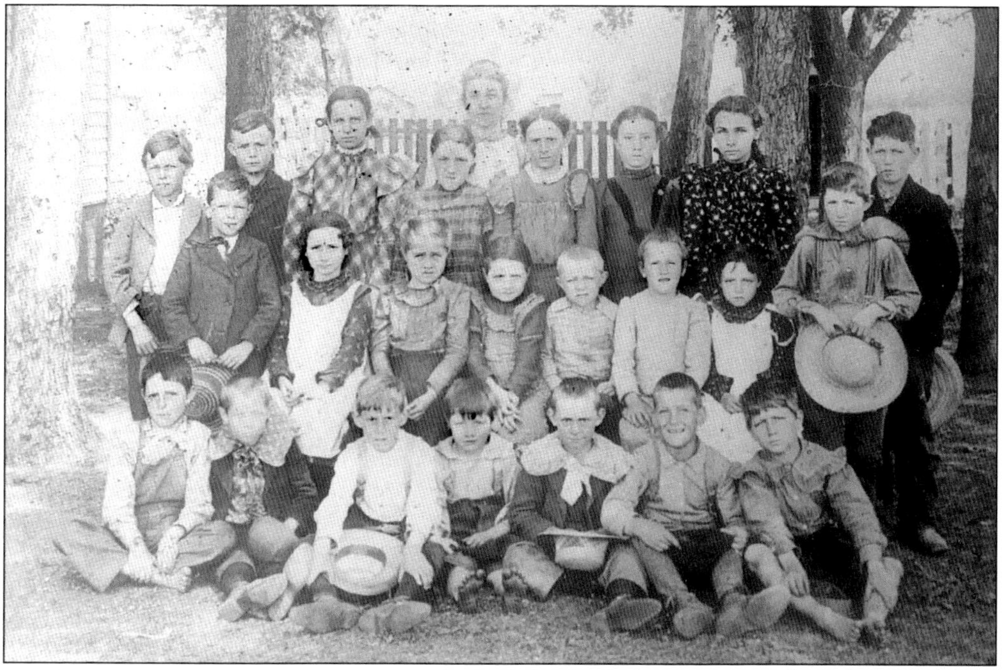

The Rome School is pictured here on May 11, 1899. (Courtesy of the Lawsons.)

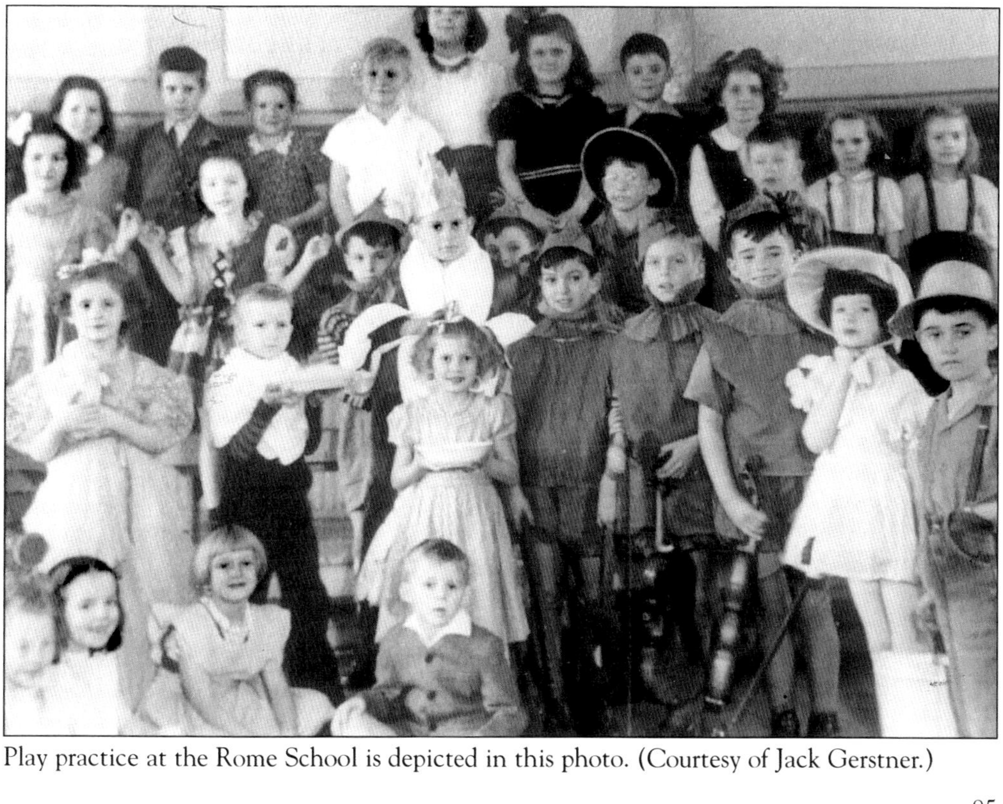

Play practice at the Rome School is depicted in this photo. (Courtesy of Jack Gerstner.)

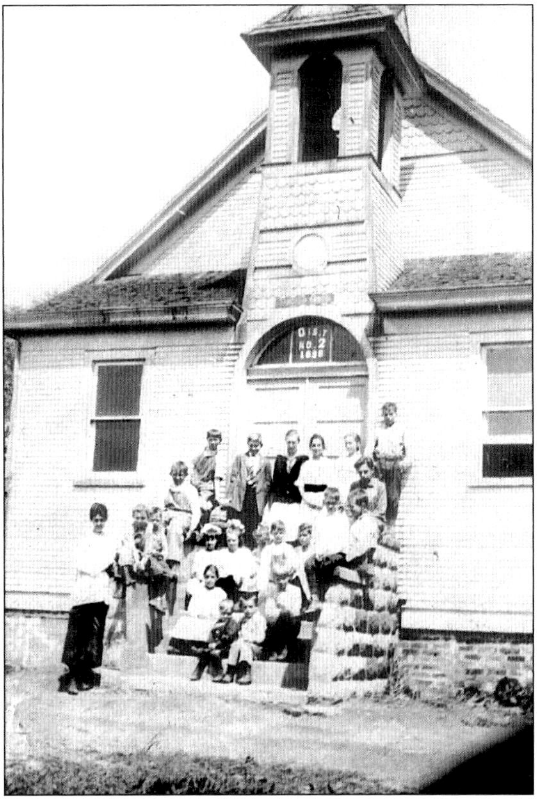

The teacher and students of the Hallock Township School District No. 2 are pictured here in Northampton after 1896.

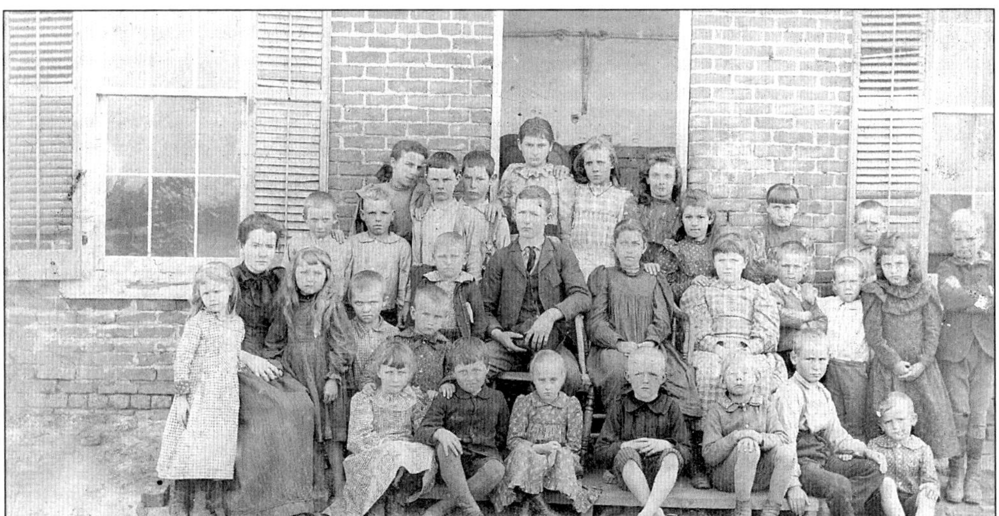

The teacher and students of the old Hallock Township School District No. 2 in Northampton are pictured here. This brick building was replaced by a wooden building in 1896.

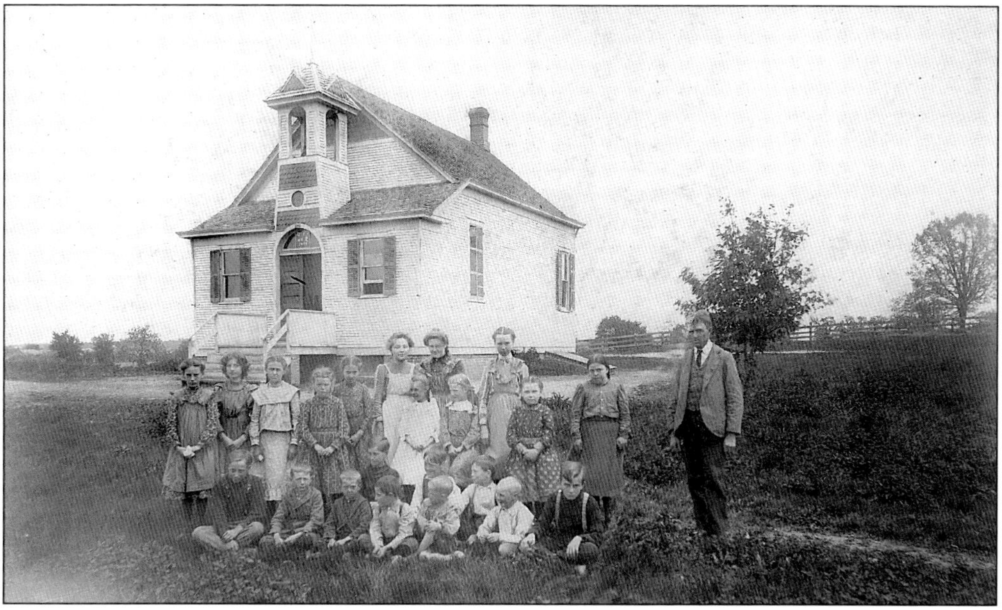

This photo depicts Hallock Township School District No. 2 in Northampton. This wooden building was built in 1896 and serves as a home today.

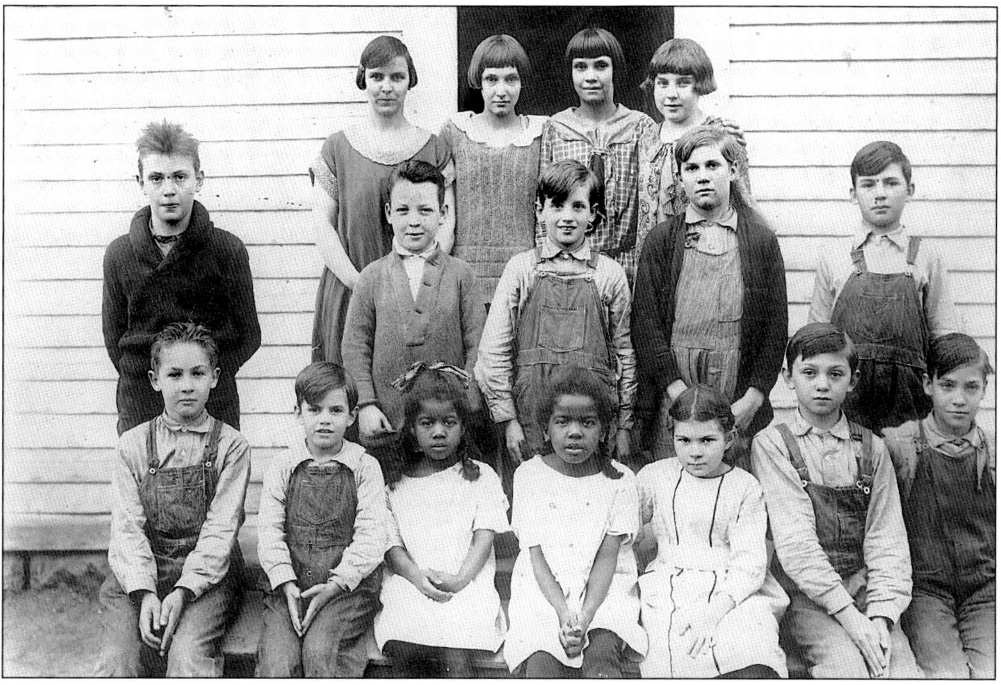

Teacher and students of the Blue Ridge School District No. 32 are pictured here in September 1924. They are, from left to right: (back row) Dora Kilmer, the teacher, Lulu Reynolds, Lola Williams, Edith Nurse; (middle row) Roy Bridgeman, Donat Lappin, Richard Gallup, J.D. Reynolds, Everett Gallup; (front row) Howard Nurse, Robert Gallup, Bernadine Moody, Vivian Moody, Katherine Bahret, Eugene Stotler, and Warren Reynolds. This photo was taken by L. Clark, a Chillicothe photographer. (Courtesy of Katherine Anderson.)

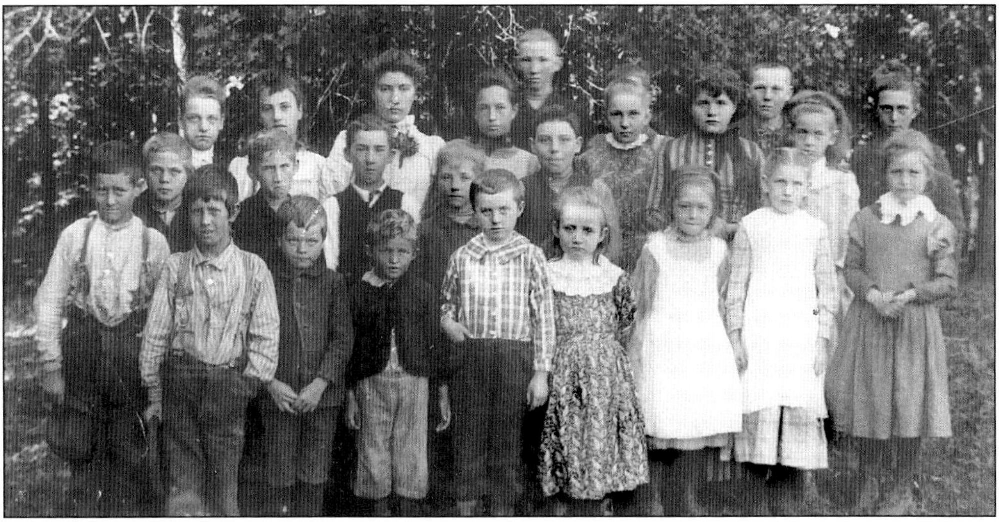

Students of the Blue Ridge School are pictured here. They are, from left to right: (top row) Alice Wait, Gertrude Root, teacher Anna Durkee, Susie Burns, Lyman Robinson, Julius Root, Guy Nurse, Bert Wait; (middle row) John Babcock, Warren Stowell, Charles Rowe, Herbert Briggs, Elbert Nurse, Mabel Robinson, Emma Babcock, Myra Wait; (lower row) Charles Weaner, Abe Weaner, Alva Babcock, Bob Cook, Charles Crady, Agnes Briggs, Alma Manoch, Jesse Manoch, and Virginia Gallup. (Courtesy of Mary Nurse Meyer.)

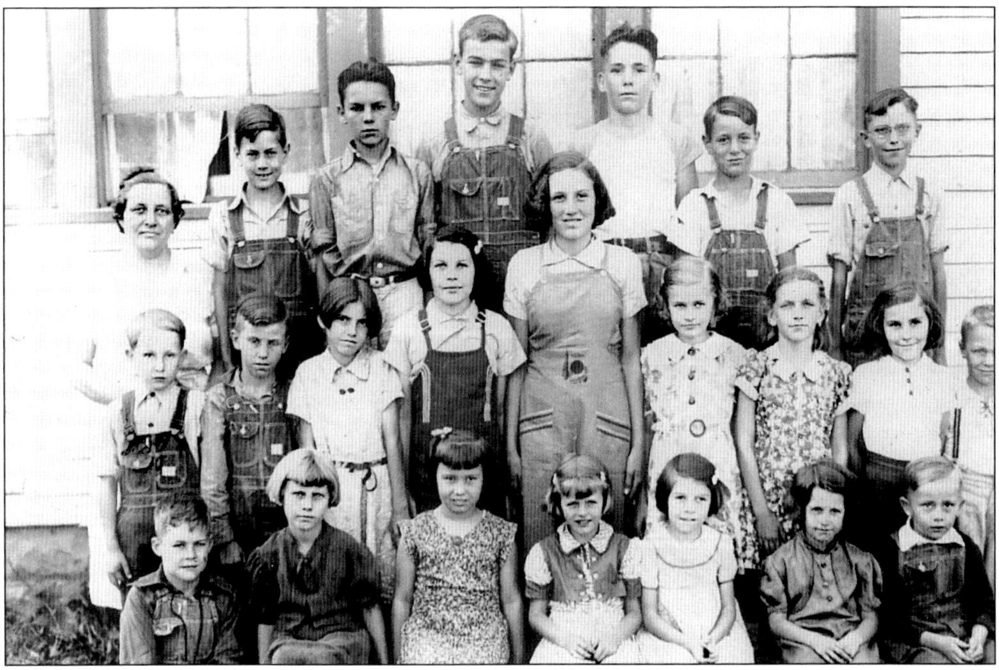

Students of the Blue Ridge School are pictured here in 1939. They are: (top row) teacher Edith Shimp, unidentified, Kenneth Perry, ? Lewis, Ira Placher, Arthur Trowbridge, Mike Colwell; (middle row) unidentified, Charles Colwell, Mary Colwell, Audrey Nurse, Wilma Trowbridge, Marilyn Miller, Alice Placher, Joanne Davis, unidentified; (bottom row) Bob Miller, June Colwell, Darlene Stotler, Janice Harkin, Mary Nurse, unidentified, and Freddy Stotler. (Courtesy of Mary Nurse Meyer.)

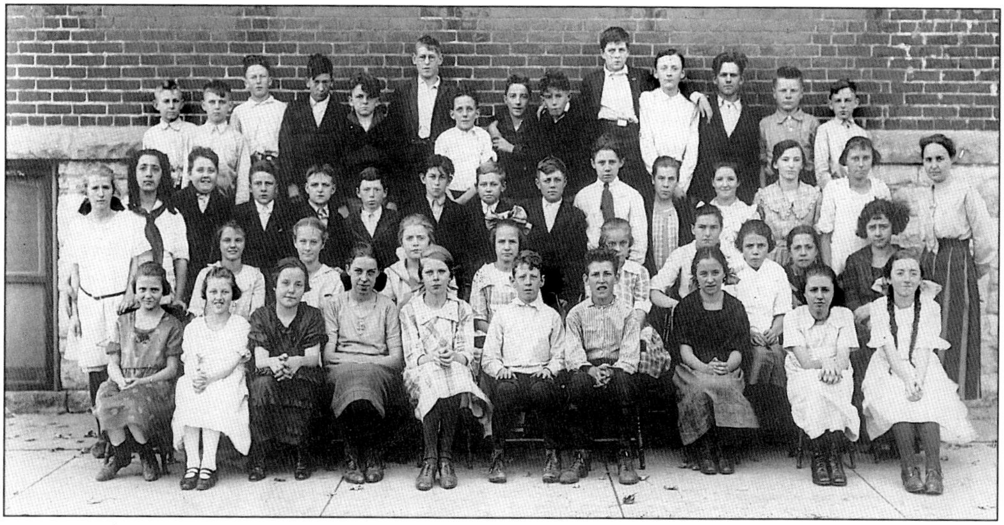

Miss Goodwin's seventh grade class at the old Chillicothe Grade School is pictured here. They are: (first row) Lois Hammett, Fern Tucker, Marguerite Westfall, Lois Schmidt, Irene Bayles, Howard Hinman, Charles Adams, Florence Welcome, Pearl Wood, Norma Stallings; (second row) Lucille Lucas, Alberta White, Edna Harris, Dorothy Murphy, Berniece Beaumont, Neva Robins, Katherine Daugherty, Helen Pasdik, Grace Rose; (third row) Dorothy Anderson, Josephine Rashid, Richard Zinser, Virgil Anderson, George Stumbaugh, Maurice Guyer, Herbert Edminister, Winfried Scott, Lewis Staab, Calvin Bradford, Geneva Pearson, Leona Stillas, Marian Harvey, Pearl Niggermeyer; (fourth row) Clifford Wisenburg, George Cleveland, Richard Williamson, Calvin Foote, Russell Bell, Clement Shupert, James Davis, Carl Wright, Ephraim Davis, Russell Paris, Herman Lucas, Raymond Wolfe, and George McLaughlin.

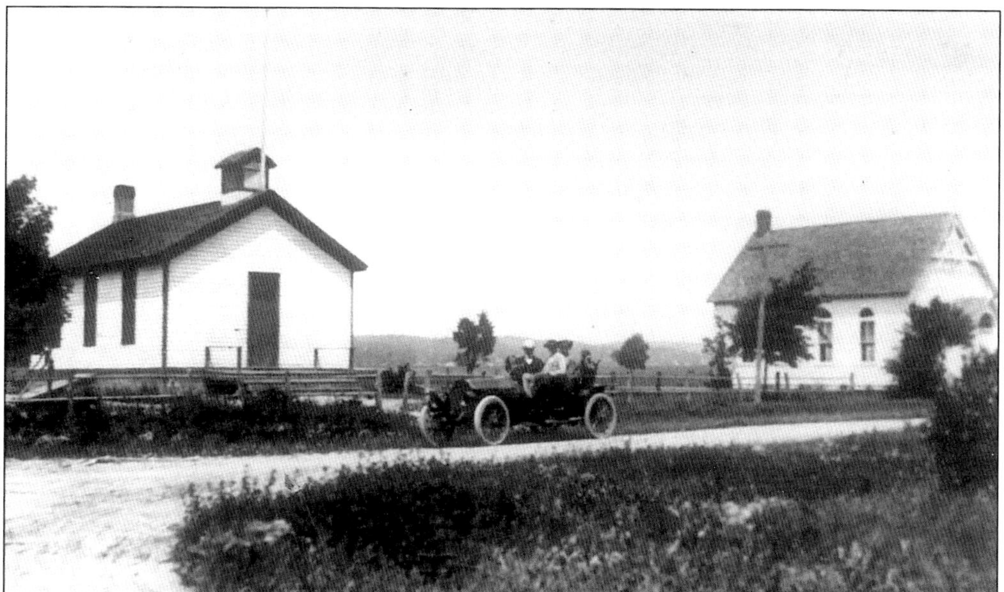

The Boylan School and the Central Christian Church were both located at the intersection of Old Galena Road and Bristol Hollow Road (now Cedar Hills Drive), where the Caterpillar Technology Center is located today.

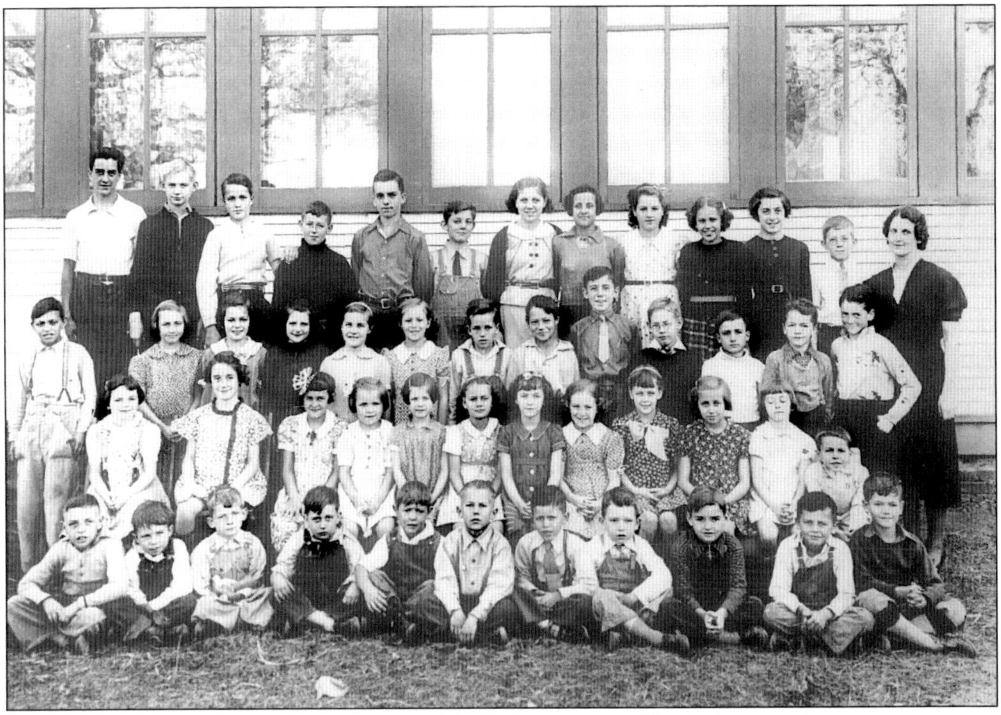

Students at the Rome School are pictured here. (Courtesy of Jack Gerstner.)

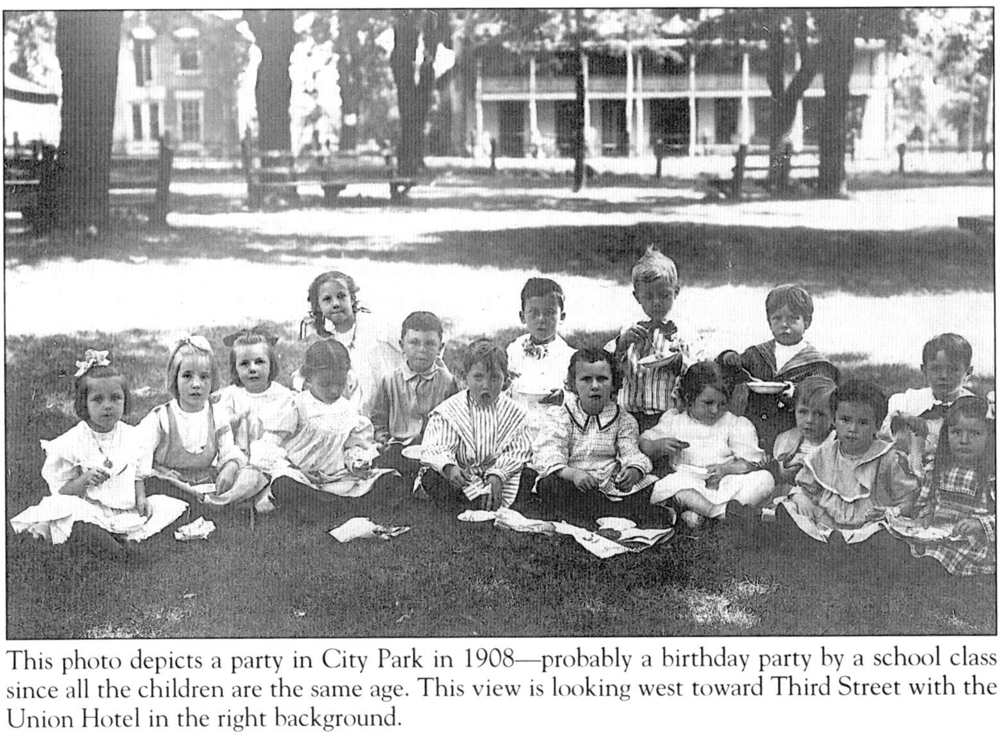

This photo depicts a party in City Park in 1908—probably a birthday party by a school class since all the children are the same age. This view is looking west toward Third Street with the Union Hotel in the right background.

Five

SPORTS

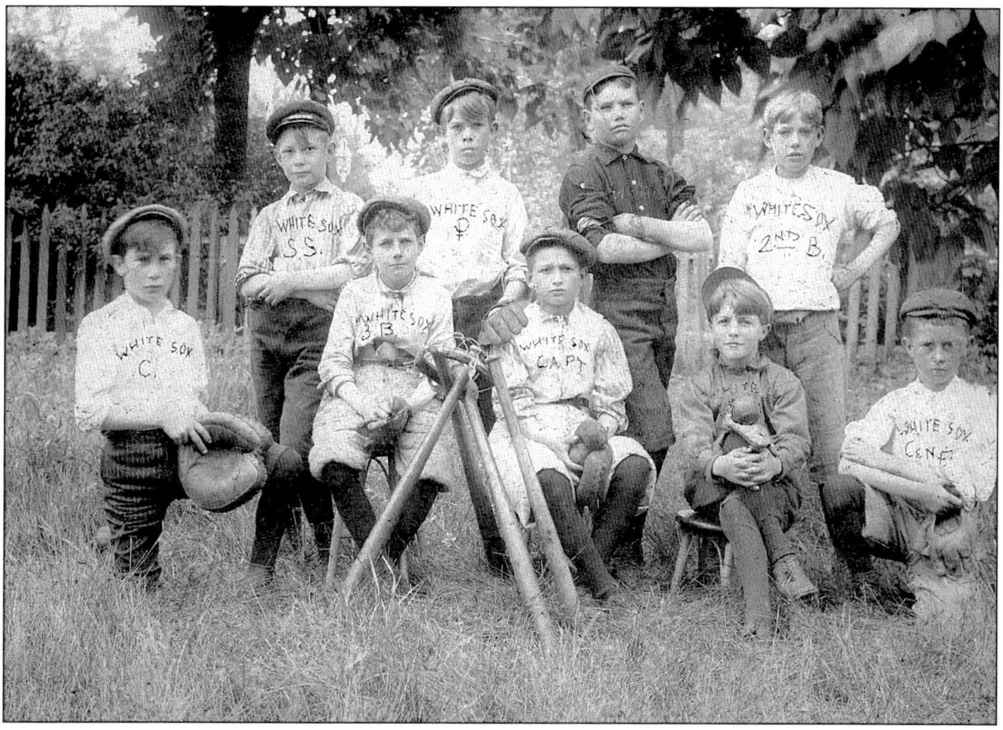

This photo depicts some young White Sox fans, since the team name and position was added in ink to the photo.

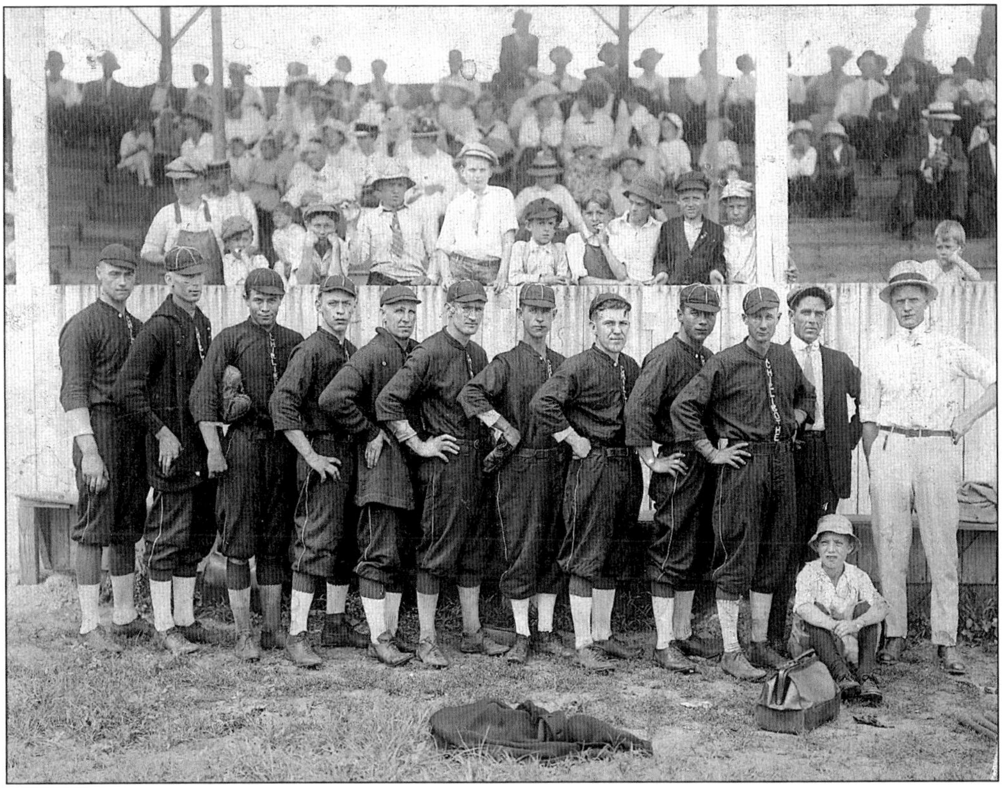

A 1915 Chillicothe baseball team is pictured above.

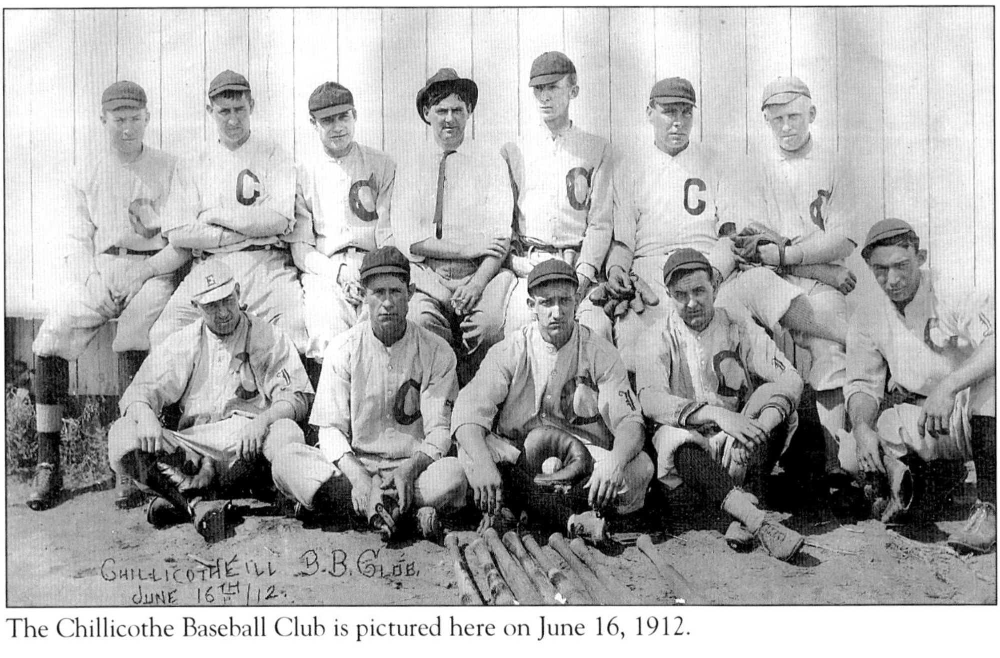

The Chillicothe Baseball Club is pictured here on June 16, 1912.

Pike Camp is waiting to bat in this photograph.

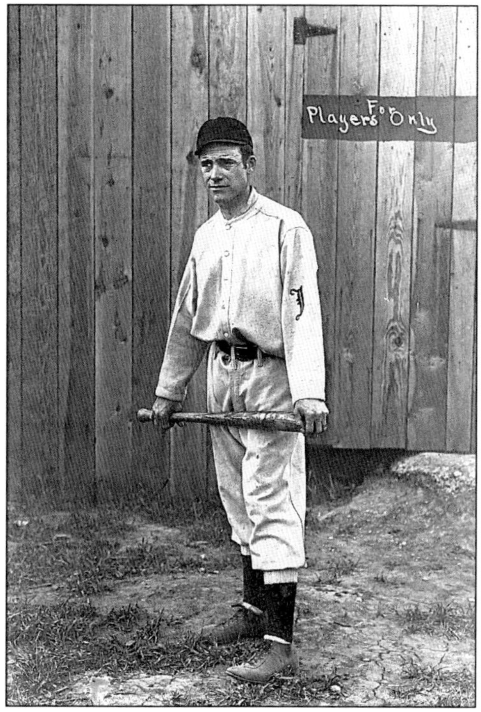

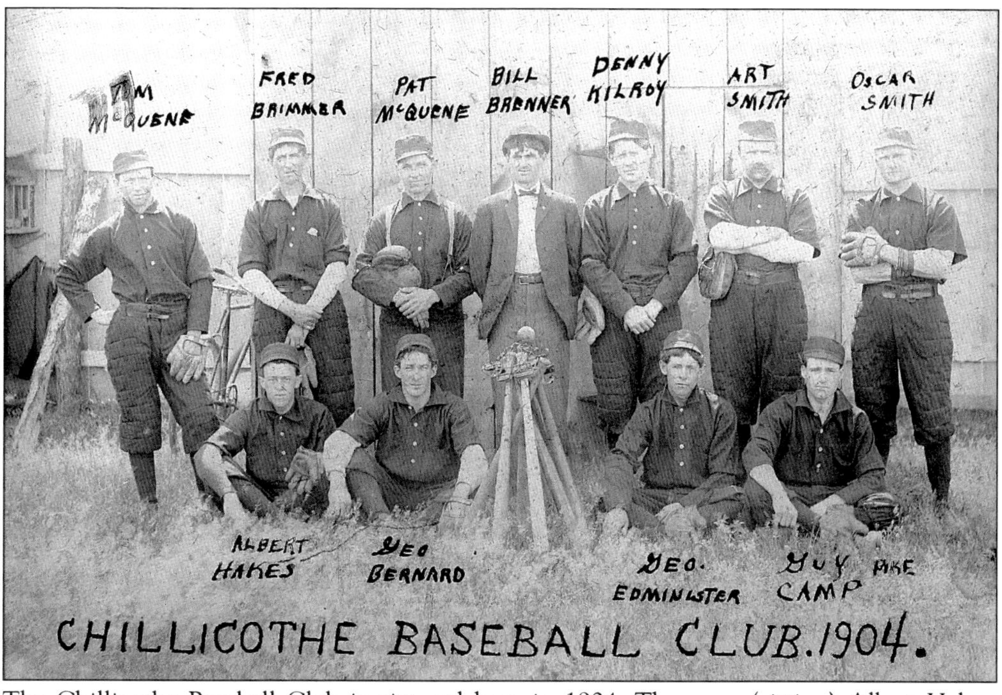

The Chillicothe Baseball Club is pictured here in 1904. They are: (sitting) Albert Hakes, George Bernard, George Edminister, Guy "Pike" Camp; (standing) Tom McQuene, Fred Brimmer, Pat McQuene, Bill Brenner, Denny Kilroy, Art Smith, and Oscar Smith.

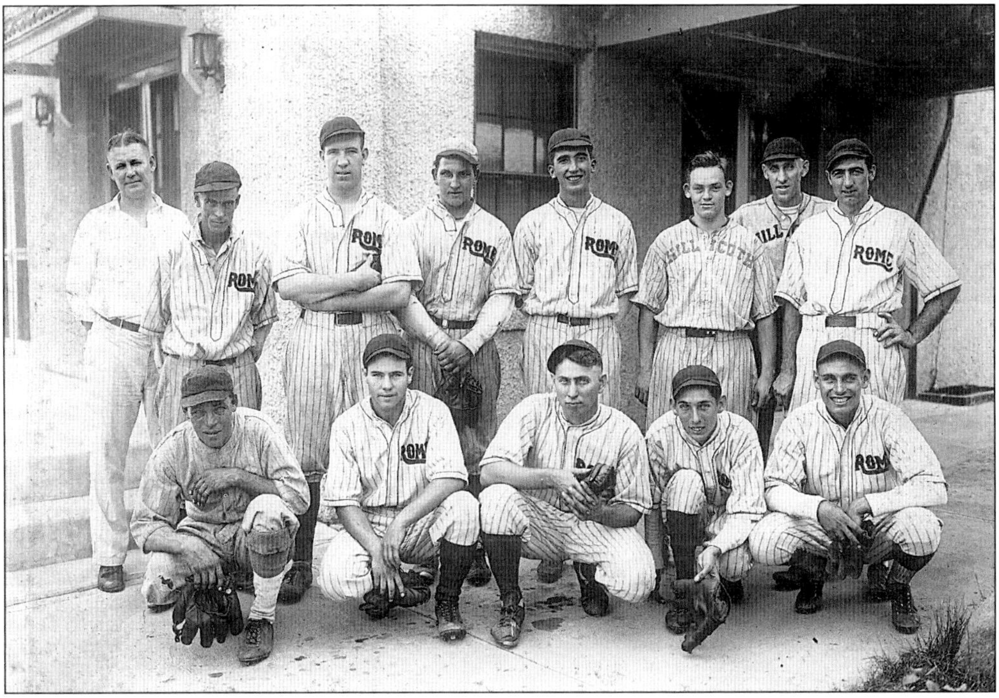

The Rome Baseball Team (with two Chillicothe uniforms) is pictured above in the 1930s. They are: (bottom row) Alfred Zie—, Everett Rose, Charles "Steamboat" Defoe, Leonard Defoe, Don Defoe; (standing) Elmer Lawson, manager, Bruce Dickison, Stanley Rose, Ted Woodruff, Leslie Wilson, Jake Perry, John Huss, and Roswell Ferguson. (Courtesy of Doris Dickison.)

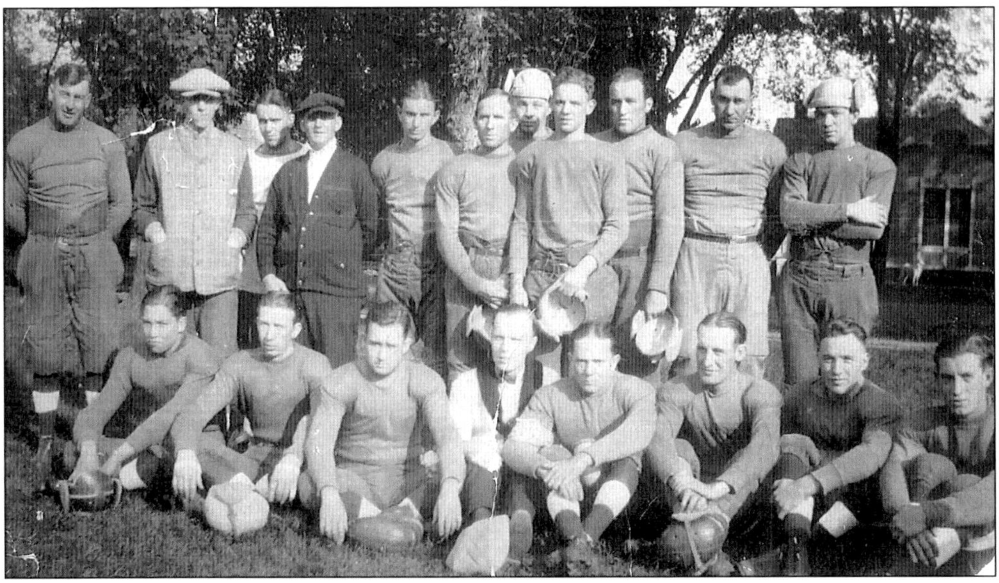

The Chillicothe American Legion Semi-pro Football Team is pictured here on October 17, 1923. They are, from left to right: (front) Gene Collins, Tom Hayden, Chuck Kennington, Nelson Israelson, manager, George Fleetwood, unidentified, Wilber Short, Willard Pearce; (back) Ross Carter, James Ingles, ? Ripley, Fred Thomas, Ora Carroll, Ed Suggett, Oscar Sweeney, Richard Cleveland, James Clyde, Floyd Shepard, and Hugh Moffitt.

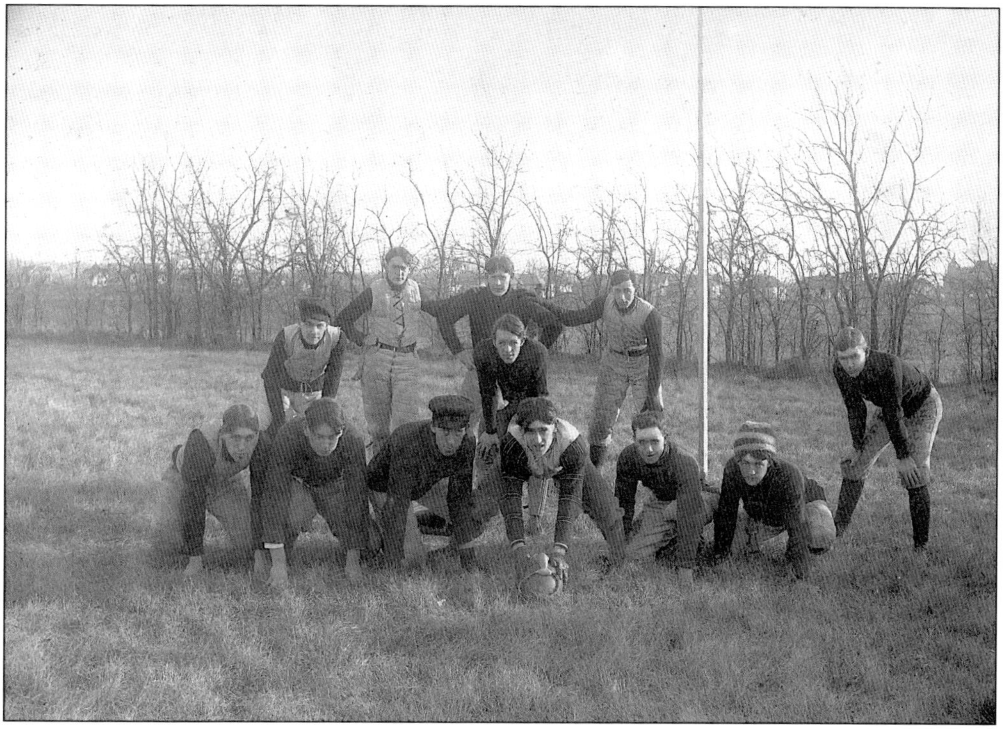

This photo depicts football in the early 1900s. Players listed here are S.A. Smith, Earl Breese, T. Bungard, Harry Hoyt, Cecil Beaumont, R. Donahue, Joe Gullett, Lance Anderson, Phil Matthews, Willie Piper, and Denny Kilroy.

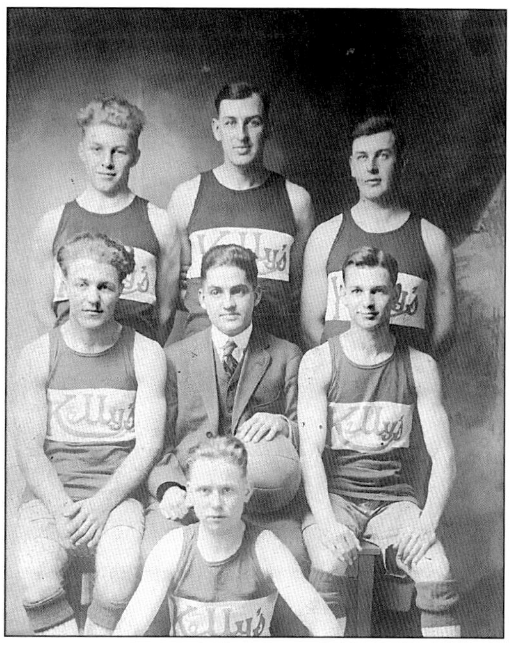

Basketball players for Kelly's pictured here are Oscar Sweeney, Ross Carter, Edward Carter, Gene Weber, Rudy Kelly, unidentified, and Leo Ennis.

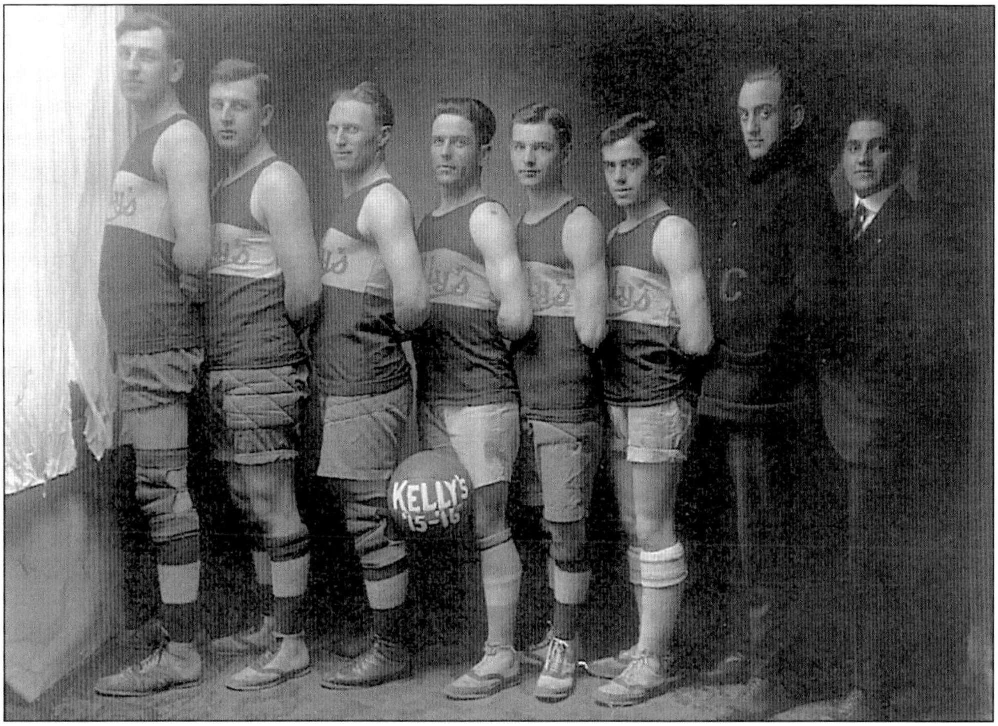

The 1915–1916 Kelly's Basketball Team is pictured here. They are, from left to right: Rudy Kelly, Kenny Mills, ? Pierce, unidentified, unidentified, unidentified, E. Carter, and Ross Carter.

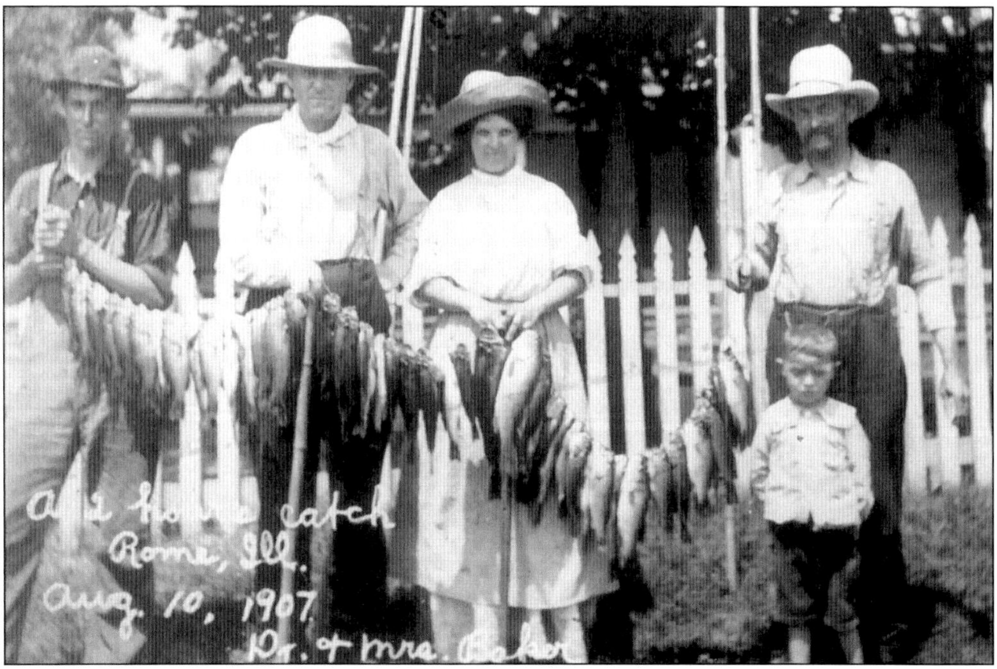

An hour's catch at Rome on August 10, 1907, is pictured above. (Courtesy of Dr. and Mrs. Baker.)

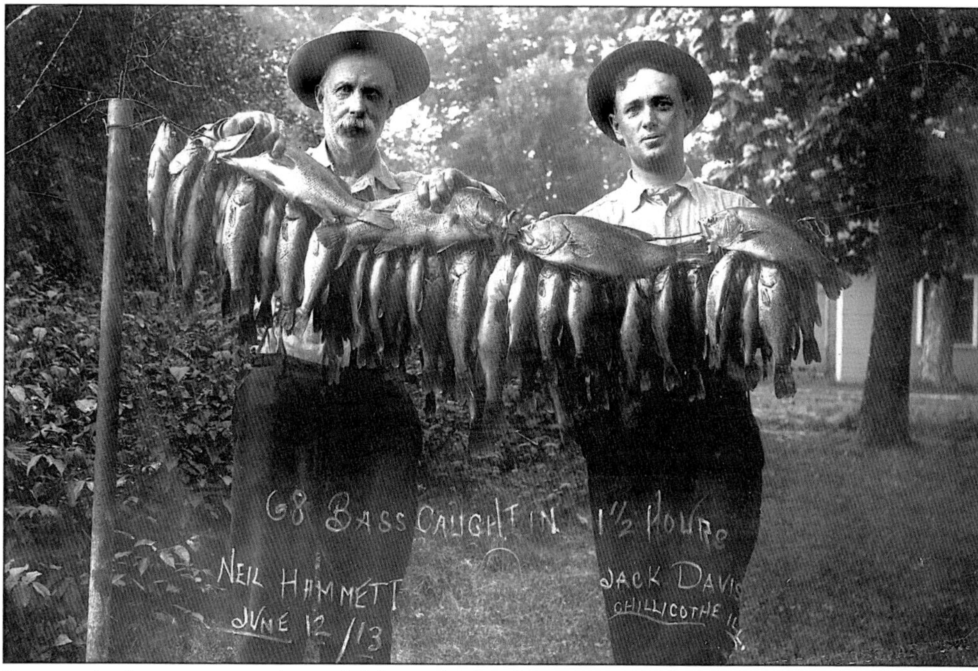

Sixty-eight bass were caught in 1.5 hours by Neil Hammett and Jack Davis at Chillicothe on June 12, 1913.

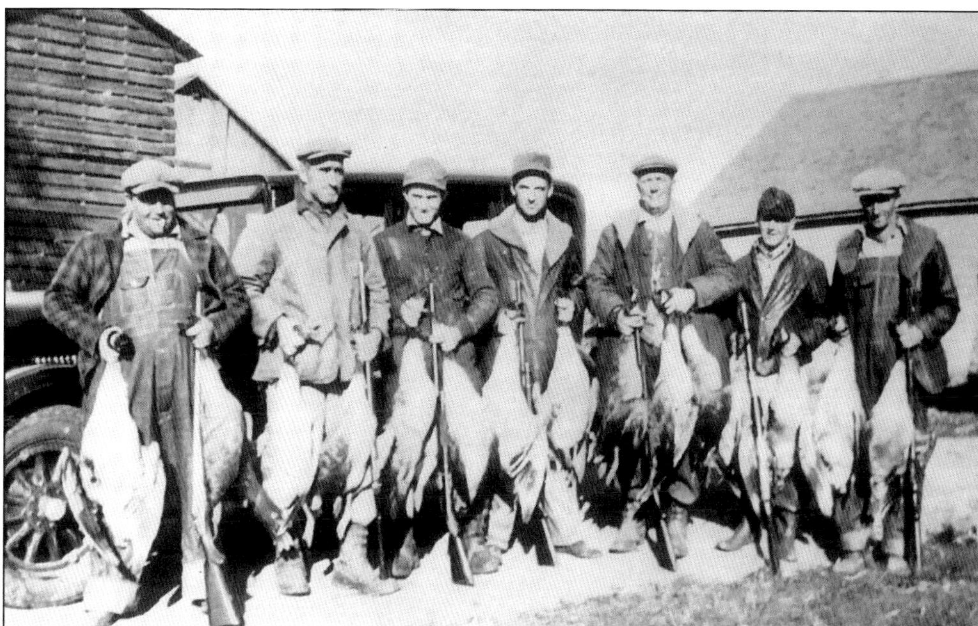
This photo depicts a successful goose hunt in the olden days. Pictured here, from left to right, are: Bill Spillman, unidentified, Ed Pennington, unidentified, Gene Cooper, Earl Van Petten, and unidentified. (Courtesy of Hank Foster.)

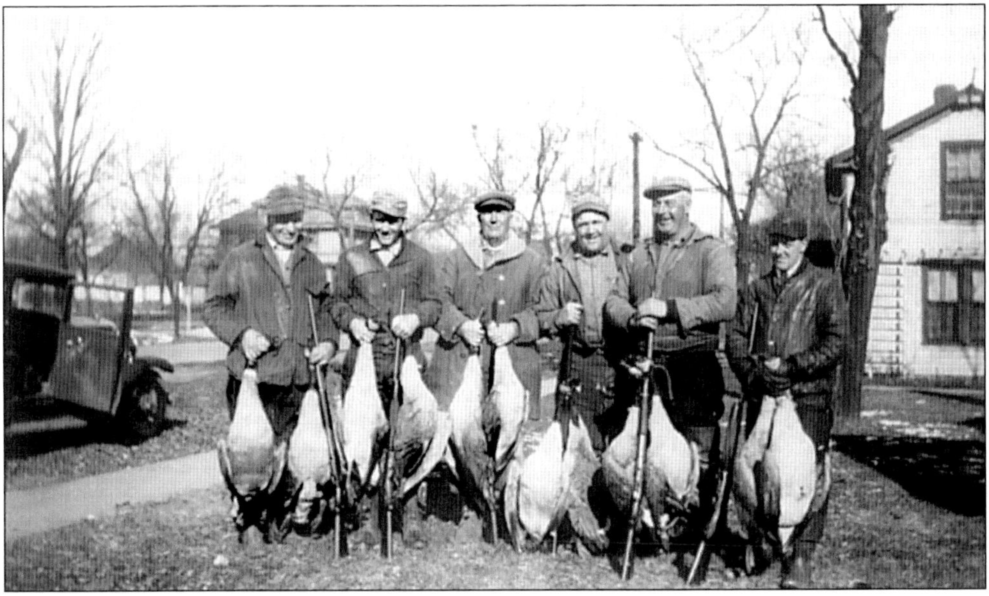

Another successful goose hunt is pictured here. The hunters are Otto Woodruff, Ed Pennington, Gene Cooper, Logan Harbican, Edward Carter, and Earl Van Petten.

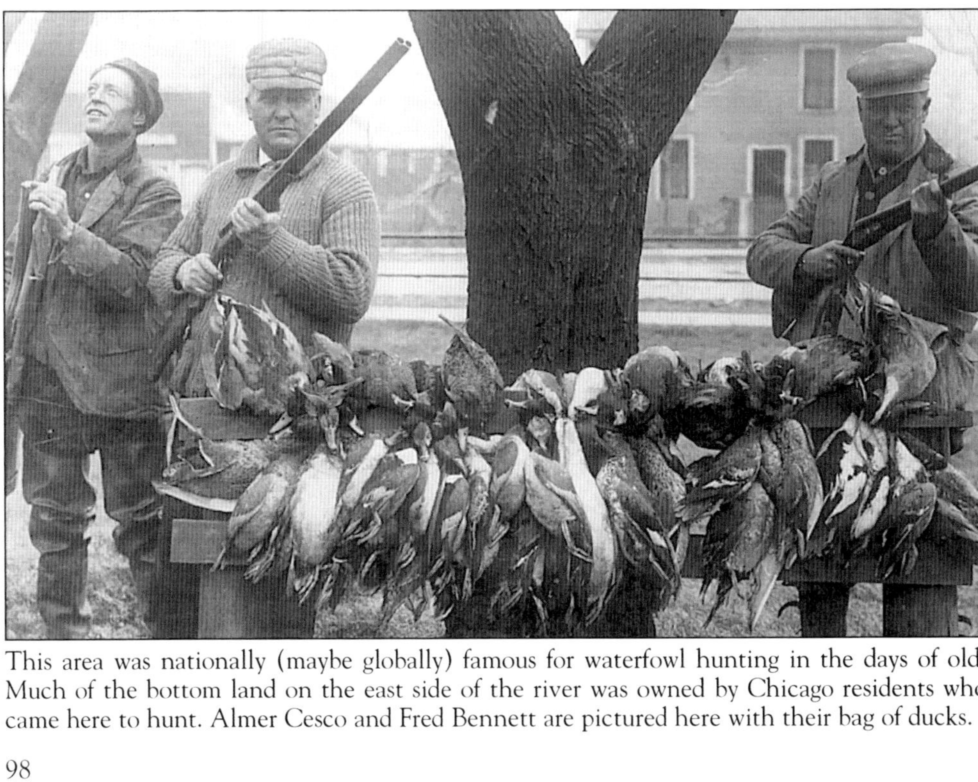

This area was nationally (maybe globally) famous for waterfowl hunting in the days of old. Much of the bottom land on the east side of the river was owned by Chicago residents who came here to hunt. Almer Cesco and Fred Bennett are pictured here with their bag of ducks.

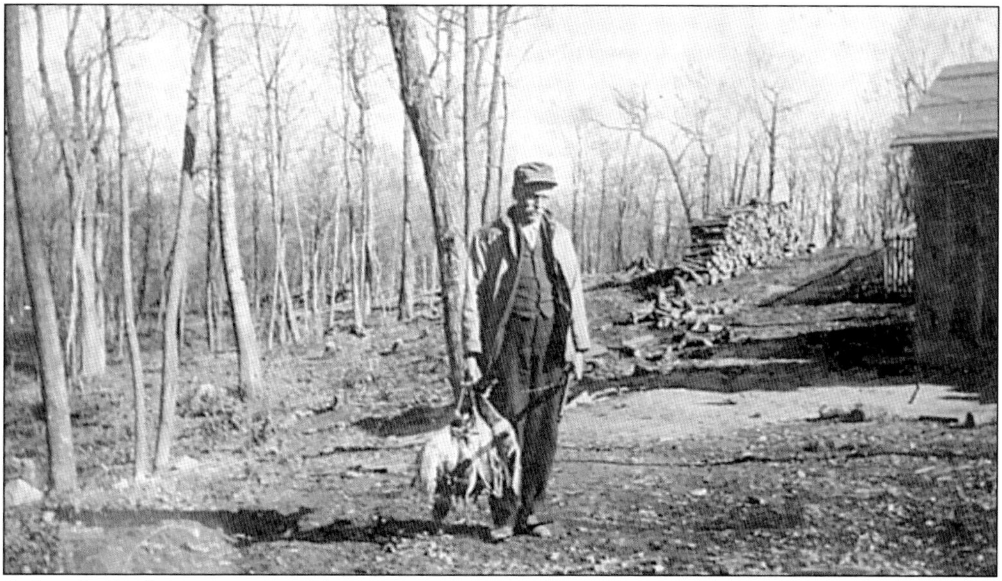

Robert B. Dickison is pictured here returning to the farm building (on the west side of the river) with the results of a successful hunt in the early 1900s. (Courtesy of Doris Dickison.)

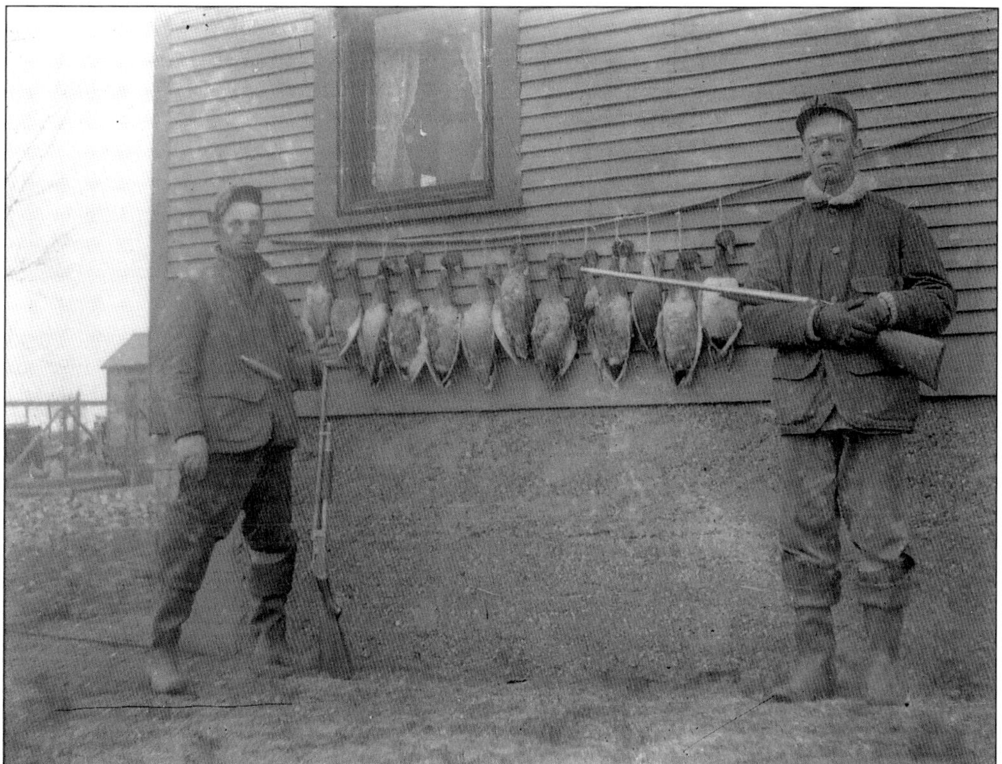

Frank Holmer is pictured here on the right in 1899 holding a double-barrel shotgun with his shooting friend and an hour's worth of mallards from around Rome. (Courtesy of Homer Gill.)

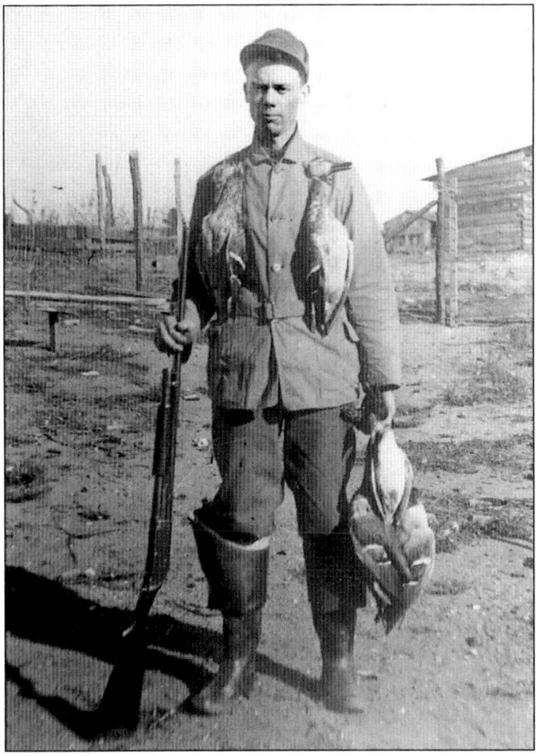

Frank Holmer is pictured here with a new 1897 Winchester model shotgun and mallards. (Courtesy of Homer Gill.)

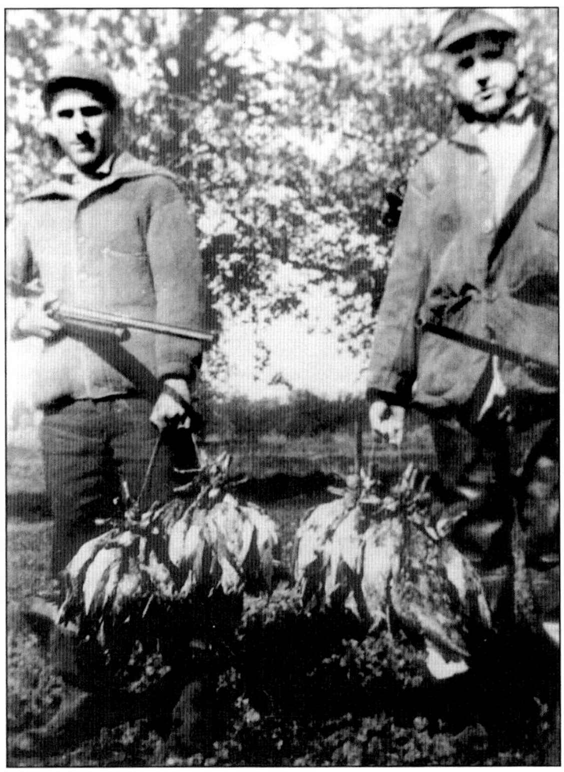

Another successful hunt is pictured here. The man on the left has a Browning Patent autoloader, and the man on the right has a pump action. (Courtesy of Jack Gerstner.)

Six

Transportation

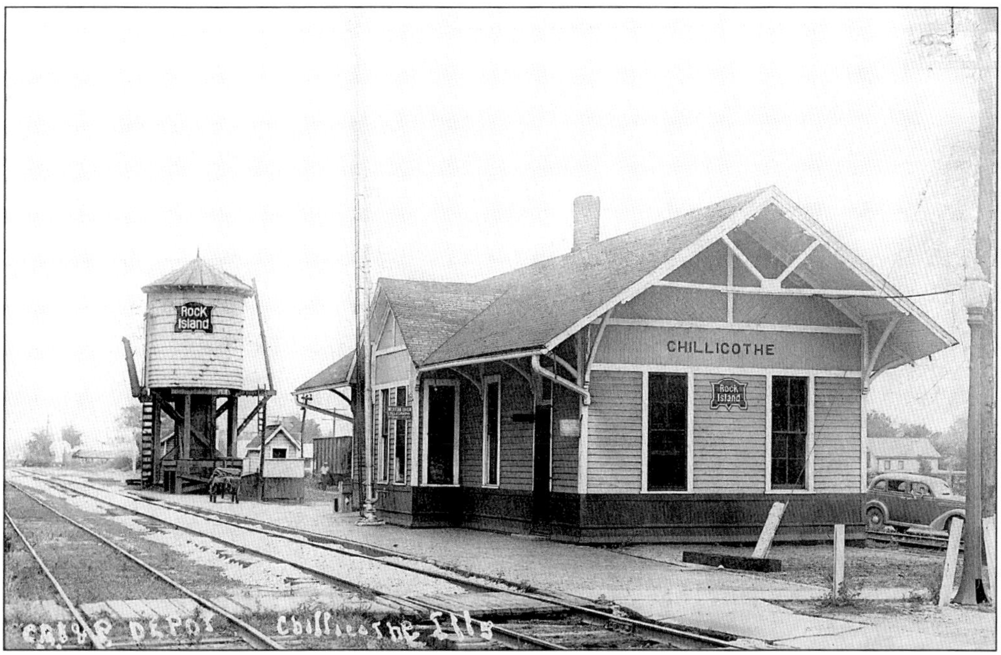

The Chicago, Rock Island, and Pacific depot in Chillicothe is pictured here. The foundation of the water tower is still located north of the depot. Note the siding to the west of the mainline track and another siding east of the depot. The lumberyard has not yet been constructed in this photo.

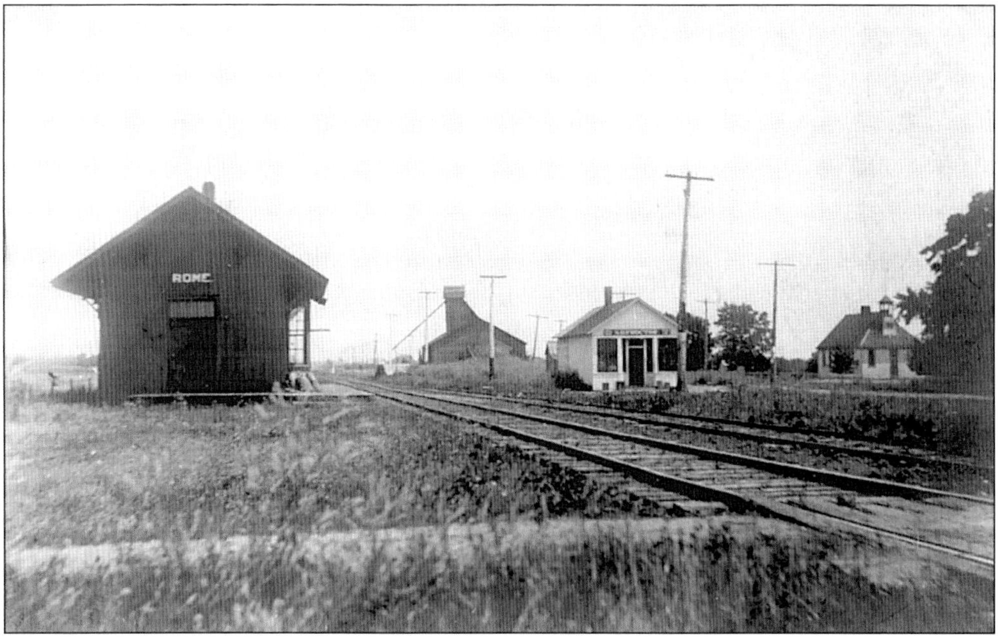

The Rome Depot stood on the west side of the tracks. On the east side was N.O. Proctor's store and grain office, which was moved to the south side of Knox and is now owned by Lawson's. Farther east and north was the old Rome School, while north along the tracks was the grain elevator. The depot burned in 1926—the fire was believed to have been caused by sparks from a passing steam train.

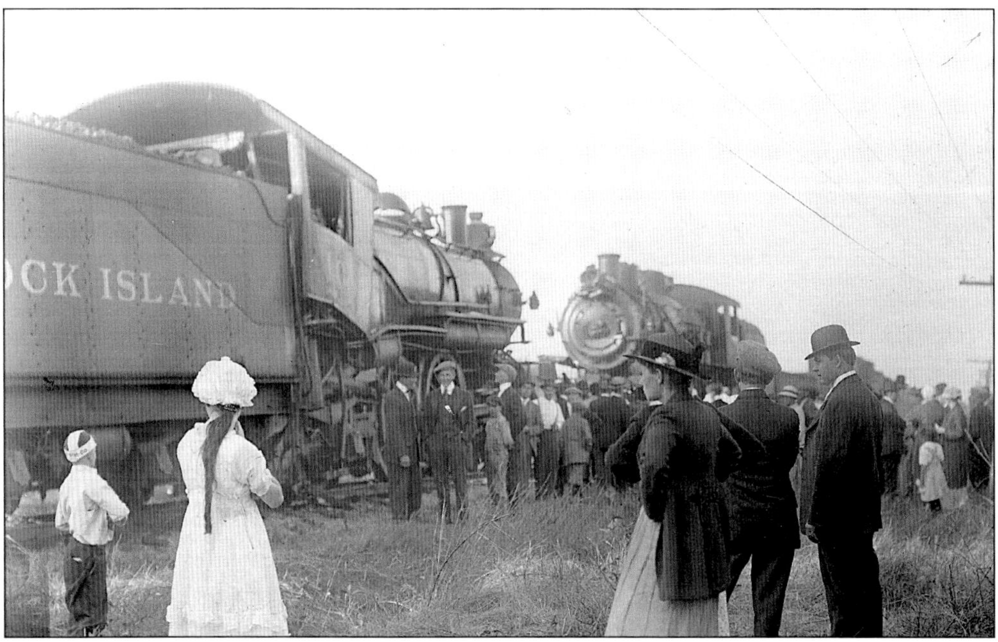

This photo depicts a 1915 train wreck at Rome. It is hard to comprehend how this could have happened on the straight, flat, open area at Rome.

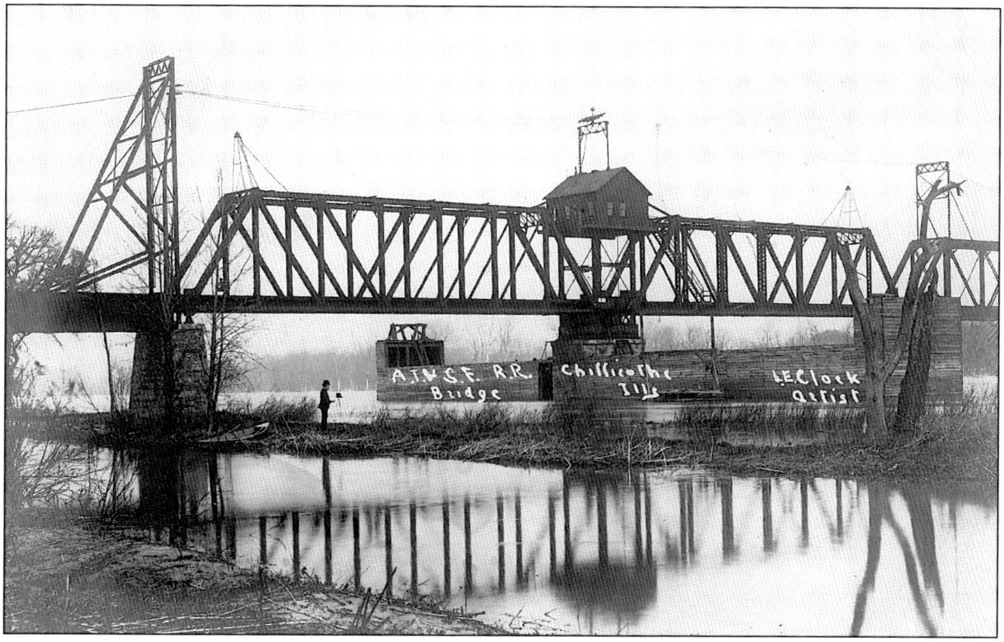

The original swinging Santa Fe drawbridge at Chillicothe is pictured above. The swing span was on the west end of the bridge.

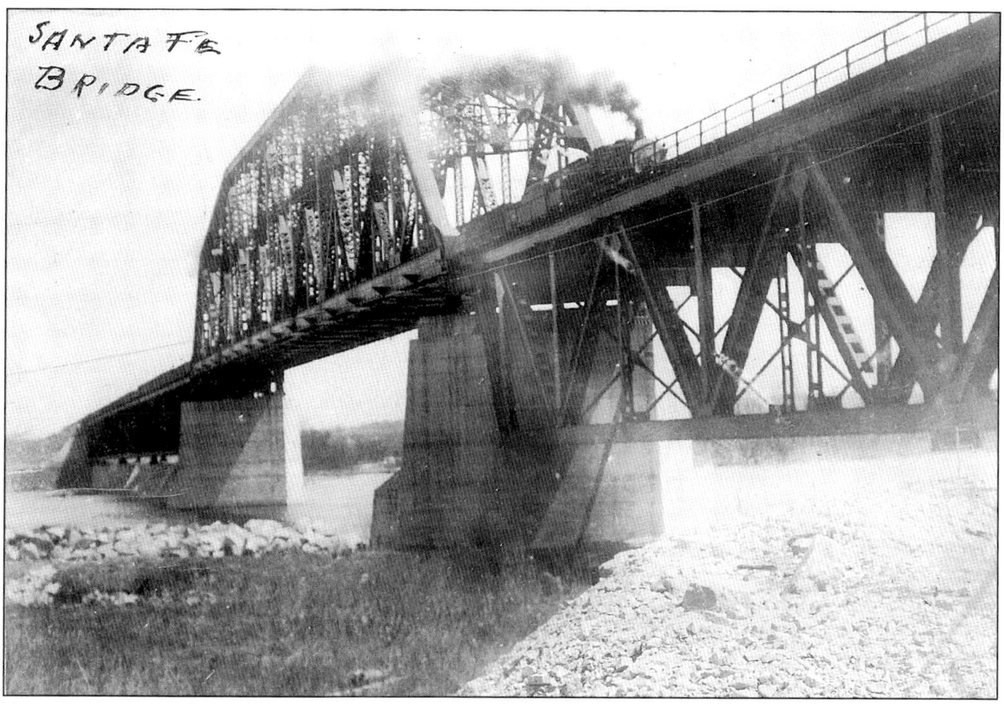

A steam train is shown here crossing the current Santa Fe bridge at Chillicothe.

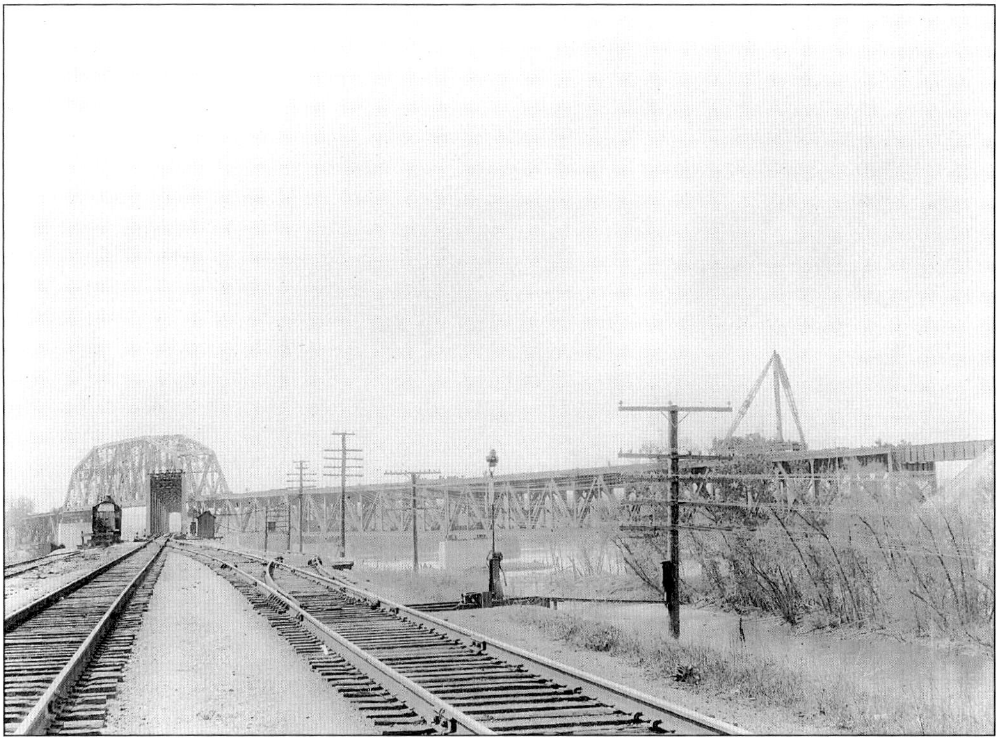

The current Santa Fe bridge was built above, and at an angle to, the earlier drawbridge, crossing over the swinging span with the higher center span of the new bridge. The photographer is standing beside the track to the old bridge.

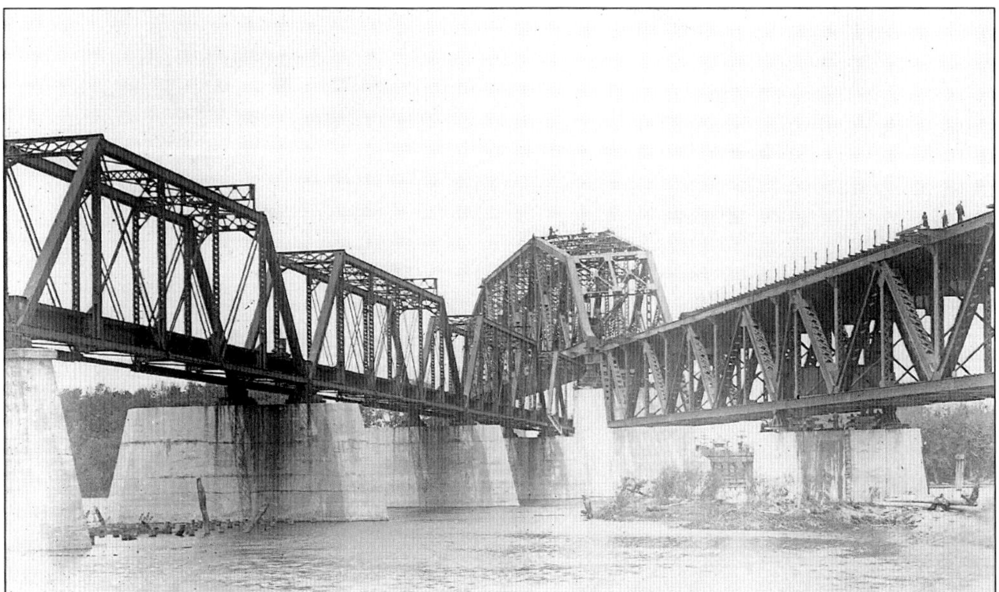

Construction of the new bridge (on the right) is pictured here in 1906. By building the new bridge over the old one, it was only necessary to halt train traffic for one day.

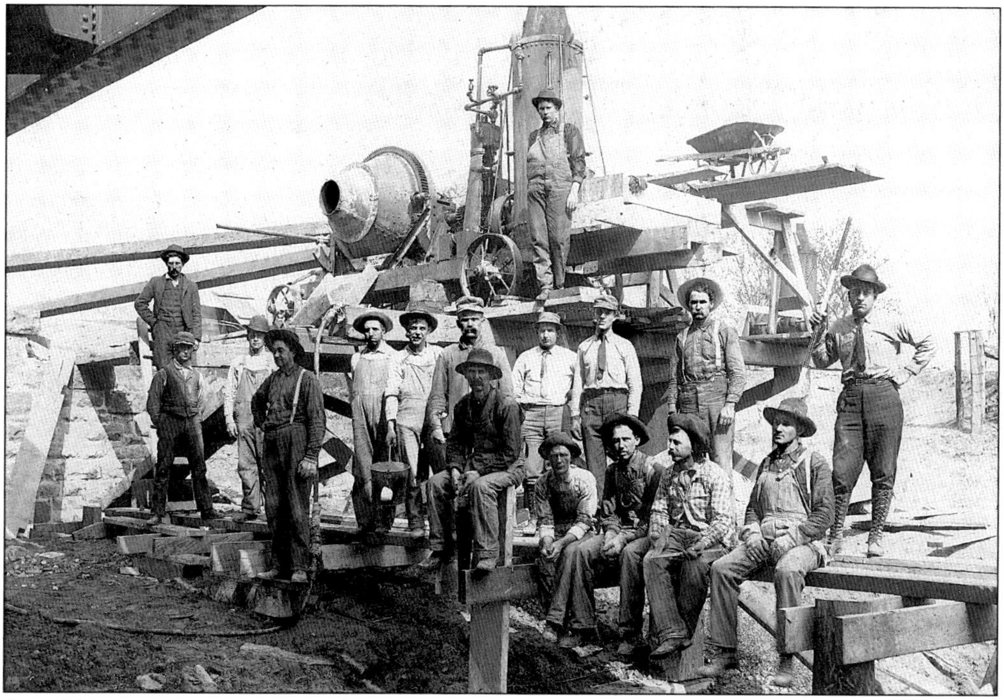

An 1896 construction crew, with a steam-powered cement mixer, is pictured here working on a bridge or overpass. The materials were wheeled up onto the platform via the planks seen in the background. After mixing, the concrete was dumped in the sluice box where it ran into a wheelbarrow. The wheelbarrow was then pushed across the planks on which the men are standing out to the supporting form.

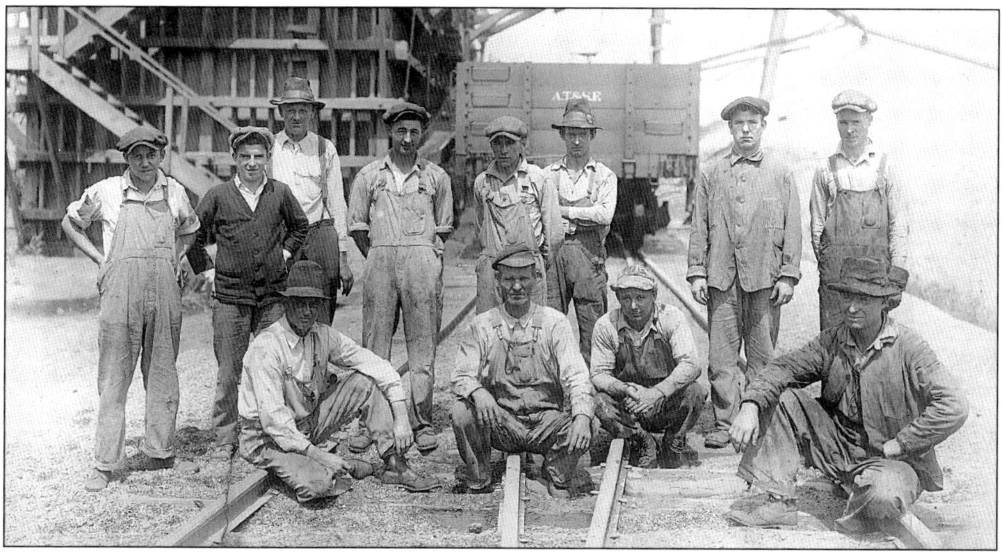

Workers at the McGrath Sand and Gravel Company are pictured here in 1923. The Chillicothe plant opened in 1914 and averaged 25 workers on the payroll. They are pictured here, from left to right: (standing) Lonnie Thompson, Charles Hoyt, George Davidson, ? Beaumont, Art Bornsheuer, unidentified, ? Anderson (Link's son), Joe Kennington; (sitting) ? Huffmen, unidentified, Chubby Taylor, and Fred Allington.

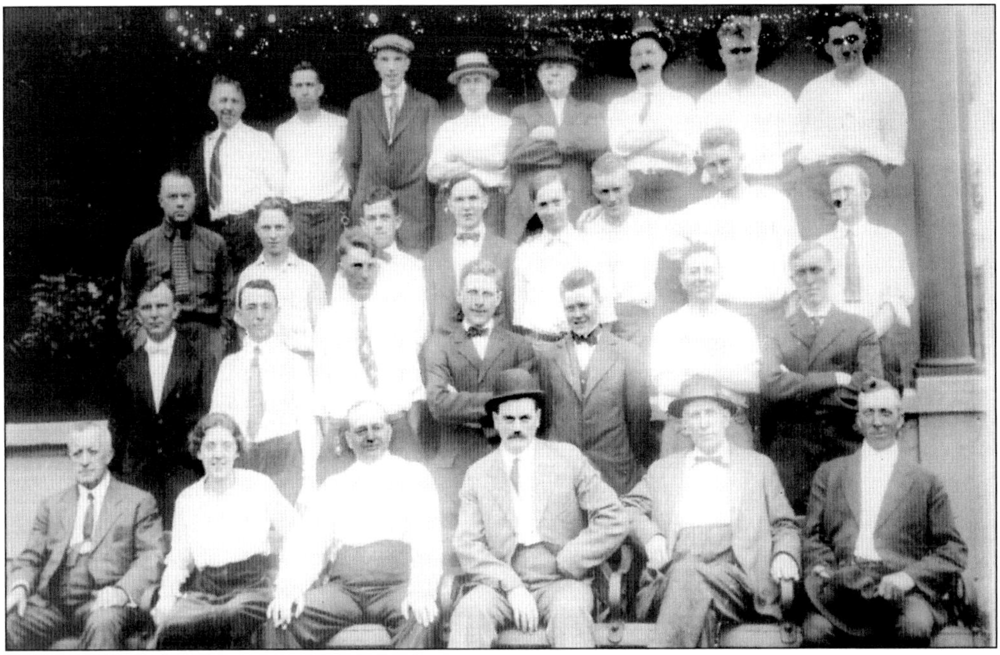

Santa Fe office employees are pictured here in 1918. They are: (front) F.M. McFarland (agent), L.E. Ravenscroft (clerk), H.H. Forsythe (chief dispatcher), John Henberger (roadmaster), John Bruner (general bridge and building foreman), C.A. Cotton (signal supervisor); (second row) I. Anderson, F. (Deacon) Gilyeat (chief clerk to superintendent), D.J. Veerman, Henry A. Nagel, Karl Bewlah, G.I. (Buttons) Jones, C.A. Beach; (third row) J.W. Brunner, Leo Ennis, W.E. (Bill) Auge, Gene M. Uhden, C.E. Edwards, Frankie Behrens, Chuck Kennington, L.H. (Nosey) Thomas; (fourth row) William Scarry (head timekeeper), Elmer E. (Slats) Thomas, C.J. Braum, R.F. (Bonny) McGregor, A.J. (Foxey) Jones (chief clerk to trainmaster), Richard O'Toole (division accountant), John Harris, and Al A. Blazina (telegrapher).

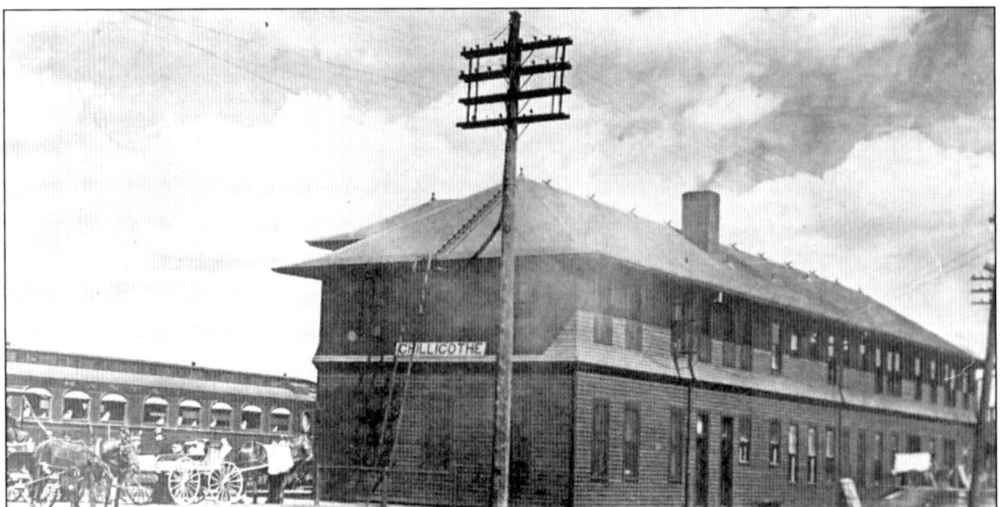

The second Santa Fe Depot in Chillicothe is pictured here. The first depot was built between the tracks in 1887. It burned in 1901 and was replaced by this building, which burned on June 13, 1963.

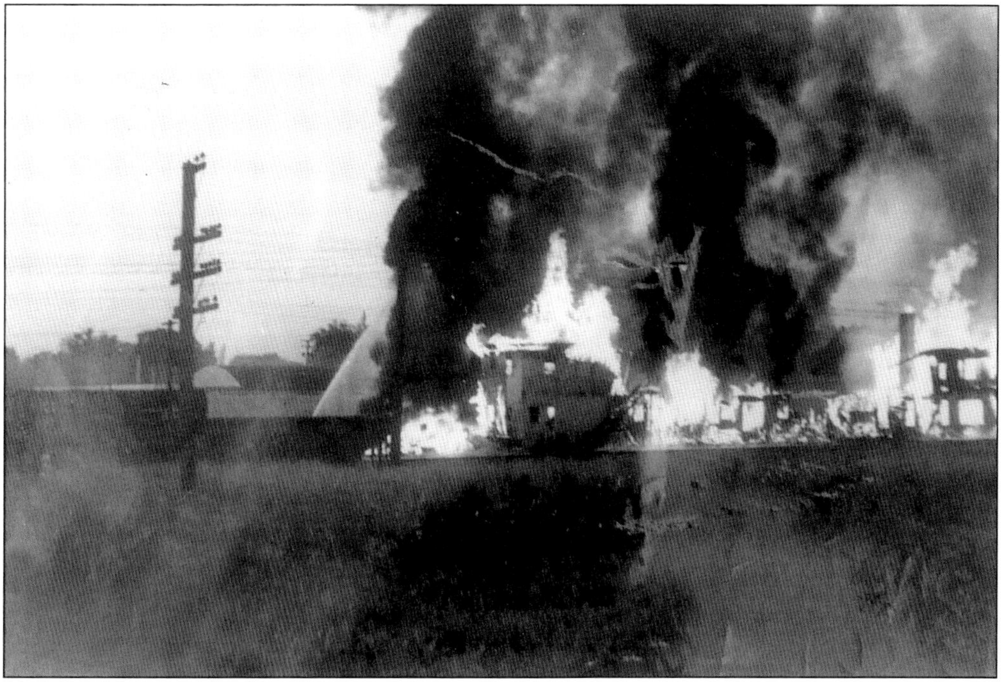

This photo depicts the Santa Fe Depot fire on June 13, 1963. (Courtesy of David Herron.)

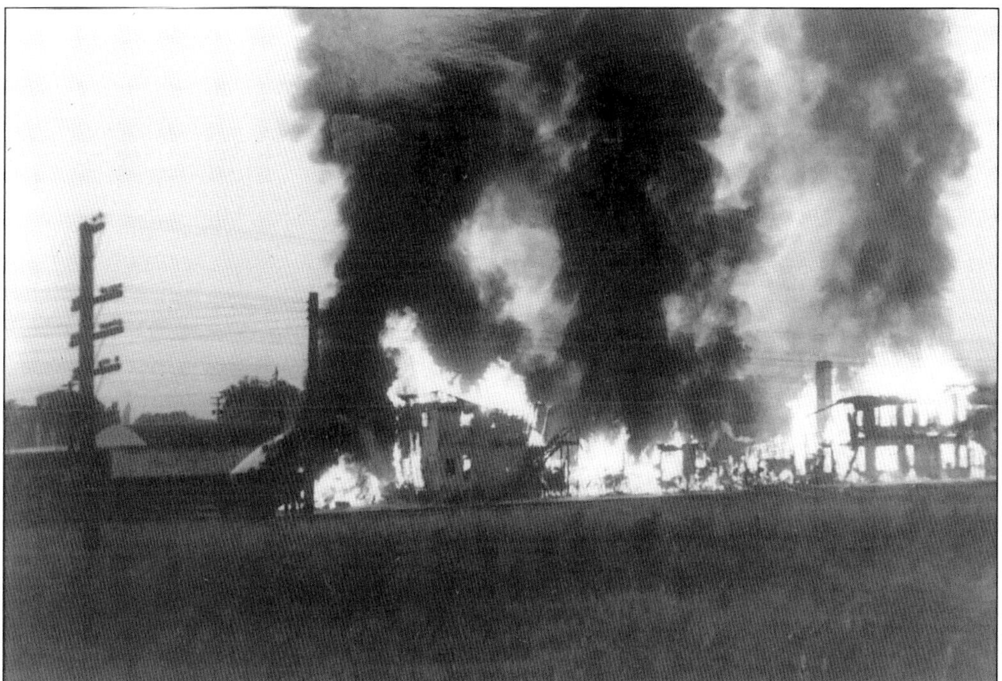

This is another view of the Santa Fe Depot fire in 1963. (Courtesy of David Herron.)

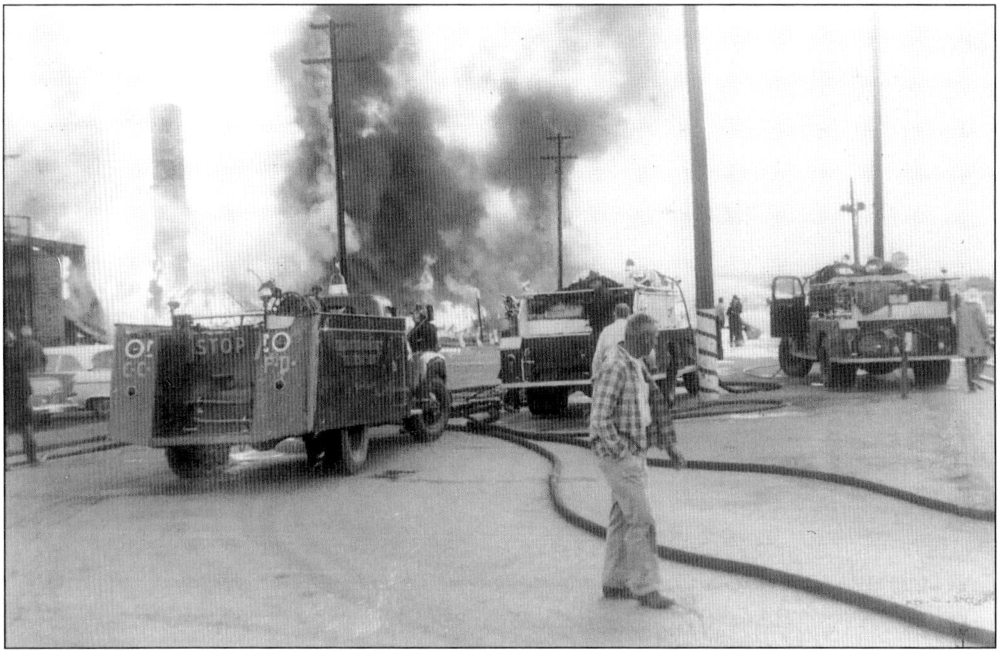

Fire trucks at the 1963 Santa Fe Depot fire are pictured here. (Courtesy of Carmen Herron.)

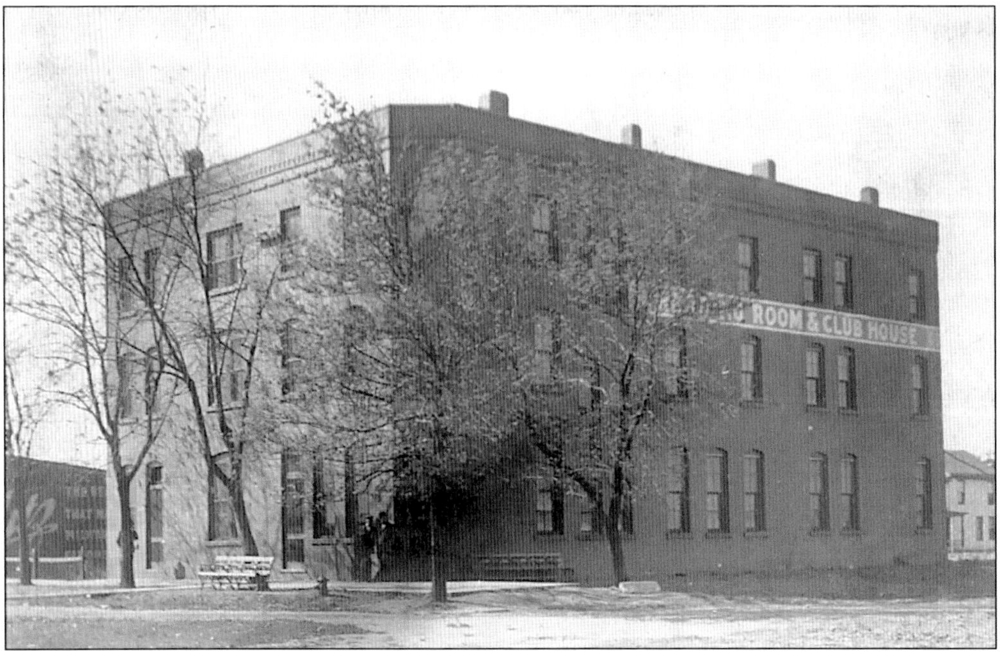

The Midland Hotel, one of the first hotels in North Chillicothe, was purchased by the Santa Fe in August of 1906 to be used as boarding rooms and a clubhouse until 1934.

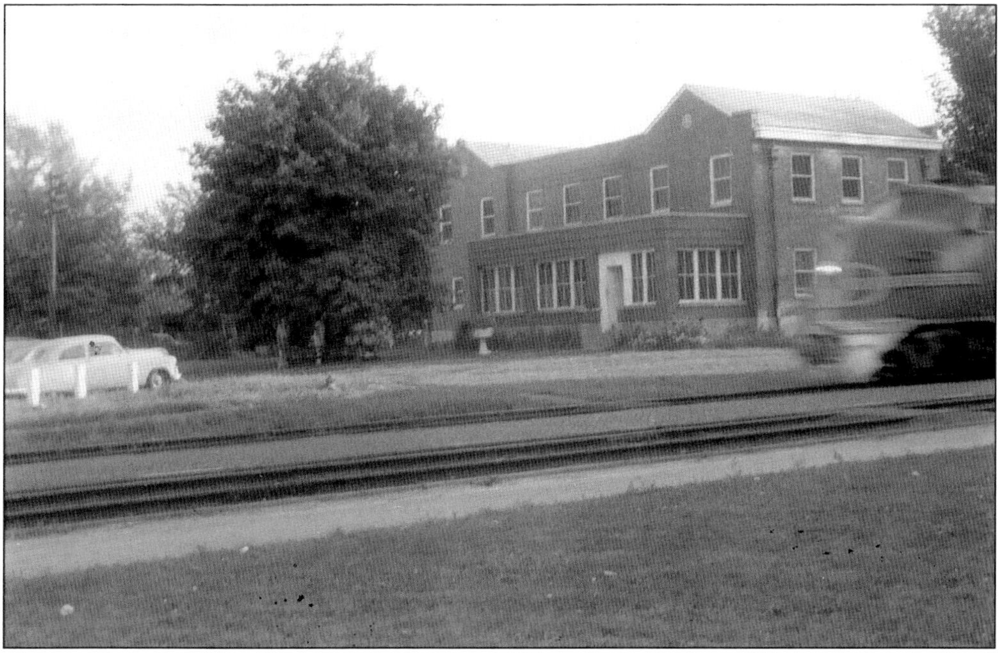

The Santa Fe Clubhouse is shown here in the 1950s. After the 1963 fire that destroyed the 1901 depot, the offices were moved to this building and remained here until the offices were moved to Fort Madison.

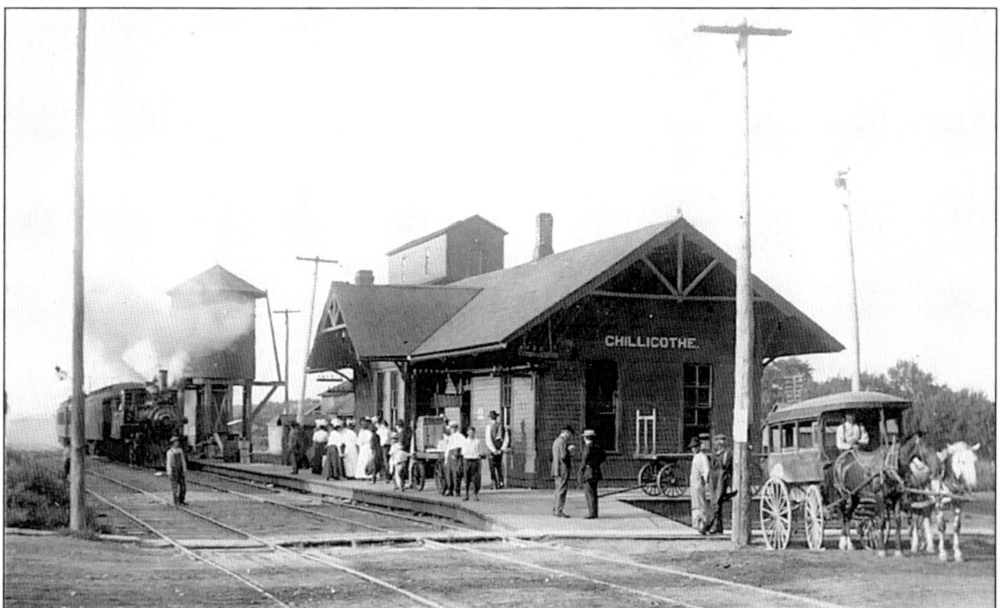

The Rock Island Depot is pictured here in August 1907. Note the steam train by the water tower, the grain elevator behind the depot, the summer crowd on the platform, and the horse-drawn omnibus waiting on Cedar Street.

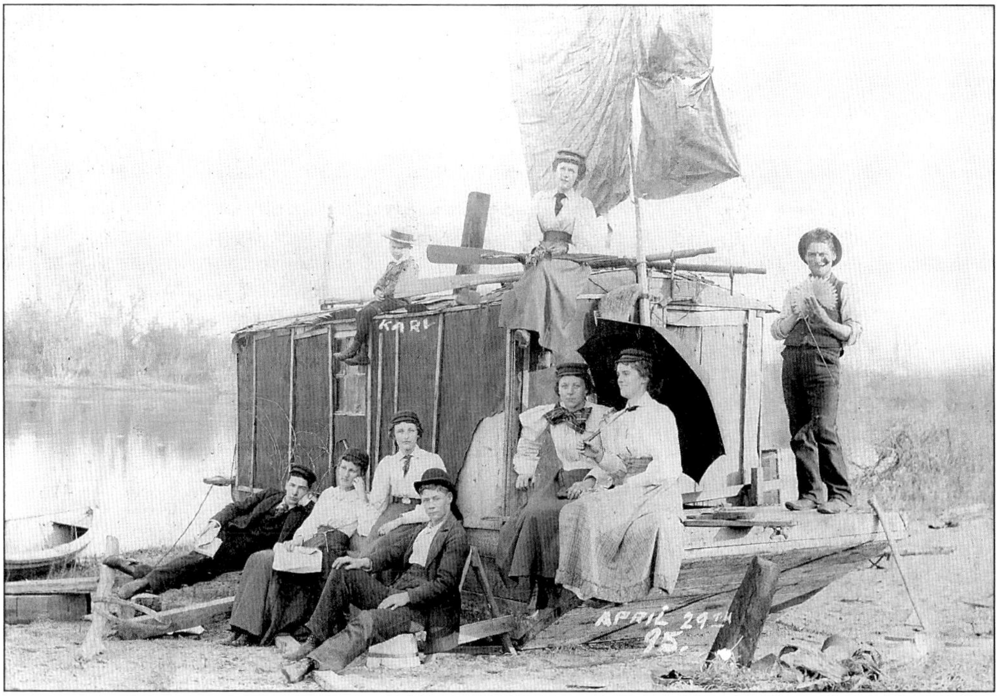

This photo depicts a group relaxing by a shantyboat on the riverfront in Chillicothe on April 29, 1895. (Courtesy of Barbara Pirtle.)

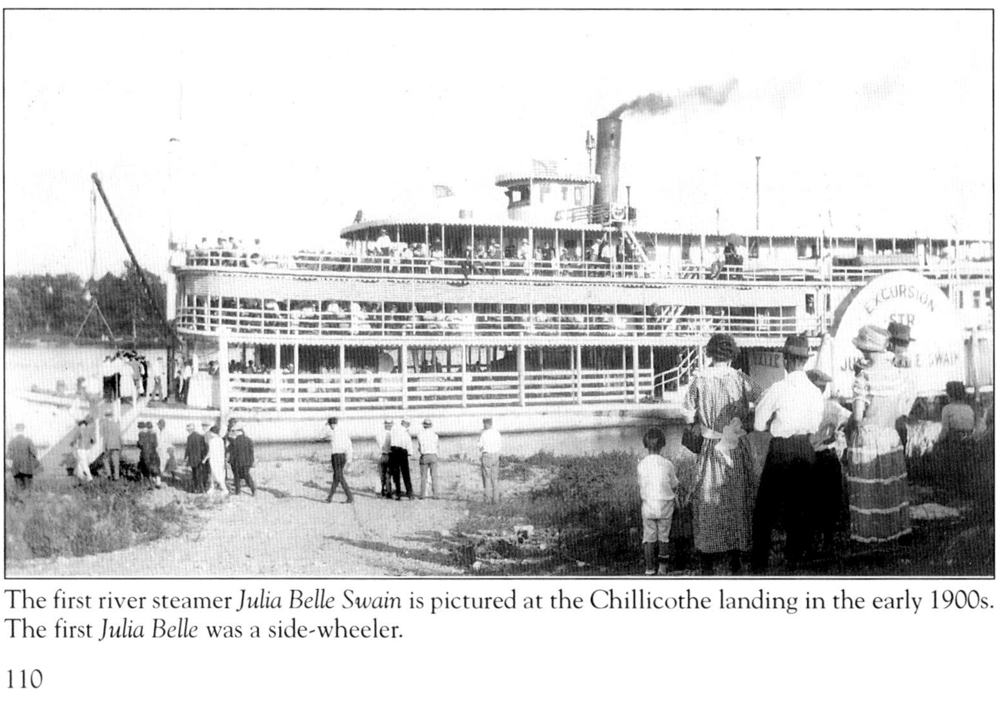

The first river steamer *Julia Belle Swain* is pictured at the Chillicothe landing in the early 1900s. The first *Julia Belle* was a side-wheeler.

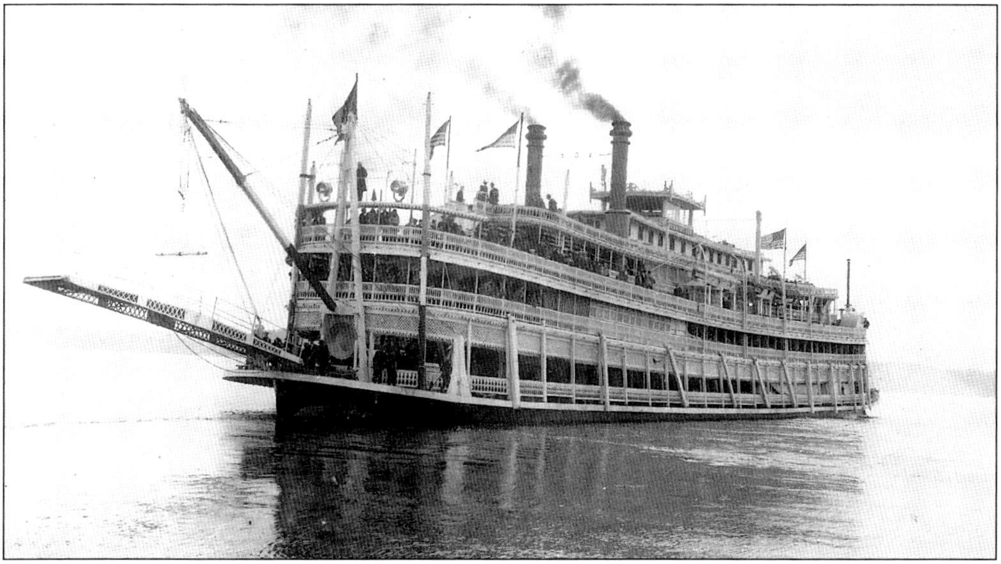

Pictured above is the steamboat *Washington*.

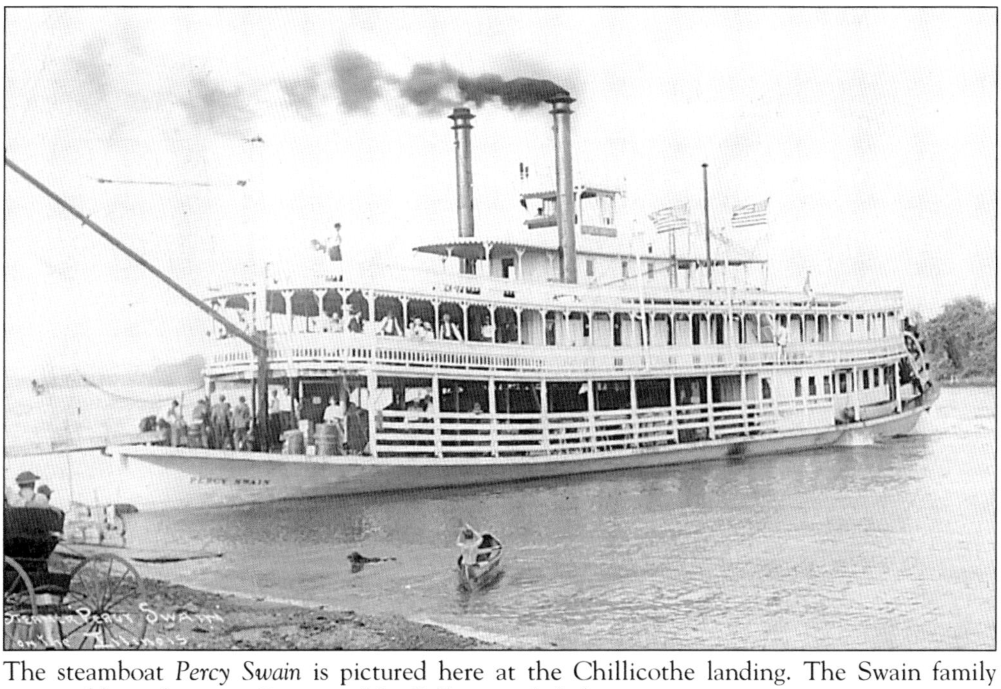

The steamboat *Percy Swain* is pictured here at the Chillicothe landing. The Swain family operated boats between Peoria and La Salle on a daily basis.

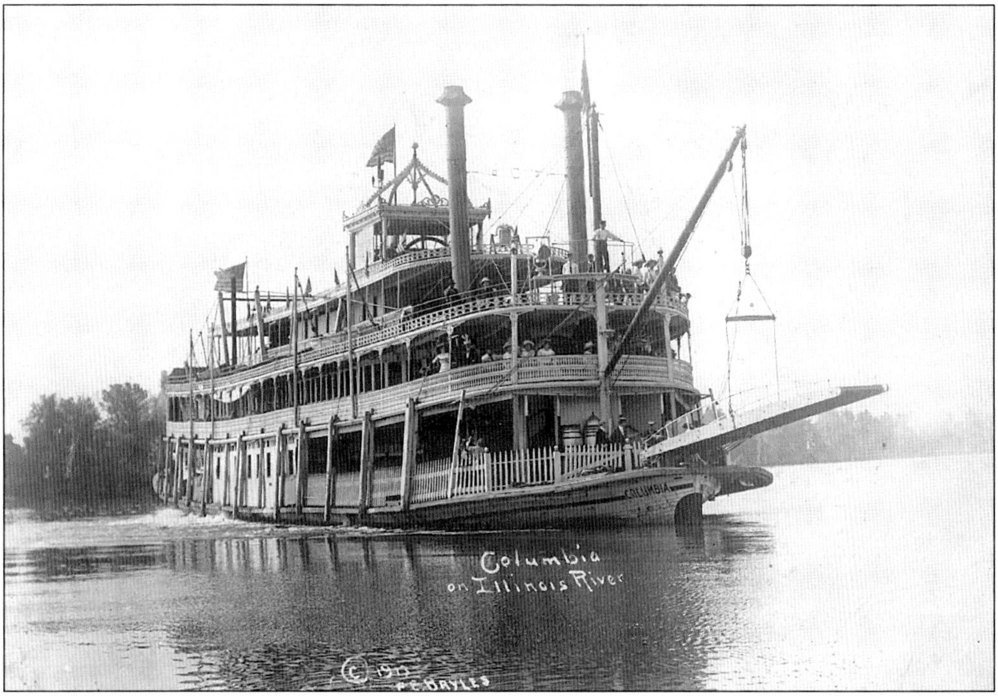

The steamboat *Columbia* is pictured at Chillicothe in 1913. This boat became famous on the morning of July 5, 1918, when she hit a snag 5.5 miles south of Peoria, taking 496 passengers—from Pekin and Kingston Mines—and crew members to their deaths.

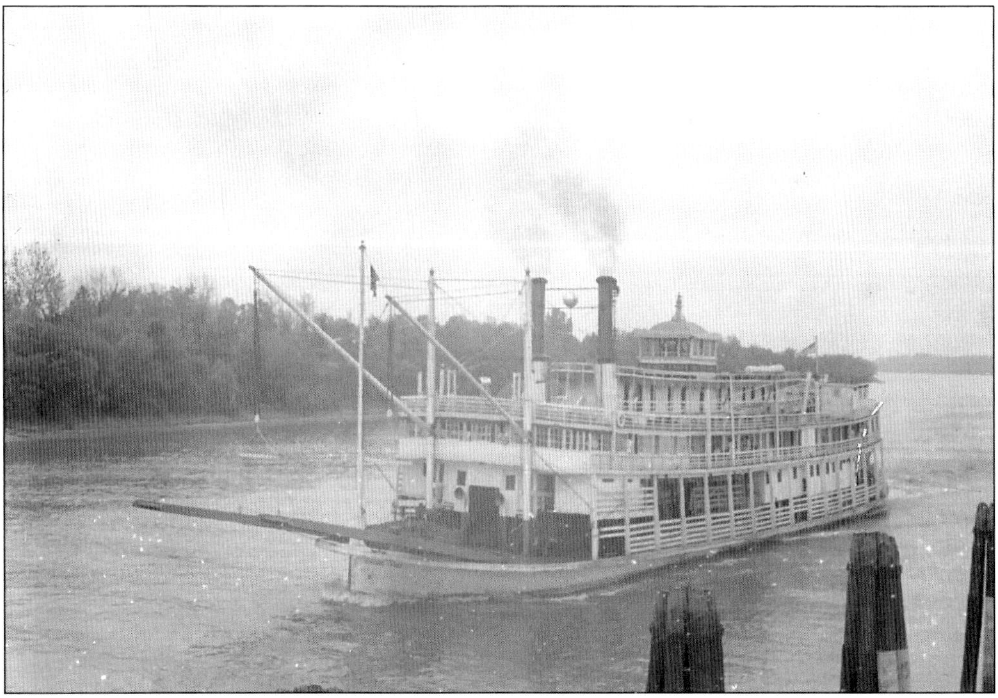

Pictured here is the steamboat *Golden Eagle*. The Eagle Packet Line competed with the Swains and Soul York for business.

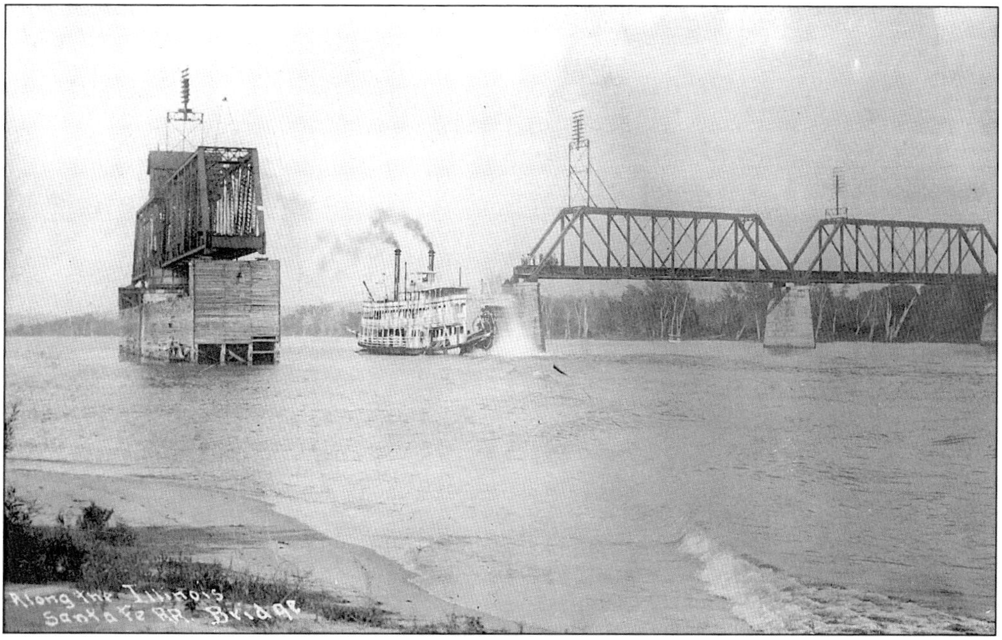

A stern wheeler is pictured here passing through the drawbridge at Chillicothe.

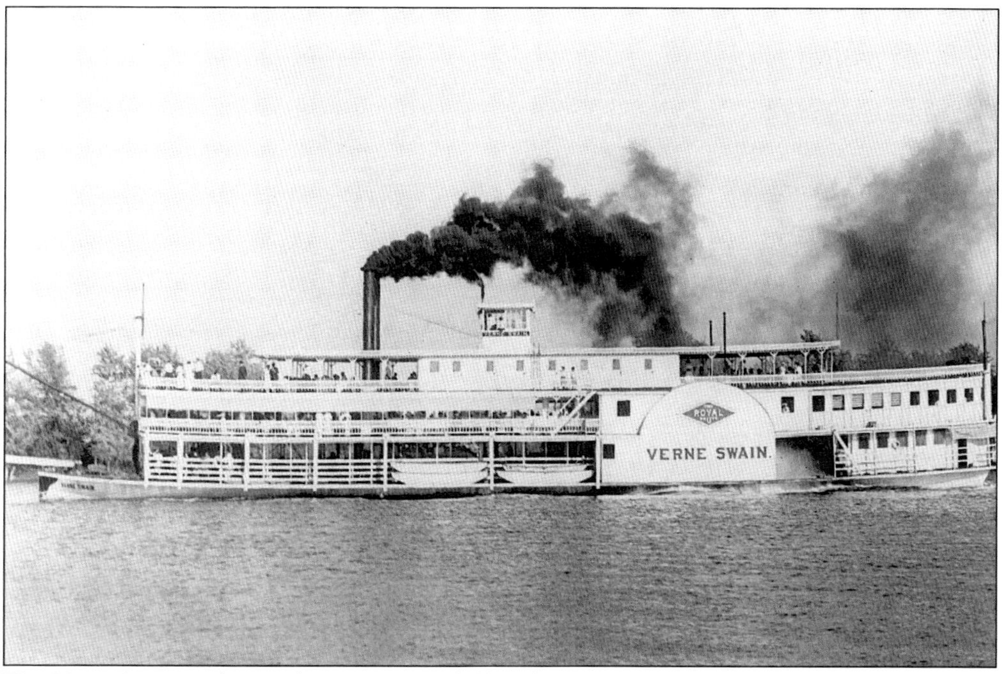

The *Verne Swain* is shown above passing Chillicothe.

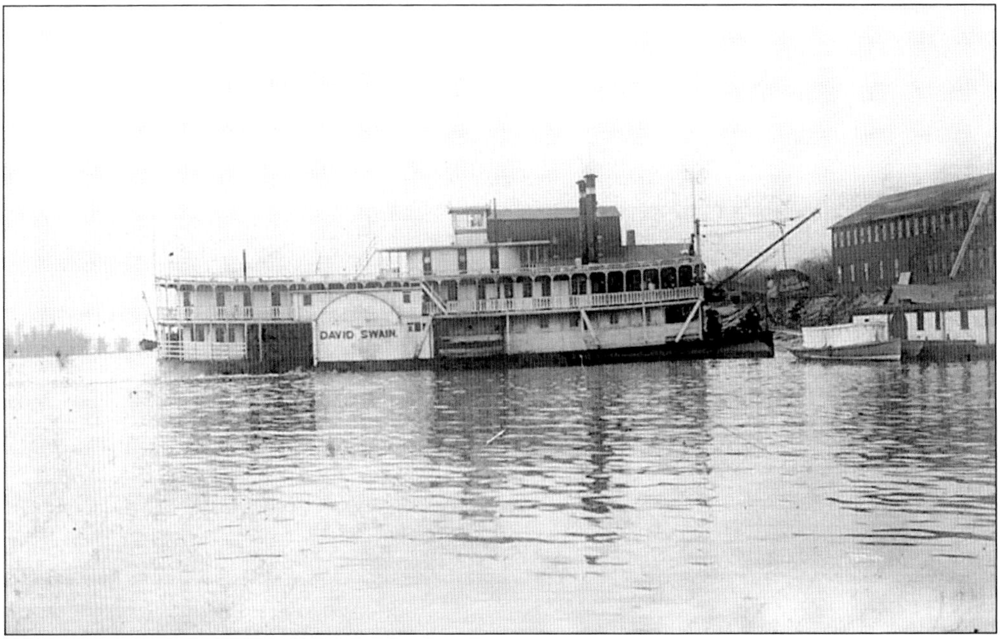

The *David Swain* is pictured here approaching the Chillicothe landing in 1906. W.S. Walker opened a fish and fur market on the white houseboat at the landing in May of 1906. Cutright's canning factory is the large building on the shore, and beyond the boat is the roof of the old riverbank grain elevator.

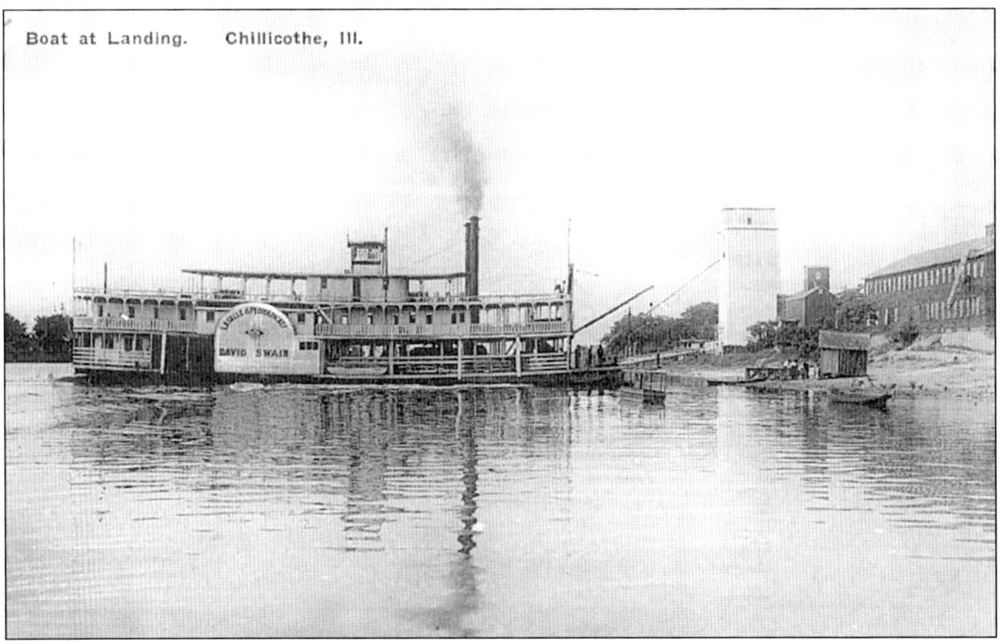

The *David Swain* is pictured here at the Chillicothe landing at the foot of Pine, after the new elevator was built in 1915.

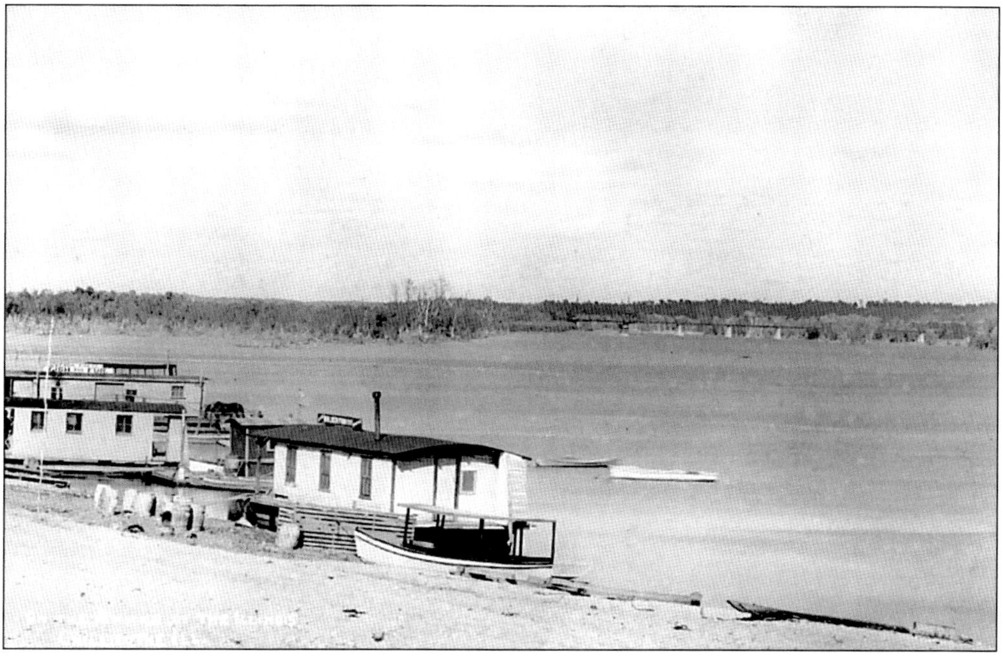

This photo depicts the banks of the Illinois River in 1908. Located closest to the camera is a steam launch, then W.S. Walker's fish and fur business in the white market boat. Just north of Walker's is a dark shanty boat, then a market boat, a harnessed horse standing on the ferry, and then the H.F. Mehl Fish Company's market boat. The Mehl Company moved to Peoria in 1921 due to a lack of fish in this area.

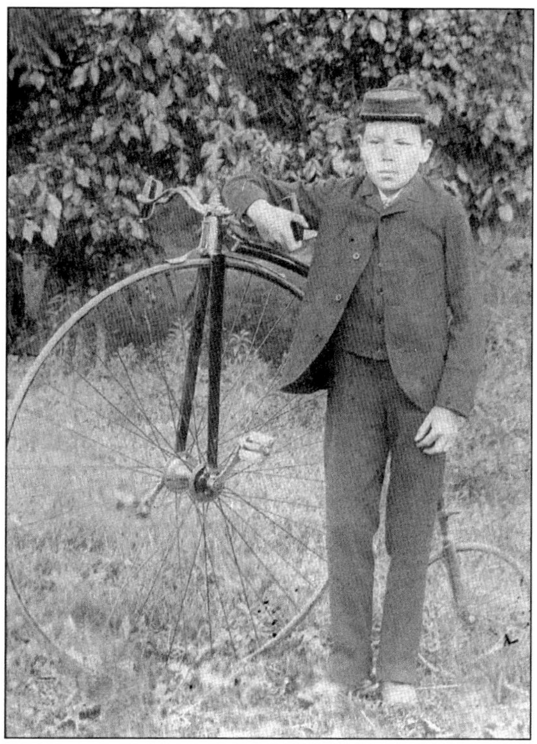

Elbert Nurse, the son of Henry Nurse, is pictured here with his bike. Bicycling became popular in the late 1880s, and the large-wheel bicycles were dangerous to ride—whenever something interfered with the front wheel, the rider would flip over the handlebar. By the 1890s, the "safety" bicycle—with two wheels of the same size—replaced the early style. (Courtesy of Mary Nurse Meyer.)

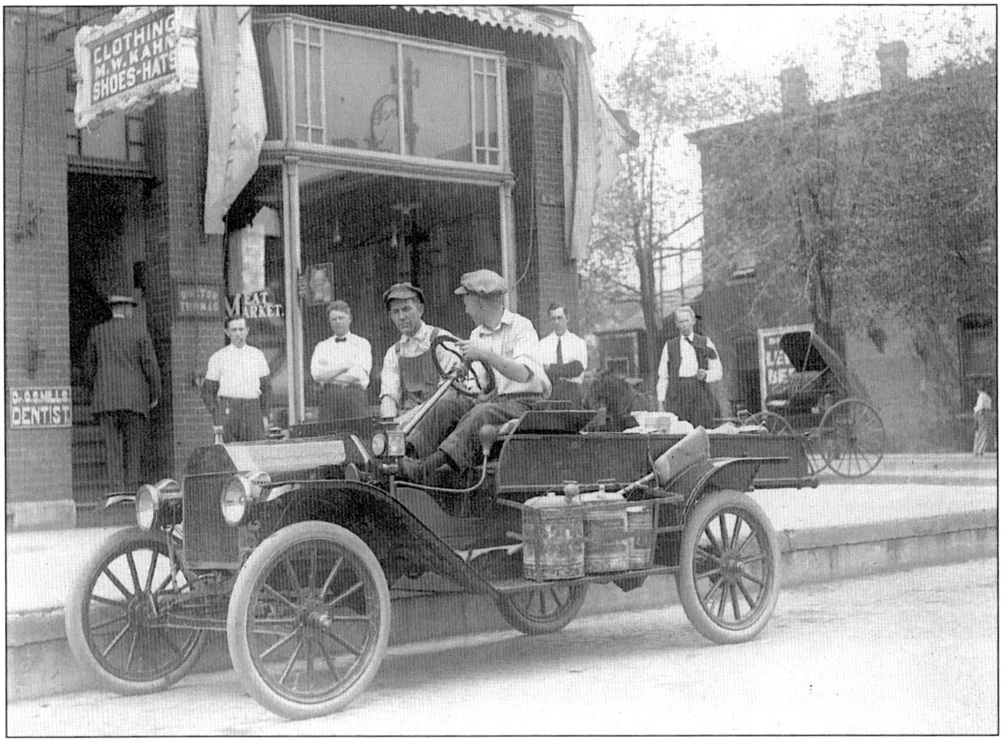

Sy Garver is pictured here in his car in front of M.W. Kahn's store at 949 Second Street in 1910. Dr. Thomas is pictured going up the stairs. Others in the background here are listed as Lee Adler, Jeff ?, Otl Bungard, Mr. Clark—selling groceries in the store at the corner—and John Johnson by the car.

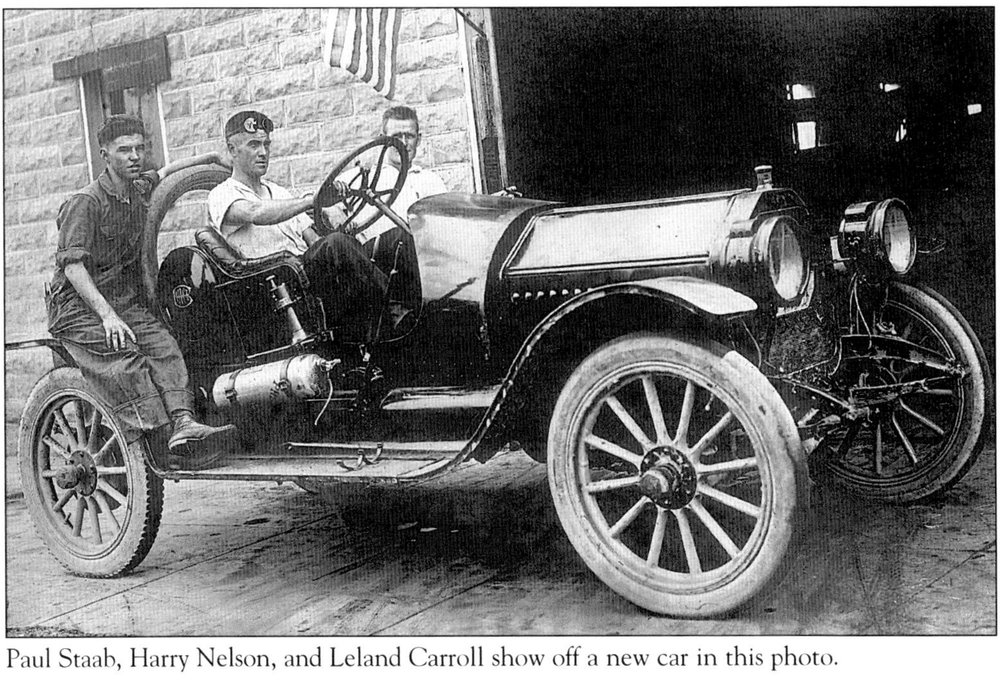

Paul Staab, Harry Nelson, and Leland Carroll show off a new car in this photo.

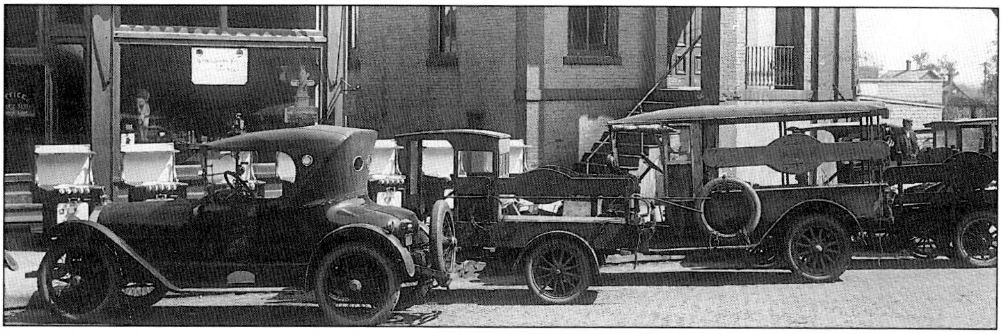

This photo depicts the east side of the south end of the 900 block of Second Street in the mid-1920s. There are five new kitchen ranges displayed in front of Frank Bacon's store. Three of the vehicles parked here are trucks. Note the steps to the old city hall porch. The store building burned in the '40s.

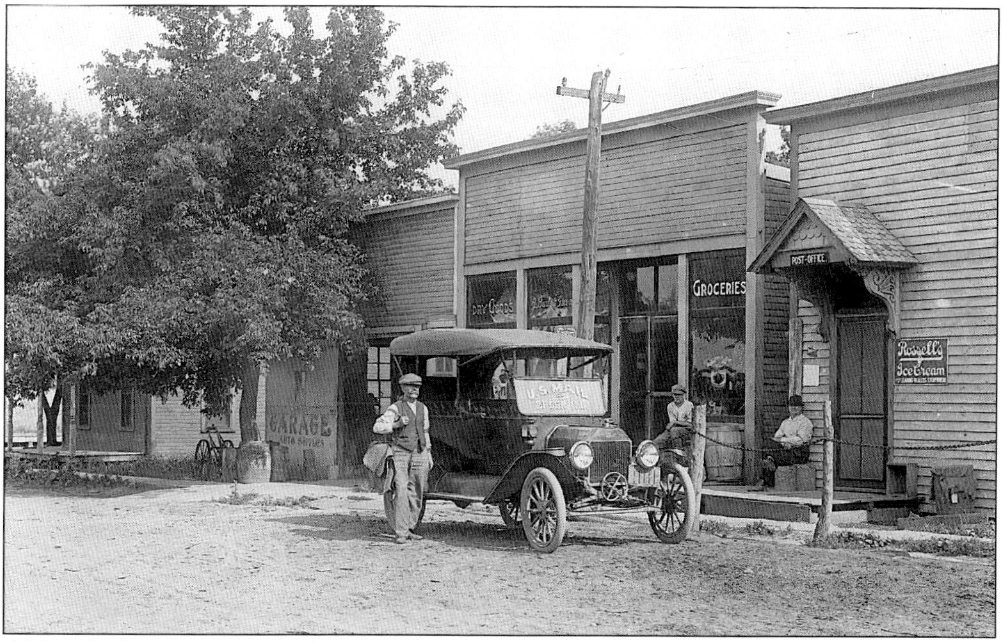

Although these pictures are from outside Peoria County, Speer is a close neighbor to Hallock Township, and the pictures are rare. The rural mail carrier is in front of the general store and post office in downtown Speer.

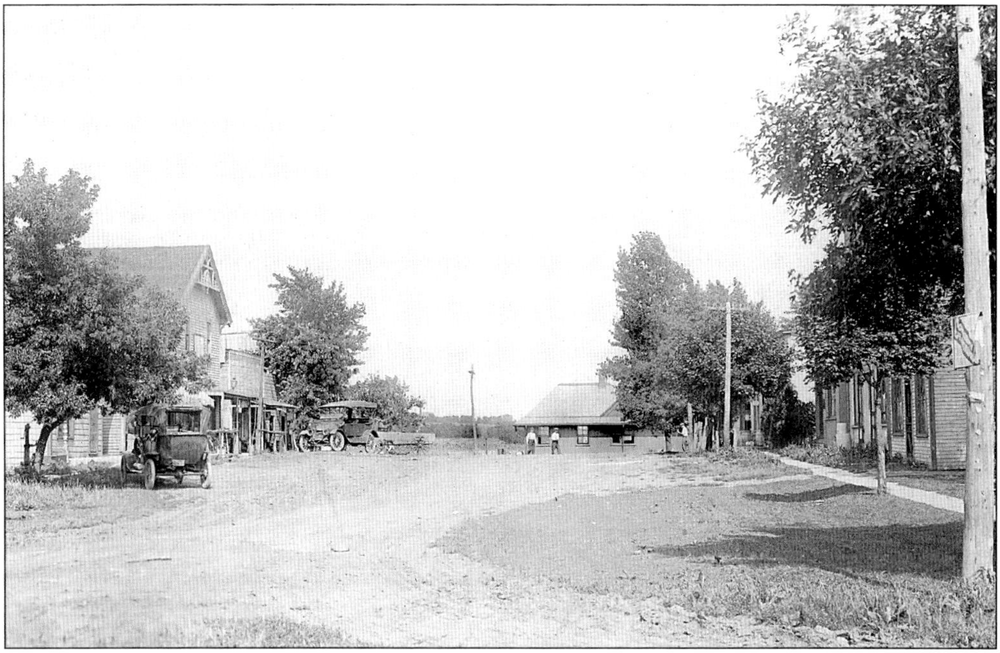

This photo depicts a view of downtown Speer. The building in the background may be the train depot.

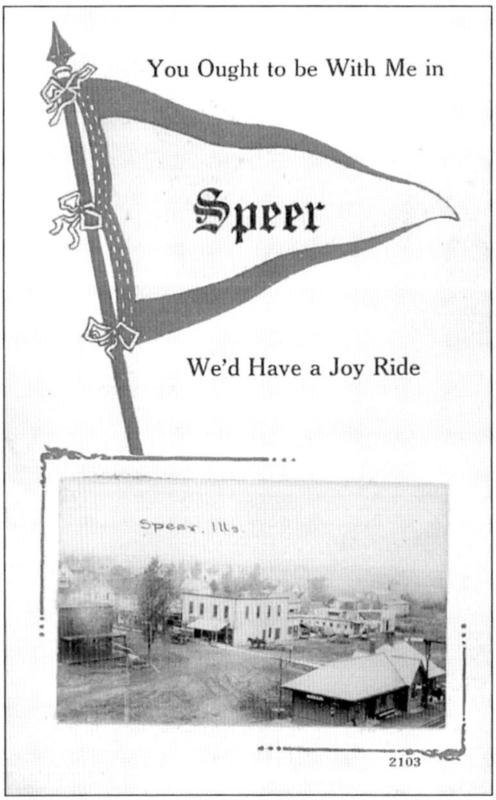

This is an earlier view of downtown Speer with the depot roof visible in the foreground.

Seven

VETERANS

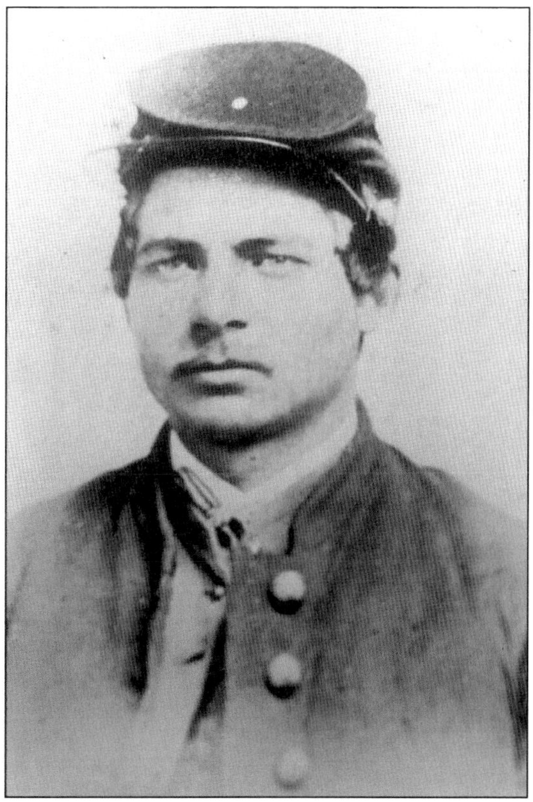

A Civil War soldier is pictured here. (Courtesy of Jack Gerstner.)

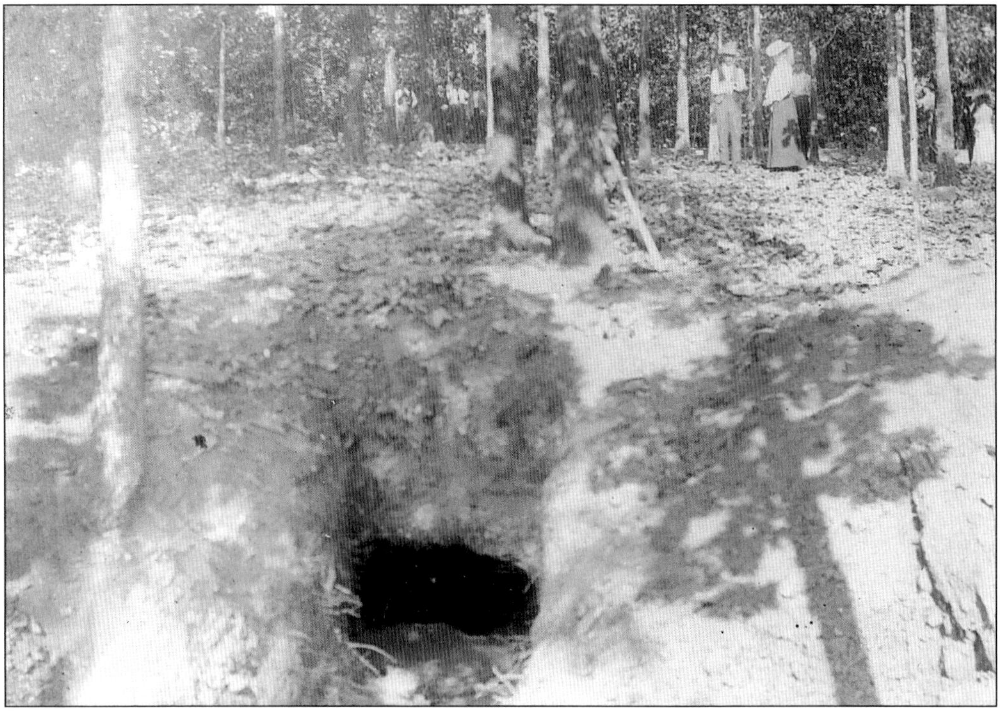

Henry Nurse, a veteran of the 86th Illinois Infantry, later returned to visit some of the battlefields where he had seen action. The mouth of the tunnel at the Kenesaw Battlefield is pictured here. (Courtesy of Mary Nurse Meyer.)

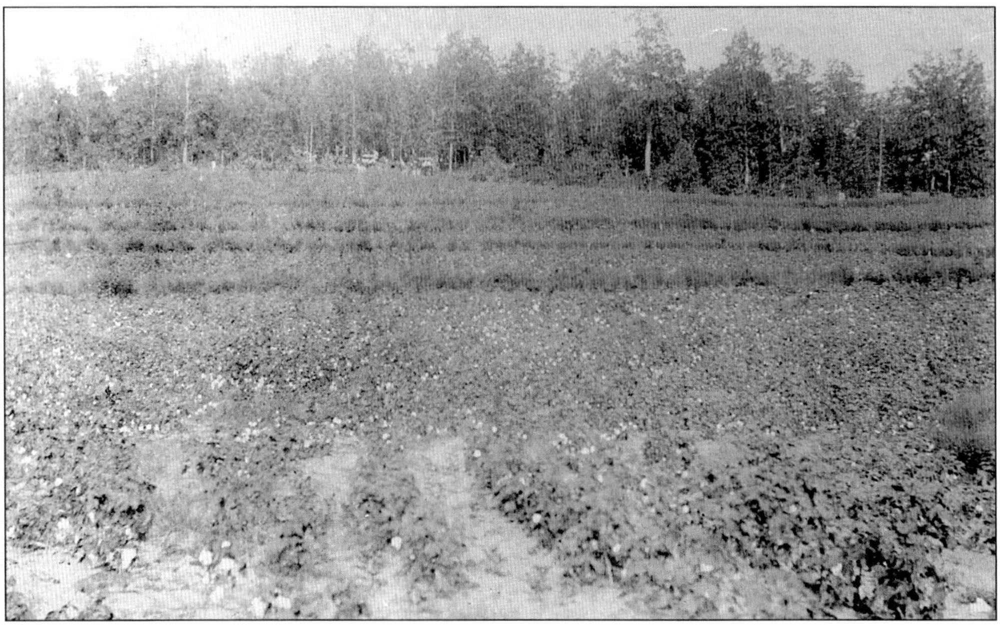

The hill at Kenesaw, up which the 3rd Brigade charged on June 27, 1864, is pictured here. This photograph is looking from the valley across a cotton field in the foreground. The 86th lost many members in this battle—26 were killed, 60 wounded and 12 missing in action. (Courtesy of Mary Nurse Meyer.)

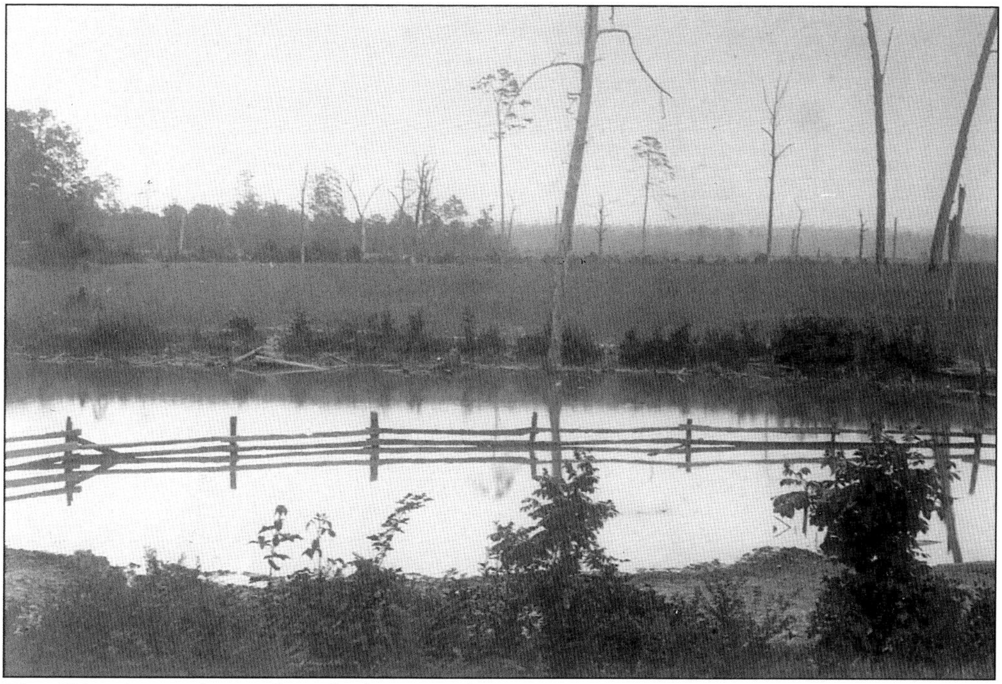

The "Bloody Pond" on the Chickamauga battlefield is pictured here. The 86th lost many members in this battle as well—one was killed, four wounded, and one was captured at Chickamauga. (Courtesy of Mary Nurse Meyer.)

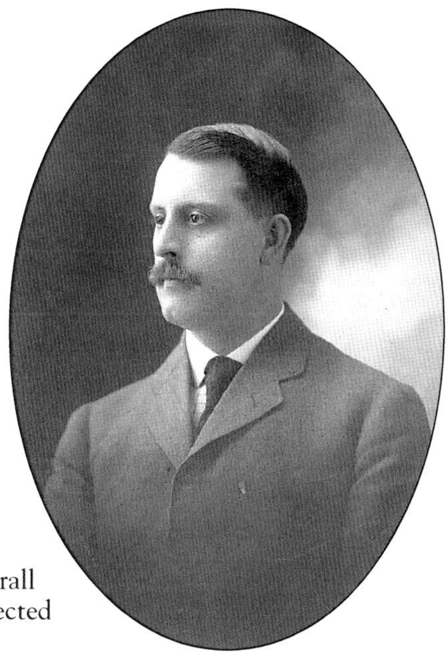

Spanish-American War volunteer Waren E. Van Dusen was a traveling salesman for the shirt and overall department of M.W. Kahn and Company. He was elected mayor of Chillicothe in 1925.

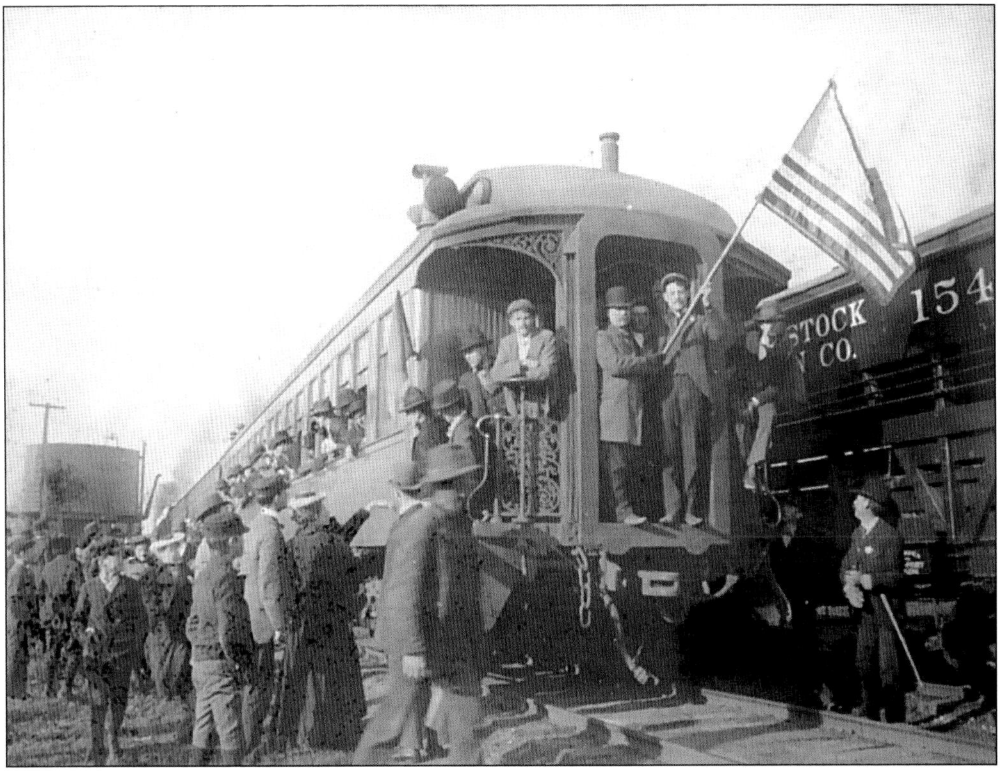

Chillicothe volunteers are pictured here on their way to Springfield during the Spanish-American War. This end coach on a southbound Rock Island train is north of the water tower, which was north of the depot. W.E. Van Dusen is holding the flag.

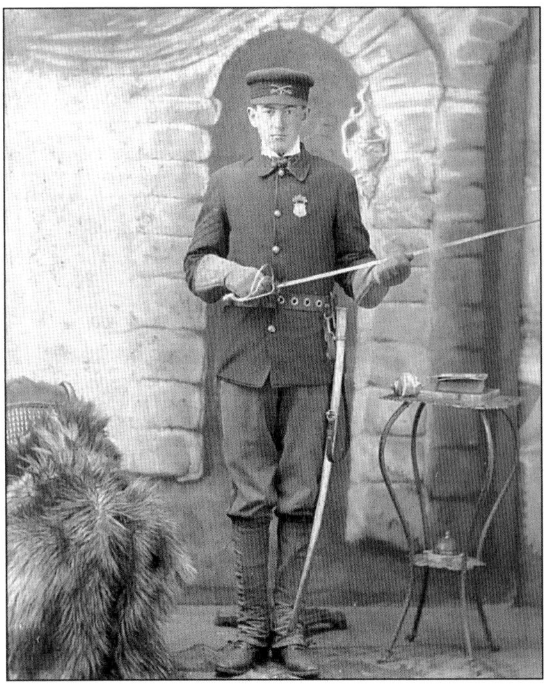

Arthur B. Wilson is pictured here in his cavalry uniform on December 31, 1898.

Captain John Kirby, Signal Corps is pictured here.

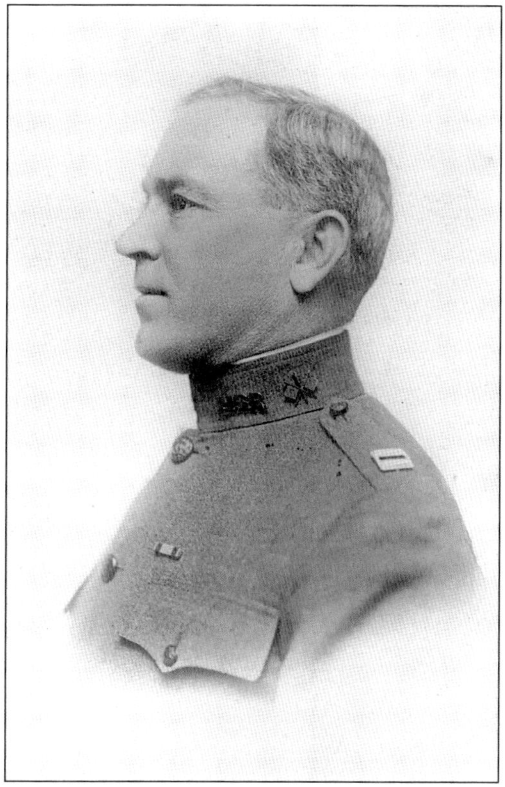

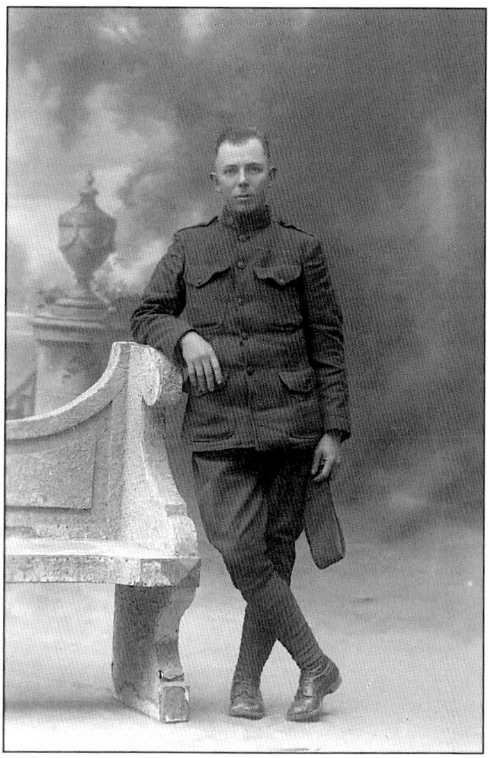

A portrait was taken for this soldier's family before heading "over there." (Courtesy of Jane Campbell.)

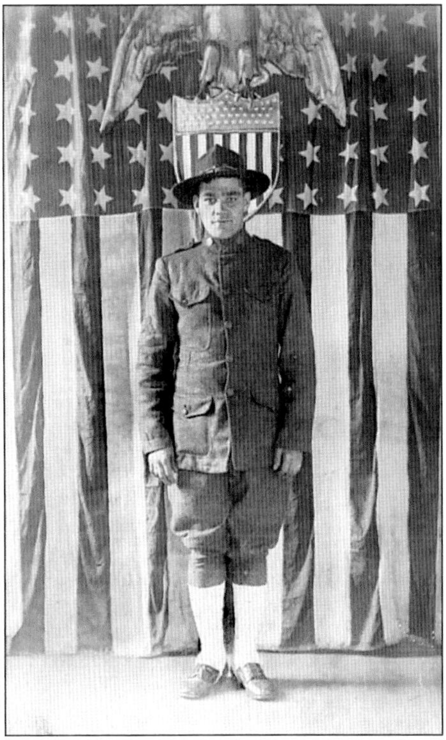

The message on this postcard reads: "Hello Mr. Mitchell, How is Peoria getting along since I left? Give this to the *Peoria Evening Star* for the public and have it in the paper, and send me one. Clyde Bowers, 20th. Co. 161 D.B. Camp Grant, Ill."

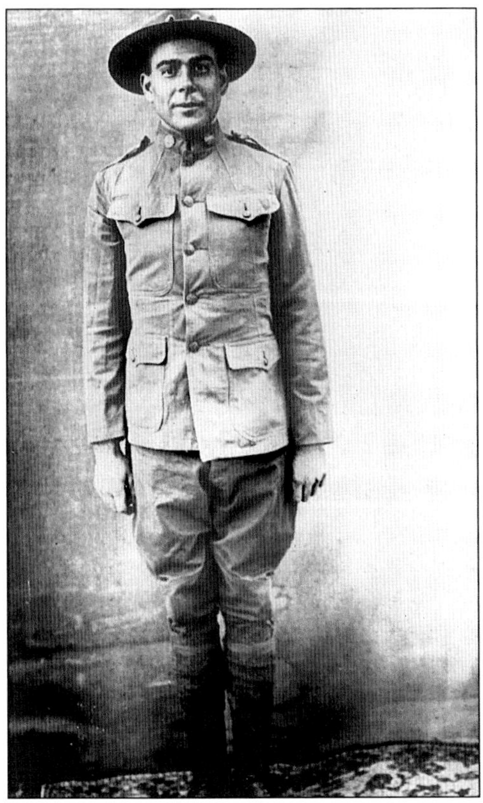

Rupert H. Nurse (Jan. 30, 1902–March 7, 1984) C.M.T.C. at Battle Creek, Michigan in 1922 is pictured here. (Courtesy of Mary Nurse Meyer.)

Leland Birren is pictured here in his uniform. The Navy hat and blouse has changed a little since World War I. Leland's brother Murrell was in the Army at the same time.

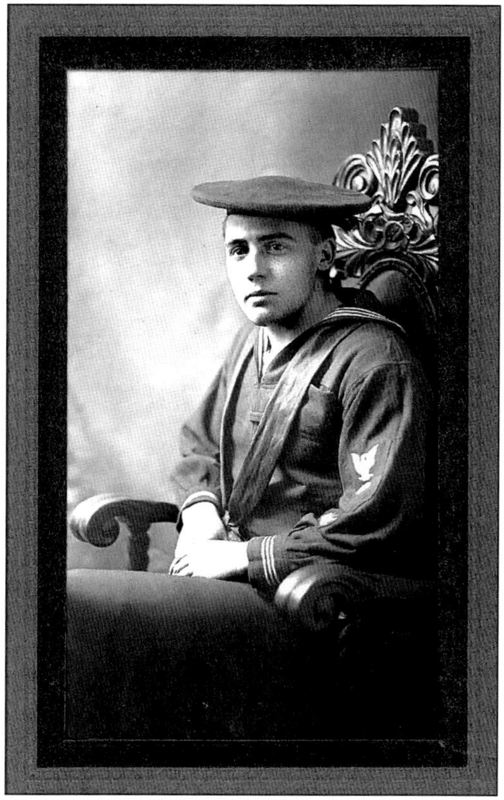

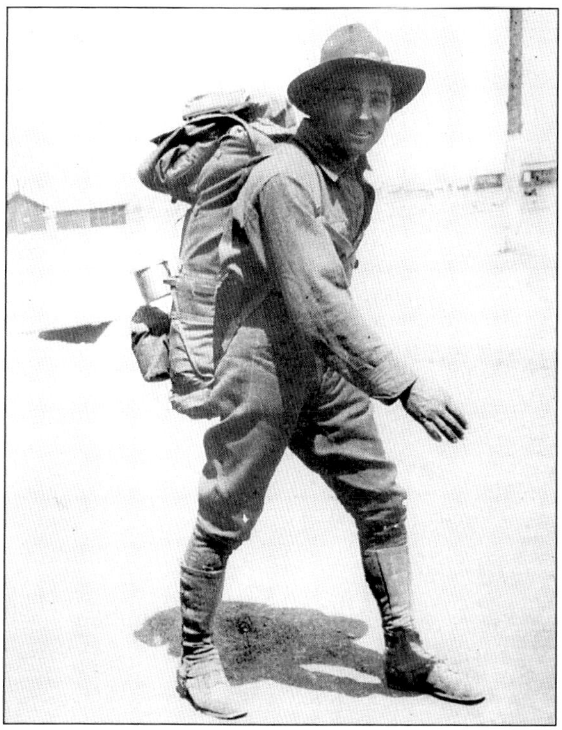

Murrell Birren is pictured on the march. Birren was promoted to Sergeant in the Headquarters Detachment, 308th Field Signal Battalion in Arenberg, Germany on the 1st of March, 1919. He made a career of the service, retiring as a major after World War II.

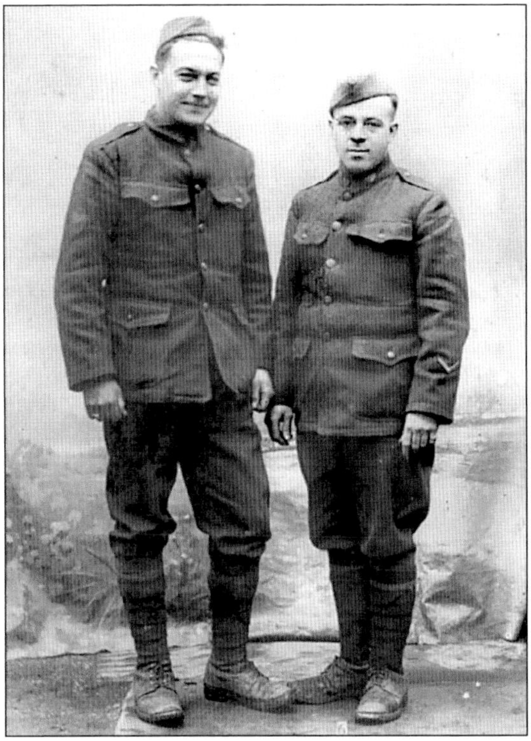

Bill Phillips is pictured on the left with his "trainer" Corporal "Chuck" Hiller.

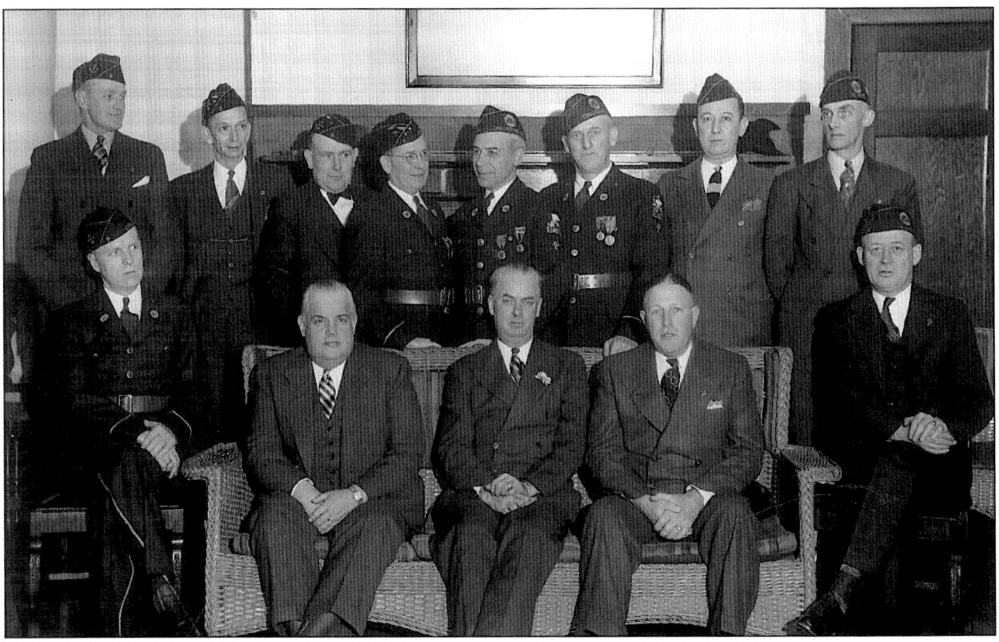

Part of American Legion Post No. 9's past commanders are pictured above. They are, from left to right: (front row) M.D. Israelson–1931, R.F. Hunter–1921, Fred Kelly–1919, Dr. S.A. Smith–1920, Raymond Cliff–1930; (back row) Ed Sheets–1935, J.F. Hubbell–1937, T.C. Anderson–1936, C.C. Edwards–1938, Dr. S.B. La Due–1940, H. Ray Hannah–1939, L.M. Wilkey,–1934, and E.E. Webb–1925.

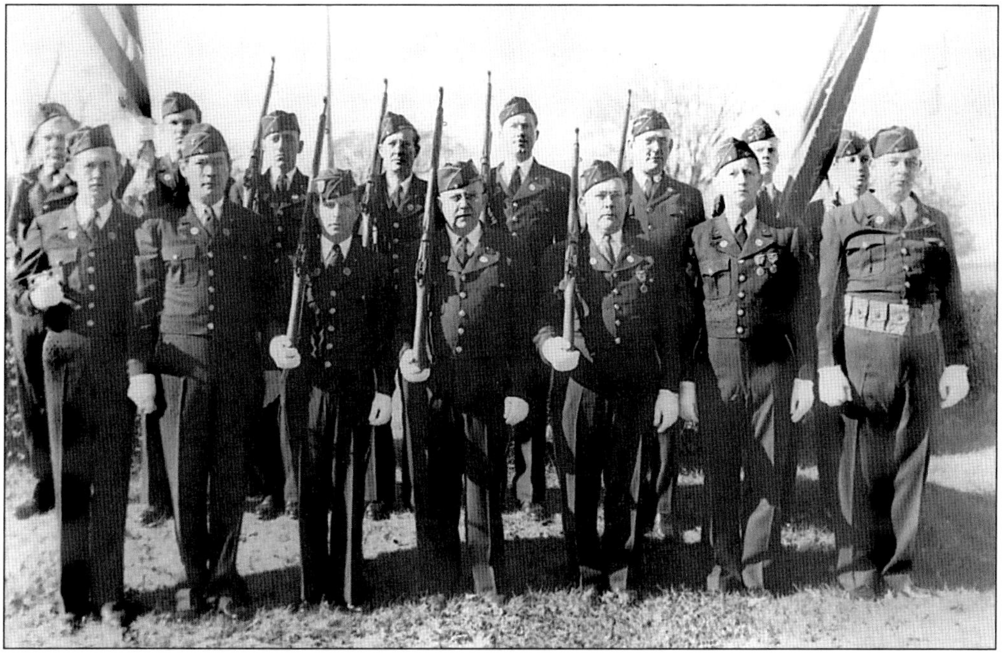

American Legion Post No. 9 color guard is pictured here in 1948. They are, from left to right: (front row) George Johnson, C.C. Chappel, L. McLaughlin, H. Camp, T. Anderson, R.E. Ward, Edward Sweeney; (back row) unidentified, unidentified, Dale Coon, C. Emerick, L.F. Parr, L.J. Carroll, L.Pierson, and Martin. (Courtesy of Post No. 9.)

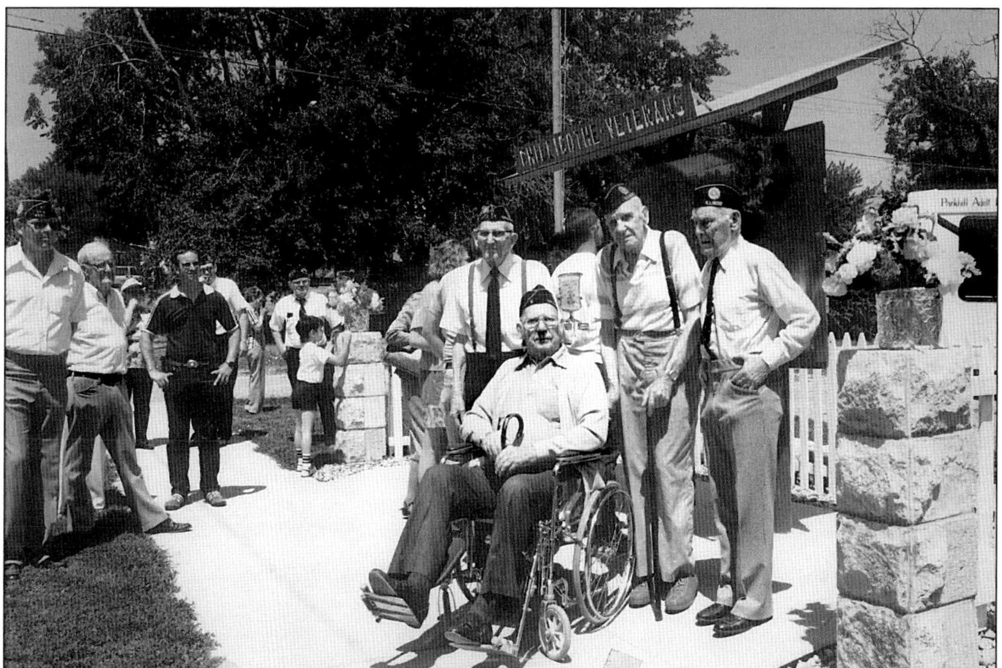

Chillicothe's last four World War I veterans are pictured here in 1990. They are, from left to right: Bill Kruger, Dr. C.F. Case, Nat Reed, and Bill Dunlap. They have all answered their final roll call since the photo was taken. (Courtesy of Post No. 9.)

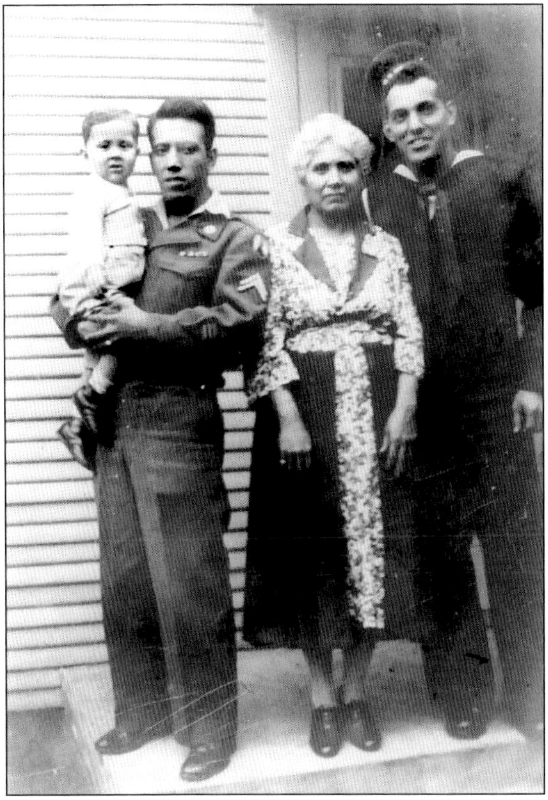

David Herron is pictured here held by Corporal John Razo, with Ruperta Razo, and Richard Razo. (Courtesy of David Herron.)

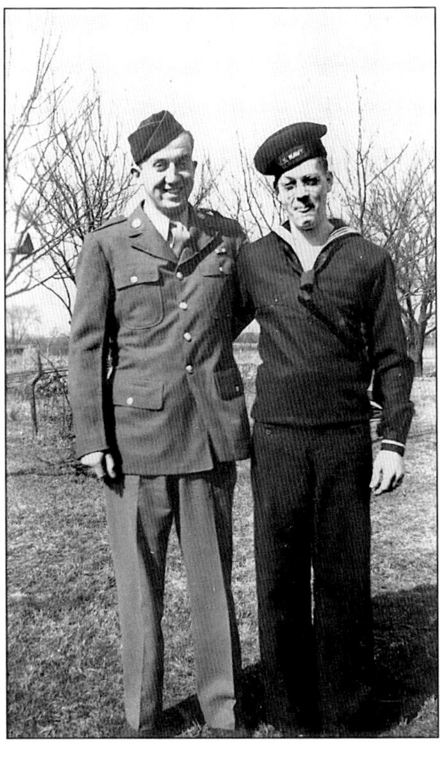

Private Don Brown and Seaman Ray Goodwin are shown here at home on leave in April of 1944.